THE IRISH SEA:

aspects of maritime history

THE IRISH SEA:

aspects of maritime history

Edited by
MICHAEL MCCAUGHAN and JOHN APPLEBY

*Papers presented at the Irish Sea maritime history conference
organised by the Institute of Irish Studies, Queen's University,
Belfast and the Ulster Folk and Transport Museum, Cultra,
County Down.
Held at the Museum, 30 September–3 October 1986.*

THE INSTITUTE OF IRISH STUDIES
THE QUEEN'S UNIVERSITY OF BELFAST

THE ULSTER FOLK AND TRANSPORT MUSEUM

Published 1989
The Institute of Irish Studies,
The Queen's University of Belfast,
Belfast
and
The Ulster Folk and Transport Museum,
Cultra, County Down

ISBN 0 85389 327 6

Printed by W. & G. Baird Ltd., Antrim

Contents

List of Illustrations

Howth Head, county Dublin, from G. N. Wright, *Ireland illustrated in a series of views* (London, 1832)

1 The Irish Sea:

The Geographical Framework

R. H. BUCHANAN

The Irish Sea is that expanse of water lying between 52–55°N and 3–6°W which separates the island of Ireland from Great Britain. To the north and south it is linked by two channels to the Atlantic Ocean. St George's Channel in the south is the wider, measuring some 44 miles between St David's Head in Pembrokeshire and Carnsore Point in Wexford, and broadening northward to 54 miles between Holyhead and Dublin. The North Channel is much narrower, only 12 miles separating the Mull of Kintyre from Torr Head in Antrim, and 19 miles to Galloway from Island Magee. Thus defined the Irish Sea measures some 180 miles in length from north-east Antrim to St David's Head, while its maximum breadth is 150 miles, between Dundalk and Morecambe Bay.

These bare facts pinpoint the essential geographical framework of the Irish Sea: they give its location, identify its relationships with the world's oceans and continental land masses, and define its boundaries and spatial dimensions. But the Irish Sea is much more than a simple geographical location: it is an area with a character of its own. Its waters differ from those of neighbouring seas, in temperature and salinity and in some of the organisms, plant and animal life which it sustains. It has its own currents and tides, of waves and even wind, for it is the most enclosed of the seas around the British Isles, and that enclosure modifies and ameliorates the formidable energy of the Atlantic Ocean which lies beyond. It is a shallow sea, most of it less than 50 m in depth; but greater depths are found in the North Channel, and extend south in a sinuous curve to St George's Channel, and the trench known as the Celtic Deep. This submarine topography, with its shoals and deeps, its muds and sediments of sand and gravel, is well-known to the fisherman but invisible from the land. Here it is the succession of beaches and cliffs, of sandy bays and rocky headlands which gives the coast its character, and the Irish Sea its great variety of enclosing landscape and scenery.

1

This natural environment is an integral part of the geography of the Irish Sea, but the sea has also a human dimension. It is a resource for man, from the earliest times providing food and raw materials, as well as a means of transport and of communication. This human dimension is emphasised in this paper, for the Irish Sea has had an important role in fostering relations between the peoples who live around its shores, in particular between Ireland and Great Britain. Economic activity, especially the demand for raw materials and markets, has been a powerful force in developing and sustaining movement by sea; but there have been other motives for undertaking voyages: the search for new home or market territory, the desire for military adventure, or the flight of refugees. Men have crossed the Irish Sea for all these reasons, but their aspirations and needs have been influenced by the vessels at their command. For example trade was strictly limited when cargoes were carried in skin boats compared with the steel container ships of today, and voyages under sail lasted longer and were much less predictable than those under steam power and screw. The changing technology of ships, one of the major themes of maritime history, explains many of the changes in the human geography of the Irish Sea, especially the pattern of trade and the dynamics of coastal settlements.

The Irish Sea Basin

Before turning to the role of the Irish Sea in history, its physical characteristics will be examined in a little more detail, for it is the reality of wind and tide which confronts the seaman of every age, and his assessment of prevailing conditions which ensures safe passages. Within the Irish Sea most voyages are likely to be relatively short in duration as well as in distance, while the enclosed nature of the basin also means that coastal features are often visible from the other shore. Such a coastline, it has been rightly said, 'is the navigator's best aid and surest compass'.[1] Across the North Channel for example, the cliffs of Kintyre are clearly visible from the Antrim coast and even houses and fields can be distinguished with the naked eye on a clear day. South from Campbelltown the sense of enclosure is accentuated on night passages, when land-based navigation lights seem to encircle the horizon; but perhaps the best view of the Irish Sea is gained from the summit of Snaefell, the highest point on the Isle of Man which itself is like the hub at the centre of a wheel. From here it is possible to see the edge of the sea at three points: Slieve Donard lies to the east, Merrick in Galloway and the Cumbrian Hills are to the north-west, and the Snowdon range to the south. From Snaefell the Wicklow Hills are below the horizon, but on some days they can be identified by the cap of cumulus cloud which sits above them.

Eighty years ago, the British geographer Halford MacKinder called the Irish Sea 'the British Mediterranean',[2] a comparison made again recently by the archaeologist Lloyd Laing although he substituted the word Celtic for British.[3] The analogy is apt, but it should not be pressed too far: both seas have a high degree of cultural unity, derived in part from easy communications, but the Irish Sea has a marked tidal regime, with heights which vary according to the changing phases of the moon and to the configuration of the coast. Mean heights of spring tides are lowest along the Irish coast in northeast Antrim and between Arklow and Wexford they are less than 2 m; but along the shallow coast of Lancashire, they range between 6 m and 8 m, a very marked difference with the Mediterranean average of 0.3 m.[4] Tides of this magnitude have an important bearing on navigations, concealing at high water dangerous offshore reefs and sand-bars, and making the building of harbours and jetties more complex and costly.

Navigation is also affected by the tidal streams which result from the Atlantic waters entering the Irish Sea from both north and south – another contrast with the Mediterranean where there is a single entry, through the Straits of Gibraltar. In the north, the Atlantic tides are constricted by the narrow entry between Fair Head and Kintyre, and here the streams are strongest, reaching on occasions up to five knots.[5] Hence the shortest sea crossing between Ireland and Britain can also be the most hazardous, especially when strong winds meet a flood tide. Southward along the North Channel the tidal stream quickly loses velocity, as much of the flood water is diverted east and north to the Firth of Clyde. Between the Isle of Man and the Irish coast at St John's Point the streams are at their weakest, and it is here, two-thirds of the way north along the Irish Sea, that the tides from the south meet those from the north. This lack of symmetry in the pattern of tidal flow through the basin is because St George's Channel is three times broader than the North Channel, and hence the Atlantic waters entering from the southwest extend much further north into the Irish Sea. The tidal streams are also weaker here than in the north, except where they are affected by local conditions. But weak or not they do have an important influence on navigation. All passages across and through the Irish Sea are affected by tidal streams, so that even given fair winds, a day's sail from south to north for example, will be delayed by meeting an opposing tide at some point in the passage.

Like tides, winds are also influenced by the enclosed nature of the Irish Sea, for the strength of the prevailing west and southwest winds is abated by the bulk of Ireland itself, lying to windward. Throughout the Irish Sea, wind strengths are rarely as severe as those of the Atlantic coasts of Ireland and Scotland, and this amelioration is signified by the designation of the Irish Sea as a distinctive area for purposes of weather forecasting. Note however that the boundaries of the area defined by meteorologists are drawn well into the Irish Sea, an indication that the influence of Atlantic weather extends well into the basin. Hence the boundary with Malin in the north is drawn between Corsewall Point and Island Magee, and in the south from Wicklow Head to St David's. The sea so defined is by no means an area of light airs and tranquil waters, but small vessels can make passages in safety in most seasons of the year. A map showing the pattern of average wave heights underlines this point, for it shows that heights within the Irish Sea are between one-third and one-half lower than those experienced off the Atlantic coast of western Ireland.[6]

The Seas Within

These differences in the pattern of wind and waves, of tides and tidal streams, show that the Irish Sea is not simply a uniform body of surface water, but rather a succession of smaller seas, each with its own hydrology and a geography derived from the character of the adjacent coasts. One of the most distinctive of these sea-regions is the North Channel, where the rugged hills of Kintyre face the bare moorlands of north Antrim across the fastest-moving waters in the Irish Sea. Because distances are short, this has been perhaps the most frequented passage between Britain and Ireland from earliest prehistory; even today there are twenty-eight crossings by ferry at peak season between Larne and Stranraer/Cairnryan. Yet apart from the sheltered sea loughs at Larne and Loch Ryan there are few safe havens on either coast, and no rich agricultural hinterlands to sustain a strong, local cross-channel trade. Contact of course has been frequent between the farming communities of Argyll, Antrim and the offshore islands of Rathlin and Islay, but the more important role of the North Channel has been to act as a throughway, linking the Irish Sea with the Atlantic in long-distance trade. This reached its peak in the later nineteenth and early twentieth centuries in the north American trade of Glasgow and Liverpool. In terms of volume it was at its most impressive during the last world war, when great convoys of merchant ships and their naval escorts steamed eastward beneath the cliffs of Rathlin Island.

South of Larne the Irish coast is breached by the broad inlet of Belfast Lough, and the low rocky coast of County Down which curves southeast to Dundrum Bay and the impressive bulk of the Mourne Mountains. The sea loughs of Strangford and Carlingford provide long and sheltered inlets along a coast which has many small havens, frequented in the past by the fishing boats which found rich catches of herring and mackerel in the relatively shallow waters where the tides meet between the Irish coast and the Isle of Man.

This northern sector might well be called the Manx Sea, for the hills of the Isle of Man are visible from most of the surrounding coastlands, and its harbours at Peel and Castletown, Douglas and Ramsey provide shelter for vessels caught on passage in the most exposed stretches of the Irish Sea. Twenty miles north of Point of Ayre lies the coast of Galloway, the shallow bays of Luce and Wigtown contrasting with the rocky inlets which form the estuaries of the Nith and Dee. Mudflats and saltings fringe the Solway, and glacial deposits mantle the older rocks of the Cumbrian coast, except in promontories such as St Bee's Head. Southward to the Isle of Walney and the dockyards of Barrow, the low coast is breached at Ravenglass and the Duddon Estuary; and beyond is Morecambe Bay, the greatest stretch of tidal sands in the Irish Sea, rich in wildfowl and in shrimps. Despite the difficulties of navigation in shallow waters, this coast has many ports. Lancaster, Heysham, Fleetwood and Preston, have each developed at different periods, but all are based on productive hinterlands, and populations which increased with the growth of manufacturing industry in the nineteenth century. Liverpool on the muddy estuary of the Mersey was to become the greatest of the Lancashire ports, its trade based on Britain's connections with the Americas and with Africa. With the silting of the Dee it succeeded Chester and Pargate as a ferry port for Ireland, while the coal wharves at Garston maintained a steady trade across the Irish Sea.

From the estuary of the Dee the coast runs smoothly west to Great Orme Head, separated from Anglesey by Conway Bay. Here is a cluster of medieval seaports – Conway, Beaumaris and Caernarvon, mark the frontier of the then English colony in Wales, and the narrow passage of the Menai Straits separates fertile Anglesey from the mountains of Snowdonia to the south. Westward, the long ridge of the Lleyn Peninsula points a finger towards the coast of Leinster, from which its name may be derived, and defines the northern limit of St George's Channel, and the second shortest crossing between Wales and Ireland. North of the Dovey estuary the hills of Merioneth form an impressive scenic backcloth to the coast, but southward in Cardigan the coast is low-lying as far as Dinas Head, where the old rocks of Prescelly form an impressive line of cliffs west to St David's Head. Here Atlantic rollers from the southwest are visible reminders that this is the southern gateway to the Irish Sea, and the main entrance from continental Europe. On the Irish shore, the ferries of the Irish Continental Line, berthed at Rosslare, underline the continued importance of the European connection.

Rosslare is an artificial harbour, developed by the railway companies in the later nineteenth century to overcome the difficulty of entering the sheltered but silting harbour of the old port of Wexford. North to Wicklow and Bray Head inshore waters are shallow and navigation is made all the more tricky by sandbars which extend like a softer version of the Great

Barrier Reef along the Wicklow and Wexford coasts, between four and six miles offshore. Dublin Bay is the one major natural inlet along this entire stretch of the Leinster coast from Carnsore Point to Clogher Head, its importance ensured by the rich agricultural lowlands which form its hinterland. In prehistory the Boyne Valley further north had greater significance, but shoals and sandbars make access from the sea difficult for all but the smallest vessels; and once the Viking colonists established their settlement on the banks of the Liffey, the pre-eminence of Dublin became assured.

The Sea and Man

To man in the late twentieth century, the sea is most often seen as a barrier, for his perception of travel is land-based, and most journeys are by road. For the road-user the sea inhibits movement: cars and trucks must be transhipped by ferry, an inconvenience which increases the cost and time taken on journeys. For many, air travel is an alternative; more expensive, but much faster and often more comfortable than sea-crossings, and now virtually the only means of long-distance travel available to the individual. Today therefore, the vagaries of wind and tide, and the realities of storm and fog are experienced by only a minority of people, by those who earn their living directly from the sea in fishing or transport, or who seek it for recreation. For most of us, even those who travel frequently in our work, the sea is a second-hand experience, a distant prospect from a plane flying at 30000 feet, or framed in the picture-window of the lounge of a modern ferry. This perspective of course belongs to the twentieth century; for most of human history the sea has played a much more important role, providing along with inland waterways, the main means of communication until the advent of the railway and motor vehicle made land transport easier and more reliable. Until then water-craft were the primary vehicles for the movement of people and goods, and the sea was the main highway, especially in an island like Ireland. For the Irish, the sea provided the means of escape from parochialism, a pathway to the resources and peoples of countries lying beyond our immediate horizon, in continental Europe and the Americas.

Obviously the role of the sea has varied through time according to man's immediate needs: to the demands of the economy by which he relates to other people, and the technology available to him. For mesolithic man for example, the sea was the only means of travelling to Ireland, the island of which he was the first human inhabitant. For him it also provided an important source of food, and along its shores he found in flint the raw material from which to manufacture tools and weapons. Later in the neolithic age, the sea acquired greater significance as goods and raw materials were exchanged over greater distances by people with a more diverse economy and more sophisticated technology.[7] The polished stone axes, quarried at several major sites along the Irish Sea – Tievebulliagh and Rathlin in Antrim, Langdale in Cumberland, Craig Lloyd in Caernarvon and Prescelly in Pembrokeshire – form perhaps the best surviving indicators of a trade which was to flourish and expand in later periods as new resources were exploited, living standards improved, population increased and mechanisms of exchange became more formal and permanent. During the Bronze Age for example, local resources of copper and gold were being fully exploited in Ireland, and exported to many places overseas, possibly as raw materials, certainly in manufactured form.

Other contributors to this volume will develop the theme of man's use of the Irish Sea as a resource and as a means of communication in the context of specific times and places. I will simply highlight by way of example, two periods when the sea had a role of particular importance in the lives of the people who lived around its shores.

The Celtic Seaways

The Roman occupation of Britain provided an overlay of continental influences which for more than four centuries caused a divergence in culture between Ireland and Britain,[8] despite the trade recorded by Tacitus towards the end of the first century A.D., and confirmed by archaeological evidence.[9] Closer interaction began soon after the withdrawal of Roman military forces, and Irish influences on mainland Britain became increasingly important, a consequence both of the movement of people and of the missionary activities of Christian churchmen.

Irish settlement in mainland Britain is indicated for example, in the legends which describe the expulsion of the Deisi tribe from Ireland and their movement to Pembrokeshire.[10] Similar colonies may have been established in the Lleyn Peninsula, in Cornwall and the Isle of Man[11], while in the late fifth century A.D. Ulstermen from north Antrim settled in Argyll and established the petty kingdom of Dalriada.[12] Its territory included land on both sides of the North Channel, an early political recognition of the close ties that continue to link Ulster with Scotland. Evidence from place-names and from archaeological data gives credence to these legends. In Wales for example, are found the only Ogham inscriptions known outside southern Ireland, their distribution in south Wales providing tangible evidence of links with south Leinster and Munster during the early Christian period.[13] In Scotland, the Irish presence is indicated by the distribution of the place-name *sliabh*, meaning a hill, whose major concentration is to be found within the Scottish territory of Dalriada.[14] The extent of these colonies may never be known, but Charles Thomas has speculated

that the total of Irish settlers in west Britain during the fifth and sixth
centuries may have equalled or even exceeded that of Germanic tribes on
Britain's eastern and southern shores.[15]

The contacts implicit in such movements must help to explain the
increasing uniformity in material culture which becomes increasingly
evident in the latter half of the first millennium A.D. Itinerant craftsmen
rather than merchants engaged in trade, are thought to have provided the
main links[16] across the Irish Sea, with exchanges occurring in the form of
ideas and skills rather than of goods. This type of cultural intercourse is
exemplified and recorded best in the travels of the preachers and missionaries of the early Christian Church, in men like Columba in western
Scotland, Machaoi in Strathclyde and Galloway, or St Sampson, whose
journeys between Brittany, Wales and Ireland have been described by the
late Emrys Bowen.[17] These men represent the forefront of the great surge of
activity within the Christian Church of the fifth and sixth centuries, which
in Laing's words: 'was the main factor that united the scattered groups in
all parts of the Celtic west.[18] A similar point was made by Nora Chadwick:
in a review of the surviving literature of the period she wrote 'we find the
Irish Sea a busy thoroughfare of criss-cross routes'.[19] Today the most
visible reminders of that early traffic, most of it presumably undertaken in
the skin boats whose modern descendant is the curragh, are found in the
ruins of distinctive churches and high crosses found throughout the
coastlands and offshore islands of the Irish Sea. Many of these are monastic
sites, but the church of the time was much more than a scattered company
of hermitic monks and itinerant preachers: rather it formed the cultural
matrix which linked the coastal communities of the Irish Sea in a particularly close relationship up to the dawn of the Viking age.

Trading Smacks and Schoonermen

A second example of the role of the Irish Sea as a means of communication, comes from the eighteenth and nineteenth centuries, a time of
economic growth, of rising population and increased production in agriculture and manufacturing industry, with a consequent need to provide
transport for raw materials, finished products and for people. Each of the
regions bordering the Irish Sea experienced major growth and contributed
commodities for trade: coal from Ayrshire and Cumberland, slate from
North Wales, grain and cattle from the ports of Ireland. In addition to this
cross-channel trade there was constant traffic along the coasts, for bulky
goods were much cheaper to move by sea than by land. Until the expansion
of the railways in the second half of the nineteenth century, and the later
development of road transport, small vessels of different rigs and sizes
carried miscellaneous goods between coastal towns and villages where

today they are transported by van and lorry. They were accommodated by the many quays built around our coasts at this time, but even open beaches could be used to discharge cargo, the vessels being run ashore at high water and unloaded into carts, driven alongside as the tide went down.

To illustrate this important period in the history of the Irish Sea, when the people around its shores were in more constant communication than at any other time before or since I have chosen a small port on the southern coast of County Down, where one of my forebears was engaged in trade in the first half of the nineteenth century. The town is Killough, built on the western side of a land-locked bay, which is open to the south but partially sheltered by offshore reefs. The bay is shallow, its bottom of mud and sand drying at low water; in the words of the *Sailing Directions* of the Irish Cruising Club: 'This harbour is little used, and not recommended for yachts owing to the proximity of the better harbour of Ardglass'.[20] Ardglass in fact has been a port since medieval times, its rocky inlet providing sheltered creeks and the hill beyond the harbour a natural site for its defence on land. But by the early eighteenth century, the port of Ardglass was in decay; while Killough Bay was seen to have potential for development by a young and energetic landowner into whose hand the property had recently come. From a greenfield site he built the town and provided it with a jetty and quays. To quote a contemporary writer, in a work published in 1744:

> Killough, now called Port St Anne, ... was of late made a town and commodous harbour by the Hon. Michael Ward, Esq., one of the justices of the King's Bench, whose estate it is; who for the encouragement of the town, built a strong kay, where ships now lie very safe. The town is agreeably situated with the sea flowing all along the backs of the houses, where ships ride in full view of the inhabitants. Some persons of condition live here, and there is a decent church and a barrack for two or three troops of horse. They have good fishing in the bay; but the principal trade of the place consists in the exportation of barley, and the importation of such commodities as are consumed in the adjacent country. Fifteen ships belong to the port that deal in foreign and domestic trade, and about twenty boats are employed in fishing.[21]

Killough continued to have an extensive trade for the remainder of the century, sufficiently valuable to encourage Michael Ward's descendant, Viscount Bangor, to spend some £17000 in improving the harbour between 1821 and 1824.[22] By then Ardglass was being revived as a fishing harbour, and although trade figures are given jointly for both ports, trade was handled mainly at Killough. In 1835 for example, exports were valued at £35161, of which grain, valued at £21770, was by far the most important commodity. Next in value were potatoes, cows and oxen, flax, tow, kelp, and horses, and a range of other goods which included bricks, butter, soap and quills. Imports were much less important, the trade being valued at only £2970 of which coal was by far the most important item, worth £2860, the remaining imports consisting of salt, tar, hardware, limestone and paper.[23]

One of the seamen engaged in this trade was William Donnan. Little is known of his early life, but between 1851 and 1855 he sailed regularly from Killough to ports in the Irish Sea, and some details of the expenses of his voyages have survived.[24] His account book tells nothing of the boat he owned, its name, size or rig, or the number of the crew; but she could carry up to seventy-five tons of coal, and may have been one of the gaff-rigged, single-mast smacks common at that time. She carried little but coal, mostly from Whitehaven but occasionally from Glasgow and Liverpool; outward trips were mainly in ballast, though a few voyages were made with cargoes of oats to Glasgow and barley to Dundalk. This pattern of trade confirms that the grain trade which had brought prosperity to so many small ports in eastern Ireland since the 1760s, had virtually collapsed by the mid-nineteenth century. As a young man, William Donnan had seen the Irish Sea at one of the busiest periods in its history; when he died in 1870, aged eighty-five, trade had declined enormously and it continued to do so. By the end of the century, Killough was connected to Belfast by a branch railway line and the last of the locally-owned smacks was a hulk, rotting just below high-water mark at the head of the bay. A few cargoes of coal and potatoes were shipped into and from the port in the inter-war years, but as a small boy at the beginning of world war two I remember the last cargo of Whitehaven coal being discharged on the quay, and the S.S. *Wilson* leaving in ballast for the Isle of Man. Thereafter the quays at Killough were deserted, becoming increasingly derelict like so many others around the Irish Sea.

In the 1840s, William Donnan seems to have made voyages at monthly intervals from Killough, a round trip to Whitehaven in winter taking up to three weeks, including time for loading. Profits were meagre, varying from £2 to £7 per voyage after expenses were paid; I suspect William must have augmented his income by working the smallholding behind his cottage on the shores of the bay. Neither he nor the brother who sailed with him was married, but many of his contemporaries in the Irish Sea trade found partners away from home, as did the fishermen who followed the herring in its seasonal migration through the Irish Sea. In my youth several men and women in Killough were descendants of such marriages, as was William Donnan's father. He was born in Carlingford in 1743, and may have come to County Down as a seaman, marrying a local woman, Elizabeth McCullough, who subsequently inherited an uncle's farm. Through ties of kinship like these, formed through sea trade and fishing, the coastal communities of the Irish Sea became closely interlinked in the last century.

Today the pattern of trade is very different, goods and passengers are carried across the Irish Sea in large vessels operating between only a few ports. Coastwise trade is minimal, much of it carried in foreign vessels, and even through traffic has declined dramatically for few ships now leave the one-time great ports of Liverpool and Glasgow for destinations in Africa or the Americas. The Irish Sea today is still an important resource for man: its tides bring nutrients that sustain its population of fish, and its deeps provide receptacles for unwanted rubbish – perhaps to our future detriment since some of the waste contains material that is radioactive. It still provides an important means of communication, but its routes resemble motorways rather than the close network of lanes and byeways which on land once linked villages with market towns: the old connections built on trade disappeared with the small ships sailed by men like William Donnan. Today these routes are being revived, if only a little, by the yachtsmen who sail the Irish Sea, not to make a living but for recreation. Some of the older harbours are being adapted for their use, providing an opportunity for new economic growth and the renewal of community life.

Gokstad ship *c.* 850–900 A.D., preserved in the Viking Ships Museum, Oslo, Norway. Photograph courtesy of Universitetets Oldsaksamling, Oslo.

2 Vikings in the Irish Sea

ARNE EMIL CHRISTENSEN

The Viking age (800–1050 A.D.) was a period of change and turbulence all over northern Europe. The Vikings, the inhabitants of Denmark, Norway and Sweden, were pagan, and their impact on the Christian kingdoms of western Europe was such that the written sources depict them as ruthless pirates and plunderers, whose military success amazed and frightened societies that were quite familiar with war and violence. This documentary picture of the savage Scandinavians is clearly part of the truth, but it must be modified by other evidence; first and foremost the results of archaeology.

The Scandinavian background for the Viking expansion was a rural society of farmers and stockbreeders, who also fished and hunted. Denmark is rich in arable land, and must have been a farmers' country then as now. Sweden and particularly Norway are less fertile, and people lived by a more mixed economy, where stockbreeding, fishing, hunting and iron smelting must have been more important than the grain fields in most districts. In addition to iron, other products of the mountains, like soapstone vessels and whetstones, were exported from Norway. Archaeological finds and place names indicate a strong increase in population in the period just before the Viking age, and population pressure on the resources at home is in all probability an important reason for the expansion abroad.

Even though the Vikings got their reputation from efficient plundering techniques, they had other abilities and other reasons for going abroad. Trade was important, and many set out with family and cattle in search of new land. The trader could turn to piracy if the opportunity arose, and the robber might bring his family on the next trip if he had found good land which was unsettled or where the inhabitants could be driven away by force. The people of Denmark, Norway and Sweden took part in ventures in various geographical directions, although there seem to have been certain divisions of interest. The Swedes and Gotlanders went east, plundering,

13

trading and settling. They traded with the Arabs, unsuccessfully attacked Constantinople and founded long-lived states on Russian soil. The Danes plundered in Frisia, France and England, settled in England and Normandy, and finally managed to conquer England around 1000 A.D. under Svein and Canute. Norwegians took part in these ventures, but they also went further west. Northern England, Scotland and Ireland were their main areas for plunder and settlement. A Norwegian kingdom was based in York, while place names indicate strong settlements in Cumberland and in the north of Scotland. The Atlantic islands and northern Scotland were probably settled before the Viking age, while Iceland was settled around 800 A.D. and Greenland about 1000 A.D. Settlement in north America was also attempted by the Vikings.

Place name evidence points to Scandinavian, probably Norwegian settlement on Shetland and the Orkneys in the early eighth century, well before the attack on Lindisfarne in 793 A.D., which is generally recognised as the opening of the Viking age. There must have been knowledge of the sea routes, both in the Baltic and the North Sea, well before 793. Swedish finds are known from Estonia, which indicate trading settlements before 800. Population pressure alone is insufficient as an explanation when we look at the expansion and the remarkable success of the Vikings against strong and well organised states like France and England. Norway and Sweden were rich in bog-iron ore, and this may have been of some tactical advantage; more iron for arms, more arrow-heads to shoot away. However, the most important tools for Viking expansion were their sailing and pulling ships. Use of the sail seems to have been a remarkably late innovation in Scandinavia. Ship finds indicate that oared ships were not equipped with a mast and sail until *c*. 700 A.D. The first trips across the Baltic or from western Norway to Shetland may have been made with rowing vessels like the Kvalsund ship, dated to the early eighth century. We do not know where the idea of mast and sail came from. Byzantium is one possibility and the area around the English Channel is another. When the sail was adopted, there must have followed a period of experimentation, but after two or three generations the combined sailing and rowing Viking ship had evolved as a fighting tool. The first attacks were probably launched in ships of the Oseberg type. This ship, now preserved in Oslo, was built around 800 and is 75 feet long. It could be rowed by thirty men, and was equipped with a mast and sail. Fifty years later, with more experience in sailing the high seas, there were improvements in hull shape and structural detail. These can be seen in the preserved Gokstad ship, which was probably built around 850 and used in a burial about 900. The support for the mast is much stronger in the Gokstad than in the Oseberg ship, for instance. As the ships developed they became seaworthy enough to take their crews on distant voyages. They were fast under sail or oars, yet of shallow draft, so that they could be easily beached. They could be taken up rivers and were light enough to be carried and handled on land by the crew. In the words of Bertil Almgren, the Swedish archaeologist, 'Viking vessels are the only ocean-going landing craft ever devised'. The ships were sharp at both stem and stern and were clinker-built by means of a 'shell technique'. Firstly, the keel backbone and the stem and stern posts were set up. Starting by nailing and riveting the first plank to the keel and stems, the shipwright built a shell of overlapping planks, riveted to one another and nailed to the stems. When the shell was ready, it was strengthened and stabilised by ribs and crossbeams. The sailing rig was one square sail on a mast amidships. Steering was by a steering oar or side rudder placed on the starboard quarter. Although the rigging is mainly known from iconographic sources, traces on the surviving hulls give some information, while the traditional single square sail rig of boats from western and northern Norway has been widely used as comparative material. The picture stones from the Swedish island of Gotland show a number of sailing ships, many with a complicated net of ropes below the sail. This has not been convincingly explained, but it may be a complicated system of sheets or ropes for controlling the sail. Rigging traces on the hull of the Danish Skuldelev wrecks from *c.* 1000 A.D. indicate a simpler rig, much like that still used by fishing boats in northern Norway less than a century ago. The effectiveness of their ships is the reason why small bands of warriors from the edges of northwestern Europe were able to terrorise large, well-organised kingdoms like France and England for two centuries.

At first the activity of the Vikings was restricted to small scale raids. However, the experience gained led to the organisation of larger ventures for military conquest. In many places Vikings settled peacefully and permanently. Shetland must have been sparsely populated when the settlers from western Norway first arrived. Most of the place names have Scandinavian roots. The place names in Orkney are both Scandinavian and Celtic, and may indicate a mixed settlement, also in all probability peaceful. In parts of northern England there are indications that the Scandinavian settlers preferred different soil from that used by the Anglo-Saxons as the latter were probably grain growers, while the new settlers concentrated on stockbreeding. The Viking settlement to the west and further south was probably less intense. The name of Sutherland for the northern tip of Scotland and Suderøyaer for the Hebrides indicate that the main weight of settlement was further north. Nevertheless, there seems to have been a considerable Viking settlement in the Isle of Man and early enough for burials in pre-Christian heathen graves. Heathen graves have also been found in Scotland and on the western islands, with one as far off the main sailing routes as St Kilda. This is a female grave with a good pair of oval brooches, and may well indicate a Viking settlement.

When we move into a discussion of the Irish Sea proper, Dublin is the natural place to start. Its status as a Norse kingdom is well attested in the written sources, both Irish and Scandinavian. The Islandbridge/ Kilmainham cemetery and other grave finds in Dublin, including reports on lost finds, indicate at least forty male and a minimum of six female burials. The small number of female burials may be due to the fact that swords and spears are larger and more easily recognised than relatively small bronze brooches. The weapons would have much greater chances of survival in a non-scholarly excavation. It may also be that relatively few Scandinavian women settled in Dublin. In addition to the arms and jewellery, the Islandbridge cemetery finds include pins, belt equipment, hammers, tongs, knives and spindle whorls. All these objects are familiar from Scandinavian Viking age finds. Significant finds are lead and bronze weights and four small balance scales. These were used for weighing out silver, and were the most important tool of the merchant in a society where silver by weight was the standard currency. Small as they are, the weights and scales are good symbols of Dublin's importance as a trading centre. There are numerous other finds of Viking character from Ireland, both graves and stray finds. Among the latter are a group of swords and axes from various rivers, which may indicate battles where the Vikings came by boat. Stray finds of Norse silver, mainly armlets, may have been lost or hidden by Irish owners as well as Norse. Not all battles were won by the Vikings and silver may have been captured by both parties. A large silver neckring from Limerick, but displaying clear Scandinavian workmanship, is a good example of this group of objects.

This is not the place to give a report on the recent excavations in Dublin. They have given a very rich picture of Viking city life, of material culture, and of a society where the organising talent of the Vikings can be seen, for example, in the orderly layout of the city. Maritime activity is attested by ship fragments, ship graffiti and models. The number and quality of the Dublin finds rank with anything in the Viking world, be it Birka, Hedeby or Smolensk. Even before the large scale excavations in recent years, there was sufficient evidence for Dublin to have been regarded as the most important Viking settlement in western Europe outside Scandinavia. The written sources concentrate mainly on the Vikings in Ireland as city dwellers, well protected behind fortifications, and mainly occupied with crafts, trade and plunder. The countryside remained Irish, or at least this is the impression the sources convey. However, the female graves found outside the cities must, in my opinion, be explained as indications of Viking rural settlement. A firm rule in Viking burial custom was that people were buried near their homes. Female graves, like those from Three-Mile Water, Arklow, County Wicklow and Ballyholme, County Down, are in all probability those of settlers' wives. The pair of oval brooches found in each grave are typically

Norse. These brooches are found in most female graves in Scandinavia, and are the most common of all Viking age jewellery. In these cases, at least, the settlers evidently came fully equipped with a family.

To the finds in Dublin and elsewhere in Ireland and the written sources of Viking settlement in other Irish cities, we must add the graves, crosses and place names of the Isle of Man, the settlement in Cumberland and on the islands of western and northern Scotland, besides the place names on the Wirral peninsula in Cheshire, which clearly indicate a Scandinavian colony, probably settled from Dublin rather than from Scandinavia direct. From the Hebridean island of Eigg comes a bog find, which is clear evidence of maritime activity of Norse character. In the bog were found two unfinished stems of oak for a fairly large boat or small ship. The size indicates that they were intended for the same boat, even though one is only roughed out, while the other is nearly finished. The closest parallel to the finished one is the Danish wreck, Skuldelev 3, dated to *c.* 1000 A.D. The principle of cutting steps for the strakes is attested from a number of finds, the oldest being the small boat found with a Gokstad ship. This boat has a stepped and hollowed stem like the Eigg example, but for three strakes only. Finds from western Norway show that the stepped stems were in use at least until the middle of the fourteenth century. It is at present not possible to date the Eigg stems within this period.

The custom of storing oak keels and stems in an unfinished state in bogs or lakes, is well attested by west Norwegian finds from the Viking and early medieval periods. Furthermore the wet storage of oak has been used by Norwegian boatbuilders to the present day. Taken together, the sources clearly point to the Irish Sea as being an important part of what can be called Viking territorial waters, in the period 800 to 1000 A.D. Their maritime supremacy must have been total. No matter how large a currach was, it can have been no match for Norse vessels, and there seems to be no indication of a maritime defence based on wooden ships, like that organised by Alfred in Wessex. Viking maritime supremacy was maintained until 1170, when Norman forces from Britain crossed the Irish Sea in ships of roughly the same type as that used by the Scandinavians. Although the Viking kingdom in Dublin came to an end, Scandinavian influence and interests in the Irish Sea did not disappear completely. Ties with Norway remained strong. In particular the kingdom of Man had close ties with Norway. The bishopric of Suderøyar and Man was under the archbishop in Trondheim from 1153 to 1536 and the last king of Man fought on the Norwegian side in the battle of Largs in 1265. Today the organising gifts and good statesmanship of Viking rulers is evident in the annual Tynwald parliamentary ceremony in the Isle of Man.

In seafaring terms, the Viking heritage is evident in the tradition of building boats of double-ended form and clinker construction, a technique which still survives in some localities. Warfare by means of Viking-type galleys continued in the Scottish western isles until the sixteenth century. The ship depicted on the tomb of Alexander McLeod in St Clement's Church at Rodil on Harris is, apart from the stern rudder, a very good representation of a vessel of the Gokstad type. Seven hundred years after the first Viking attacks in the Irish Sea, Viking-type vessels were still being used for the transport of fighting men going into battle.

Medieval ship on the municipal seal of Youghal, county Cork, *c.* 1527 from Richard Caulfield (ed.), *The council book of the corporation of Youghal* (Guildford, 1878).

3   A Survey of Early Irish Maritime Trade and Ships

JOHN DE COURCY IRELAND

Until the development of regular airline flights to the European continent and the opening of regular direct passenger services by sea to French ports, which occurred only recently, well after the end of the second world war, Irish people for some one hundred and fifty years had grown used to the feeling that to reach the European mainland the natural route was through Britain. In the years after 1945 even trade between Ireland and the continent had almost ceased to be carried in Irish ships, and it has been mainly the growth in the last few years of a fleet of short-sea traders in Arklow, Ireland's most famous maritime town, that has restored this situation.

It is in fact quite natural that Ireland, a European off-shore island, should be, and in fact was, in regular maritime contact with the European mainland. However, historical events cut off the Irish people from this natural sea-borne association, and its past existence was only dimly if at all realised by generations of inhabitants of Ireland, including elements in the present population.

However, even in the time of the Roman empire there was continual if irregular contact by sea between the people of Ireland (all of whose ancestors had of course come to Ireland by sea from various starting-points) and the mainland of Europe. Irish sea rovers played a part in the overthrow of the Roman empire, and after that Christian missionaries regularly sailed between Ireland, Britain and the continent. This traffic in course of time gave rise to the Brendan legend, which by the late middle ages had taken root in all countries of western Europe, including Venice and much of central Europe. Medieval representations of the ships in which the Irish saintly scholar – or more likely, in fact, a great number of such individuals who are epitomised in his legend – is supposed to have made his

21

sixth century voyages are interesting for research workers seeking to trace the evolution of ship design in medieval northern Europe. The islands which Brendan is supposed to have discovered in the Atlantic began to appear on the increasingly accurate cartographic representations of the coastline of western Europe and the mysterious ocean beyond it. These maps in turn played their part in stimulating the urge for oceanic voyaging which marked the end of the medieval period.

Most of the existing seaports of Ireland, ranging from the capital Dublin to small ports like Arklow and Wicklow, Wexford and Annagassan, were created by the Norse, whose settlements in Ireland from the ninth century onwards were important factors in the cultural development not only of Ireland, but of Europe in general. Previously these ports were at best small settlements, usually monastic, where vessels, probably characteristic Irish skin boats or currachs, were brought ashore for shelter. With the Vikings new quays were constructed, and Dublin and Limerick in particular became important elements in an intricate commercial network created by the Norse, linking western, northern and north-eastern Europe. Norse-Irish accompanied by Gaelic-speaking Irish were involved in the settlement of Iceland, to where Irish saintly scholars of the Brendan stamp had preceded them long before. The Norse-Irish were also in contact, sometimes peacefully, sometimes not, with Moorish Spain, where scholars were remarkably well informed about the geography of Ireland and describe among other things whaling off the south Irish coast.

The Norse settlers not only greatly influenced boat and shipbuilding in Ireland, but also imported many nautical terms still in use with the Gaelic language.

The arrival of Norman adventurers primarily from Wales in the seventh and eighth decades of the twelfth century not only established a nominal lordship of the English kings over Ireland, shadowy as a rule except round Dublin, and in the fifteenth century generally fragile even there, but brought in improvements in shipbuilding and ship-design and reinforced the maritime commercial relationship built up in previous centuries between Ireland and the continent.

By the end of the fifteenth century Ireland was thoroughly integrated into the general pattern of European late-medieval seaborne trade. The oldest known English 'rutter', dated by experts to the early fifteenth century gave elaborate instructions for shipmasters sailing to Ireland. A Venetian 'rutter' of 1470, a Genoese document of 1435 and the French 'grant routtier' of 1484 all testify to the frequency of passages by sea between Ireland and the European continent as well as Britain. Early maps, from the Catalan map of 1375, by way of such masterpieces as Fra Mauro's map of 1457–9, Juan de la Cosa's map of 1502, Vesconte Maggiolo's Atlante Nautico del 1512, to the great maps of the Breton cartographers of Le Cônquet a few years later, show an ever-increasing knowledge of the coast of Ireland and its ports. It was not until the second half of the sixteenth century, that the great strategic importance of Ireland in the new age of the Atlantic seaways began to be clearly realised. Certainly it was a major factor in motivating the English conquest of Ireland in the late sixteenth and first years of the seventeenth centuries.

During the later middle ages the seaport towns of Ireland (except for Dublin, where the English monarchy exercised some limited control) and coastal areas, for example in west Cork and Donegal, ruled by local chiefs, had a maritime life of their own. They developed their commerce and fisheries without needing to pay much heed to the shadowy nominal overlordship of the English king or to each other.

At this time the leading Irish ports were Waterford, Ross, Drogheda, Galway, Limerick, Dublin, Youghal, Cork, Kinsale, Sligo, Dingle, Dundalk, Ardglass, Carlingford, Carrickfergus, Arklow and Wexford. In addition numbers of small towns such as Rosscarberry in County Cork or Malahide in County Dublin carried on a lively trade by sea. It is estimated that there were up to eighty active ports in Ireland.

Irish ships traded with Seville and Lisbon, Galician ports, Bordeaux, ports in Brittany and Normandy, Bruges and Antwerp, Hamburg, Lübeck and Gdansk, Reykjavik in Iceland, Chester, Liverpool, Welsh and Cornish ports, Bristol, Bridgewater and Gloucester, and ports in west Scotland. Exports were fish, hides and leather, woolfells, woollen cloth and cloaks, woollen yarn, tallow, linen yarn, timber, grain, some livestock, brass and re-exported French and Iberian wine. Imports included wine, honey, iron, manufactured products like knives and weapons, tin, nails, spices, silk clothing, soap, hops and salt and a new and increasing import, coal. There were pilgrimage routes to Santiago de Compostella via La Coruña or Bordeaux from Galway, Dingle, Kinsale, Waterford, Wexford and Dublin.

It is evident that during the fifteenth century the Irish had a generally favourable balance in their trade with England. During considerable periods there were perhaps more Irish ships than English involved in the important exchanges with Chester, the most important port in northwest England, and Bristol, the greatest port of medieval England after London. In their trade with continental ports, the ports of Ireland provided a proportion of the ships involved, but not a high one, whereas in their exchanges with southwest England and Wales the Irish provided a high percentage of the shipping concerned (for example 34 per cent of ships sailing from Bridgewater to Ireland in the period 1484–97) and, in the case of the Welsh coal trade, probably a majority of the shipping.

Although limited, there is quite continuous written evidence of the extent of shipbuilding and, less specifically, of the types of ships built in Ireland. Possibly the earliest documentary evidence is Adamnan's sixth century life of St Columba, where mention is made of planked vessels, dug-out log boats and currachs (skin boats). There are records of wooden rowed galleys being built in Ireland in the thirteenth century, and cogs in the fourteenth, to be superseded by carvel-built round hulled vessels late in that century, or at least outmatched by them.

Irish vessels arriving in foreign ports from the early fourteenth century onward are categorized as 'cog', 'navis', 'nef' or simply ship. Irish-owned 'hulks', 'barges', 'balingers' and 'pickards' appear in later medieval documents, while 'galleys' for military purposes were built in several Irish ports, but 'carracks' recorded from time to time in Irish waters all seem to have been foreign-owned.

The manuscript by Antoine de Conflans, Faiz de la Marine et Navigaiges* dated *c*. 1540, declares that Irish 'nefez' are just like French ones, and built in Ireland or in 'Bisquaye', which at that date was turning out particularly stout whaling vessels that were involved in whaling and fishing off the newly-found coasts of north America, a fact of which Irish shipowners can hardly have been ignorant. A paragraph of this manuscript is devoted to the traditional Irish skin boats (currachs). It was during the fifteenth century that flotillas of sea-going 'cottes' were built at Wexford not only for carrying fish to Bridgewater in southwest England but also for engaging in the new trade of importing coal from Wales to Ireland. Each 'cotte' would load eight to ten tons of coal. The Hebridean 'galley' evolved from the Norse longships and in similar form was in common use till the end of the sixteenth century on Ireland's north and west coasts.

Illustrations of Irish medieval ships are scarce, but important examples include graffiti on planks from eleventh century Norse Dublin (where four model boats were found in the same excavation); a single-masted double-ended ship on a round tower at Roscrea; a fourteenth century manuscript with a representation of the building of Noah's Ark, by Adam O Cianain, and a pen-and-ink picture of a single-masted, double-ended ship on the flyleaf of the late fourteenth century Book of Ballymote, now preserved in the Royal Irish Academy.

Regarding ship-sizes, it is known that fifteenth century Limerick handled and evidently built ships of 200 tons, and that the approaches to Dublin had become so dangerous by that time that ships of more than 100 tons could not enter, but discharged at the southern end of Dublin Bay off Dalkey. A quite typical list of twenty-seven Irish ships requisitioned, or chartered, in 1301 to carry stores for Edward I's campaign against Scotland, includes ships varying in size from the 22 ton *Nicholas* of Dublin and the 40 ton *Mari Cogge* from Youghal, to the *Grace Dieu* of Cork and *Sante Crucis* of Youghal, both of 140 tons. No wreck of a medieval ship has been identified in the coastal waters round Ireland or in the country's many inland waterways.

* Ms français 742 of the Bibliothèque Nationale, Paris.

Nevertheless it is hard to believe none exists and it seems inevitable that with increasing maritime archaeological activity, primary structural evidence will be found.

An examination of the names of Irish shipmasters, ship-owners and merchants engaged in maritime commerce in the middle ages reveals people of Norman, English, Welsh, Celtic-speaking Irish and occasionally, continental descent. It is clear that a homogeneous Irish nation was evolving, and distinctive architectural achievements in the fifteenth century seem to emphasise the strength of the maritime relationship with continental Europe. But the absence of a centralised Irish state proved disastrous in the following period for the evolving nation.

Medieval Irish ship, from *The book of Ballymote* (*c.* 1400), facsimile edition edited by Robert
Atkinson (Dublin, 1887).

4   Trade and Shipping on the Irish Sea in the Later Middle Ages

TIMOTHY O'NEILL

In this brief survey of traffic on the Irish Sea in the fourteenth and fifteenth centuries attention is focused on the activities of a group of individuals rarely mentioned by the political historians – the merchants and mariners of the ports.[1] These men were accustomed to the sea and ships, whereas the ordinary medieval traveller dreaded the sea and avoided long voyages, preferring instead the hazards of overland routes. This fear was due in part to shipboard conditions, the dangers of piracy and the risk of shipwreck.

The crossing of the Irish Sea was the longest sea voyage that most English and Irish officials, soldiers, clerics and messengers had to face. In contrast to the short hop across the English Channel the Irish Sea crossing meant at least a day and night sailing and often longer.

Giraldus Cambrensis wrote in the twelfth century, 'the Irish Sea surging with currents and that rush together is nearly always tempestuous so that even in summer it scarcely shows itself calm, even for a few days to them that sail'.[2] Symon Semeonis, travelling from Clonmel to Jerusalem, referred 'to the very stormy and dangerous Irish sea', which he crossed just before Easter 1323 and the Italian traveller and poet Fazio degli Uberti, writing *c.* 1360 must have had a rough passage as he wrote: 'Still varying winds with hiss and hideous roar blow thru that sea coasting the dangerous shoal of isles and monstrous rocks a mass confused'.[3]

Crossing from Ireland to England was usually easier, due to the prevailing winds, but the east–west voyage could be much more unpredictable. Laud's Annals tell of John Curcie who in 1204 'attempted fifteen times to sail over to Ireland but was always in danger and the wind evermore against him wherefore he waited awhile among the monks of Chester. At length he returned into France and there rested in the lord'. Richard Fitz Ralph, archbishop of Armagh, 1346–60, once commented that he knew

27

men who had to wait four months for a favourable crossing.[4] Far worse must have been the fate of those on board the wine ship which left Dalkey, the deepwater outport of Dublin, in November 1307 bound for Scotland. This vessel was blown around the northern Irish sea until 'about the feast of Epiphany' (6 January), by which time, we are told, the wines were gone bad,[5] while the condition of the crew can be left to the imagination.

In the early fourteenth century a great deal of traffic on the Irish Sea was directly concerned with the war in Scotland. The campaigns of Edward I and Edward II against the Scots were made possible by the constant supplies of men and provisions carried by ships along the North Sea coast of England and by convoys sailing north from Dublin and Drogheda to Skinburness (the port of Carlisle) or to Ayr. Ireland was one of the king's great storehouses of grain, if not the main one. In 1298, for example, 8000 quarters of wheat, 10000 quarters of oats and 2000 quarters of malt were purveyed and shipped from Ireland along with pigs, beef, fish and wine. Transport was provided by fleets of ships commandeered or arrested for the purpose.[6]

Commandeering was a common occurrence throughout the middle ages whenever shipping was required to bring men or supplies to or from the country. Although it must have caused a considerable disruption of normal trade, shipowners and sailors were usually paid when the period of service was over. From 1310 to 1312 the constable of a Drogheda ship was paid 12*d.* a day and thirty mariners received 3*d.* each day for twenty-four days naval service. Around the same time the master and constable of the *Aliceot* of Bristol were paid £30 in wages for a half years service 'to overcome the Scots and Irish . . . our felons and enemies by the sea coasts'. The owners of the *Aliceot* received a new mast, three cables and 'a large rope for rigging' when the ship was discharged.[7]

From the records of arrests of ships for major expeditions and convoys it is interesting to note the numbers of Irish ships commandeered. In 1301, 46 of the 74 vessels assembled at Dalkey were Irish and in 1303 about 37 of the 173 arrested were also from Irish ports.[8] Shipbuilding clearly went on in the Irish ports. Drogheda's murage grant of 1296 mentions tariffs on shipbuilding materials including masts, rigging ropes and canvas, coming to the town.[9] Shipbuilding expertise is evident in the many mandates issued by the king in the thirteenth, fourteenth and fifteenth centuries for the building of galleys. Six were ordered in 1234 and in 1241 the men of Dublin were ordered to build a new galley to go with the one they had. At the same time the citizens of Waterford were to build two and the men of Drogheda, Cork and Limerick, one each.[10] In 1408 carpenters were provided to work on the construction of a warship in Drogheda.[11] At other times local craftsmen were no doubt kept employed building the fishing vessels, lighters, ferryboats and river craft which are constantly mentioned in the records.

Towards the end of the fifteenth century some indication of the numbers of Irish ships plying the Irish sea routes emerges from the Bristol customs accounts. Wendy Childs found that over the decade 1480–89 at least 70 and probably 90 ships and at least 93 working shipmasters from Ireland were at Bristol and Bridgewater. There were about 30 more operating in the Chester trade according to that port's customs records. These figures show that Ireland was well provided with shipping on the two main trade routes across the Irish Sea to England.[12]

Throughout the period of the later middle ages Ireland's main export commodity was fish, particularly herring. There appear to have been two clear divisions in the herring trade: the fisheries of the Irish Sea, which were closely bound up with the ports of Dublin and north Leinster; and the herring fisheries off the south-western and western coasts, which were haven-based and where the crews of visiting Spanish and English fleets used the beaches to land and process their catches.

Herring were plentiful in the Irish Sea throughout the fourteenth and fifteenth centuries and there are many references to boats fishing for them. The Chester customs accounts show large consignments being shipped from Drogheda and the ports of County Dublin. Indeed herring was Ireland's chief export to Chester until the middle of the fifteenth century, while Chester's main export to Ireland at the time was salt. In the early sixteenth century the fisheries around Ardglass and Carlingford appear to have been particularly valuable. In 1535, for example, a fleet of 600 English fishing boats was in the area and the captains offered to help the lord treasurer, who was campaigning along the coast, by making available 3000 fighting men for two or three days.[13]

Second only to the fish trade was the export of cattle hides. The bulk of these were destined for the markets of continental Europe and only a relatively small proportion went to England. Hides were exported from all parts of the country and were carried in small boats as well as large Spanish and Hanseatic vessels. The trade was engaged in by English and foreign merchants in addition to merchants of the Irish ports. The main sources of records for this varied export trade are the calendars of patent and close rolls of England and Ireland. Although most of the entries from these sources refer to disputes about customs payments in English ports, whither ships had resorted owing to bad weather, pirates or war, they give details that indicate a regular and extensive trade in hides between Ireland and the continent, especially Flanders, in the fourteenth and fifteenth centuries.

A typical entry of this nature concerns the case of William White and Robert Lowys, both of Dundalk, who in 1339 loaded 1000 hides in a ship called the *Laurence* of Drogheda and, having paid the customs in Drogheda, sailed for Antwerp. Because of the king's enemies the ship was forced to come to London, where the hides were seized and William and Robert

asked to pay customs again. They protested at this and instructions came
from the king to check their letters of cocket which had been sealed by
customs officials at Drogheda. If these letters were in order, they were to be
allowed to proceed to Antwerp in a ship not chosen for the king's service.[14]
In Flanders there was a constant demand for leather to supply the needs of
the prosperous large towns of the area, which had become one of the chief
manufacturing regions of medieval Europe. Great quantities of Irish hides
also went to Pisa where, for example, in six months during 1466–7 nearly
34000 were imported and 24000 over the same period in 1482–3.[15]

Good profits of up to 30 percent could be made and returns like this
meant that large shipments were organised from all the major ports,
especially those skirting the Irish Sea. In 1353 merchants from Drogheda
loaded 3700 hides in a Spanish ship bound for Flanders. Another Drogheda
partnership was involved in an unusual incident in their home port in 1384.
These men had over 12000 hides on board three ships for export when they
found themselves left behind and the hides stolen. The cargo had been put
in the *Seyntemarie Knyght* of Gdansk, the *Christofre* of Campe (Flanders) and
the *Katheryne* of Bristol. Sailors on the Gdansk and the Flemish ships
expelled the merchants, robbed the *Katheryne* and sailed away, leaving the
Drogheda men very much poorer.[16]

Wine was another bulk trading commodity, which along with salt and
iron was medieval Ireland's chief import. The geographical accident which
placed the main supplies of western Europe's wine, salt and iron on the
shores of the Bay of Biscay was greatly to the advantage of medieval Irish
merchants and mariners who were able to organise round trips bringing out
hides, fish and corn and returning with wine, salt and iron if required.

Trading voyages were regulated by personal contacts between the
merchants and the shipmaster and agreements were reached beforehand as
to cargo, freight charges and destination. When, for example, some merchants of Chester planned in 1393 to send a ship to Bordeaux or La Rochelle
for wines to be brought back to Ireland, they stipulated that the ship was to
be unloaded and reloaded in Gascony within twenty-one days of arrival.
On the return journey the ship was to go to Dalkey and remain there for
three or four days while the merchants decided whether or not to go to
Drogheda.[17] The wine was shipped in tuns – huge 250 gallon wooden
barrels and consequently the freight charge was very high, averaging about
10 percent of the total cost. The ports of the southeast and east of Ireland
were more accessible for medieval ships sailing from Gascony than those of
the west of England and the records indicate that frequently wine ships
zig-zagged up the Irish Sea, with Waterford being a convenient first port of
call. Freight charges on the wineship *Trinity* of Ottermouth in 1394–5 were
as follows: to Waterford, 14s. a tun, to Dublin, 15s., to Drogheda, 16s., to
Beaumaris or Chester 18s.[18] The loading and unloading of the wine tuns

was a complicated task, and was especially difficult in Dublin and Drogheda where the ships were unable to berth at the quay side due to sandbanks
and silting. In Dublin the wine was transferred to small craft usually at
Dalkey and brought to the quay where the great crane hoisted the tuns onto
the quayside.

Salt and iron came in large shipments, especially in the fifteenth century.
Drogheda and Dublin merchants obtained special permission to buy and
offload from ships which anchored offshore and the Drogheda merchants
sometimes came as far south as Lambey Island for this purpose. In 1431
Italian and Aragonese merchants living in London loaded a Venetian
carrack, one of the largest type of medieval ships, with salt and iron in
Brittany to bring to Dublin, but the ship was seized in Plymouth.[19] John
Gayncote a merchant of Dartmouth combined with a group of Drogheda
merchants in 1435 in what must have been a very ambitious undertaking.
They secured a permit to bring from Brittany a fleet of eight 200 tun ships,
each crewed by up to forty men, with cargoes of salt, iron and other goods.
One reason, perhaps, for such a large undertaking was that salt imports
from Chester were dwindling towards the middle of the fifteenth century.[20]

The survival of the port towns in medieval Ireland depended on their
relations with the magnates of the neighbourhood but this was a mutual
dependence based on the exchange of commodities such as hides and fish
for wine, salt, iron and quality cloth. Drogheda merchants in particular had
frequent dealings with the Ulster Irish and their coastal trading voyages
were sometimes made more secure by safe-conducts which were negotiated
on their behalf by the archbishop of Armagh. Two Drogheda men rented
the Bann fisheries from the king in 1386.[21] In 1402 some burgesses sailed
north to purchase cattle for the meat store of the town while in the previous
year the mayor of Drogheda has been in the Carlingford area organising
supplies of firewood. Around the same time Dublin merchants ventured to
Lough Foyle and Lough Swilly and even as far as Ballyshannon.[22]

Apart from the wind and waves the major hazard for shipping on the
Irish Sea throughout the fourteenth and fifteenth centuries was the presence of pirates and rovers of one sort or another. Political historians have
dealt adequately with the disorder in the north Irish Sea during the Scottish
wars of Edward I and Edward II but the Scots still continued to menace
merchant shipping. To a large extent they were looking for food supplies,
and ransoms for captured ships were frequently paid in the form of victuals,
as illustrated by the case of John of Lyons. Around 1345 he was returning
from a trading voyage to Connacht and was driven by a storm to the
Scottish coast where his ship was captured by rebels. When hostages were
taken, John and his ship were sent to Drogheda to bring back food supplies
by way of ransom. When English ships were taken, similar demands were
made.[23]

After 1400 increasing numbers of Breton and Spanish pirates began to appear in the south Irish Sea. In 1442 Drogheda petitioned for money to repair its walls complaining that Spanish, Scottish and other rebels daily frequented the coast of Ireland destroying ships and merchants. The citizens of Waterford complained in the same year of attacks by enemies including Scots, Bretons and Spaniards.[24] Walter Dolman, a royal messenger, was captured by Bretons in the Irish Sea in August 1437. He spent twelve months in prison in Brittany and was freed on payment of a £200 ransom.[25]

The Scots demanded food by way of ransom but the Bretons were more interested in money and had evolved a system by which ransoms were paid that had quasi-legal standing. An incident in 1446 illustrates the procedures involved. A group that included two proctors of Llanthony priory was captured at sea by two Breton ships. The prisoners were divided between the ships and ransoms were agreed upon. Certain men became in effect hostages and were taken off to Brittany to be held until those who were freed raised all of the ransom money. One of these men, Davy Fleming, had to sue through parliament some of his companions who had been freed, since they did not pay the Bretons fully and he had to make up a substantial deficit in order to go free.[26]

As a result of the depredations of their fellow countrymen, Breton shipping was considered by some seafarers as 'fair game' and the Armagh registers provide a graphic eye-witness account of an unprovoked attack on three Breton vessels anchored in Drogheda harbour 1 July 1484. The crews had gone ashore *causa recreandi* when two Liverpool ships arrived and sent boarding parties to commandeer two of the Breton ships. Then they sailed away complete with their cargo of wine, salt and iron.[27]

In conclusion it can be said that although much of the evidence for Irish Sea trade in the later middle ages comes from records of legal proceedings that emphasise problems rather than prosperity, it is clear that the main participants, the merchants of the port towns, not only survived, but did well. The men of Dublin and Drogheda in particular, individually, and through their newly constituted guilds were among the most enterprising of medieval Irish merchants. They kept in touch with the general trading developments in western Europe and overcame the difficulties caused by the silting of their ports and the insecurity caused by frequent warfare on land and sea.

Shipping at Carrickfergus, County Antrim *c.* 1560, from a sixteenth century town map in the British Library (Cotton MS Augustus I, ii, 42).

5 Irish Sea Trades and Shipping from the Later Middle Ages to *c.* 1660

DONALD WOODWARD

Despite the poor survival of detailed customs records for Ireland during this period the broad outlines of trade with her mainland neighbours are well established. A narrow range of raw materials and semi-processed wares was exchanged for manufactured goods of bewildering variety and some raw materials not easily obtained from Irish sources, particularly coal. Within this framework new developments took place, especially among Irish exports in the early Stuart period, which reveal the increasingly commercialised nature of the Irish economy. Additionally there were two essentially 'invisible' trades: passengers and their personal possessions frequently crossed the Irish Sea but their movements were rarely noted by the English customs officials, while smuggling was practised up and down the coasts of the bordering countries. In the north east of Ireland, Scottish pedlars were said to take advantage 'of such creeks unguarded and swarm about the country in great numbers'.[1] As a result the customs records of England and Wales, which are invaluable for studying commercial activity in the Irish Sea, reveal only the minimum legitimate level of trade. Nevertheless, they show many of the numerous small vessels which shuttled across the narrow waters and scurried along the coasts of the four countries, carrying goods 'from port to port', although at the moment little is known about the Irish and Scottish coasting trades. However, a peep-hole is provided by the data relating to the Irish wine trade in 1614–15: 143 vessels carried wine into the country and there were 65 shipping movements of wine along the coast.[2]

During the sixteenth century the major Irish exports were fish, shipped in huge quantities from Wexford and the ports of south Munster, skins and hides, and linen yarn together with some timber and wool, and relatively small amounts of woollen cloth.[3] Among the cloth were the voluminous

35

mantles which were well enough known in England to be used for lighting effect by Shakespeare:

> But look, the morn in russet mantle clad,
> Walks o'er the dew of yon high eastern hill.
>   (Hamlet: Act 1, scene 1.)

Ports on both sides of the Irish Sea handled a variety of products although there was some specialisation: Drogheda was the chief exporter of linen yarn destined for the Lancashire textile industry, and sent mostly through Liverpool, while Dublin's major trading partner was Chester.[4] Among the Welsh ports only Milford conducted an extensive trade with Ireland; in the later sixteenth century timber products, mostly from Wexford, were exchanged for coal and some grain chiefly sent to Dublin and Wexford.[5] Bristol was the major port supplying consumer goods to Wexford and south Munster and received large quantities of fish, especially early in the century, and other products in return.[6] Other ports of south west England conducted some trade with Ireland although vessels rarely rounded the Lizard to trade with Exeter, Southampton or other south coast ports.[7]

In the absence of accurate annual statistics it is impossible to gauge fluctuations in the Irish Sea trades during the sixteenth century with any certainty, but it is difficult to believe that local feuding and attempts to increase the area of effective English control in Ireland, and the reactions which such activity stimulated, did not have a deleterious effect on trade from time to time. Scorched earth policies and the appropriation of flocks and herds must have reduced prosperity, but sixteenth-century warfare rarely caused massive structural damage to the economy and recovery could occur quite rapidly. Indeed there are signs of development in the Irish Sea trades. Shipments of coal from Milford expanded considerably during the second half of the century, and Irish trade at both Chester and Liverpool grew, at least down to the early 1590s, while Youghal enjoyed temporary prosperity 'as a port for the new plantation settlements in Munster'.[8] However, many of the ports of the south and southwest seem to have been in decline in the later sixteenth century, and this suggestion is reinforced by the relatively low level of Bristol's Irish trade compared with the early part of the century.[9] Difficulties in the southern trades were offset to some extent by the growing commerce of Dublin and Drogheda, although the evidence of the Chester and Liverpool port books suggests that the Nine Years War took a heavy toll on Irish exports. However, trade with the northern coast of Ireland was opened up with the establishment of Derry, first as headquarters of the English campaign in the north, in 1600, and subsequently as an important trading centre.[10]

Almost four decades of peace followed the settlement of 1603 in Ireland and the accompanying changes in the ownership and exploitation of Irish land helped to produce a remarkable transformation in the Irish Sea trades. The decline of the southern fishery continued,[11] but the export of four commodities – linen yarn, wool, timber, and livestock – grew substantially, marking a significant jump forward in the process of the commercialisation of the Irish economy: linen yarn poured into northwest England, a peak of 1553 packs or nearly 350 tons being recorded for 1638; wool exports especially from the ports of Munster helped to keep the looms of southwest England busy – a peak of just over 3.3 million lbs, or nearly 1500 tons of wool were shipped over in 1637; timber was consigned to England and the continent in increasing quantities; livestock, virtually a completely new trade in the seventeenth century, amounted to some 45600 cattle and 34800 sheep a year on the eve of the 1641 rising.[12] The enormous growth of trade is illustrated dramatically by the increasing number of ships employed: at Chester in 1602–3 67 vessels arrived from Ireland and 133 returned, whereas in 1639 no less than 574 vessels entered the Dee carrying Irish livestock; Minehead had very little trade with Ireland early in the century but in 1629–30 70 vessels arrived from Ireland, and 182 in 1636–7; Bristol's Irish trade grew more sedately – in 1636–7 117 vessels cleared for Ireland compared with less than 50 vessels a year in the early seventeenth century.[13] The Ulster port books for 1614–15 – rare survivals – show that 176 vessels cleared the ports of Carrickfergus, Coleraine and Derry, and that 207 vessels entered.[14]

Whether or not the expansion of exports raised the living standards of the majority of the Irish is open to question,[15] but there is no doubt that they demonstrate significant changes in the Irish economy. The extent of such change can be best illustrated by looking at the export of wool and other sheep products. In 1640–41, a year for which we have a full list of exports, wool shipments stood at 2728373 lbs and flocks at 5124 lbs.[16] By simply dividing those exports by the average weight of a fleece it should be possible to calculate the total number of sheep needed to fuel the export drive. Unfortunately, it is impossible at present to provide any estimate of Irish fleece sizes, but English fleeces are estimated to have averaged 1.9 lbs in the mid-sixteenth century while a Yorkshire farmer calculated the average weight of his fleeces at 2.33 lbs in the 1640s.[17] However, it is possible that the yield from Irish sheep was greater than that since their wool was coarse and they were sheared twice a year;[18] but it seems unlikely that Irish sheep produced more than 3 lbs of wool a year. Of course, if the average size of Irish fleeces was greater than 3 lbs a new calculation would be needed. If the total of wool and flocks exported is divided by the three estimates of fleece size the following results are obtained.

Table 1: Estimate of the Number of Sheep Providing Wool for Export from Ireland in 1640–41

Commodity	Amount	A ÷ 1.9	B ÷ 2.33	C ÷ 3.0
Wool	2728373	1435986	1170976	909458
Flocks	5124	2297	2199	1708
Total sheep		1438283	1173175	911166

In addition, substantial numbers of skins were exported together with a significant number of live sheep, which can be added to the notional sheep estimate – derived from Table 1.

A further adjustment is necessary to allow for the sheep which carried the wool used to produce the 279722 yards of frieze and 42870 dozen pairs of frieze stockings, together with some other cloths also exported in 1640–41. Thus, on the eve of the 1641 rising the produce of at least 1.5 million, and perhaps more than two million sheep was being exported from Ireland, together with large quantities of linen yarn, timber and timber products, and cattle.

Clearly Ireland, often thought of as a land teeming with cattle, housed vast numbers of sheep: both Fynes Moryson and Gerard Boate wrote of the large numbers of sheep in Ireland, and in 1672 Petty estimated that there were some four million sheep in the country although numbers had probably grown since the Restoration.[19] If, for sake of argument, there were four million sheep in Ireland in 1640 as many as 50 percent of them were helping to swell the export trade. The level of exports achieved for a number of commodities in the early seventeenth century, and especially during the 1630s, indicates an economy in which an increasing proportion of output was intended for the export market and suggests that Louis Cullen's belief about the high degree of commercialisation in eighteenth-century Ireland may have been true as early as the 1630s. We have been told recently that 'the communications system of Ireland at this time [*c.* 1600] was poor' and

Table 2: Estimate of the Number of Sheep Involved in the Export Trade in 1640–41

	Sheep Equivalents		
	A	B	C
Wool and flocks	1438283	1173175	911166
Sheepskins	311075	311075	311075
Lambskins	166775	166775	166775
Live sheep	34845	34845	34845
Total Sheep	1950978	1685870	1423861

that 'inland communication, notably by road, was notoriously bad'.[20] That may well have been the case, but internal communications were not sufficiently bad to preclude a massive and rapid commercialisation of the economy. Perhaps it is time to reconsider the suggestion that 'commercial activity was not, of course, central to Ireland's basically subsistence economy'.[21]

The rising of 1641 and the ensuing decade or more of political uncertainty brought the export boom of the 1630s to an abrupt halt. Difficulties in Ireland were exacerbated by the progress of the civil war in England, for both Bristol and Chester endured protracted sieges. Prendergast's belief that by 1650 Ireland 'was reduced to a howling wildnerness' is now accepted as unduly gloomy,[22] although the evidence to support an optimistic assessment is extremely sparse. Trade with Ireland was at a low ebb at both Chester and Minehead,[23] and no doubt had fallen at other ports. However, it is likely that a recovery in trade had begun to set in by the mid-1650s. By the end of that decade Bristol's trade was getting back to normal – eighty-three ships arrived from Ireland in 1658–9 and ninety-two the following year. Overall the high level of exports achieved in the early 1660s indicates recovery from some point in the mid to late 1650s.

A marked feature of the Irish Sea trades before 1641 was the dominant rôle played by Irish merchants: Dublin merchants controlled the bulk of Chester's Irish trade, while at Bristol Irish merchants played a very important part in the trade with their own country. Drogheda merchants controlled the bulk of the town's trade with Liverpool; and Irish merchants in general seem to have dominated most branches of the livestock trade.[24] It was only in a few trades that the Irish merchants did not have the whip-hand. By far the most significant of these was the coal trade which was controlled largely by the masters of vessels on their own accounts. Often they were also part-owners and it was common practice for most of the cattle boats entering the Dee to call at local staithes and load a cargo of coal before the return crossing to Dublin.[25]

It is possible that the Irish merchants were allowed to dominate the Irish Sea trades because English merchants were preoccupied with the more lucrative continental trades. This suggestion is supported by the appearance of a small number of lower-ranking English tradesmen in the Irish trade from time to time.[26] However, much more important was the ability of the Irish merchants, especially those in the larger ports, to control the trade by operating various restrictive practices and by securing freedom from customs payments.[27] As O'Donovan put it:

> Many of the great ports only allowed their own privileged citizens to buy from or sell to strangers, and, even when outsiders were not actually forbidden to trade directly with one another, they had to face tolls and customs and restricting regulations. In other words, the freemen of those cities were middlemen with a legal monopoly.[28]

Julian Walton's recent study of the Waterford merchant community paints a picture of a powerful and privileged oligarchy of long-established families of Norman or Old English origin exercising a tight grip on the affairs of their own city.[29] His article is a fine pioneering work which could be followed with advantage for other ports. Although not specifically stated, Walton implies that the merchants were also firmly in control of the city's sea-borne trade. That aspect of their activities could be explored through overseas customs records and especially through the English port books. Clearly, before 1641 'merchants were a prominent and powerful element in Ireland' and the merchants of Cork, Galway and Limerick, along with those of Waterford, 'were almost exclusively catholic and Old English'.[30]

Few historians have studied the ownership and operation of the vessels engaged in the Irish Sea trades. As a result, the discussion which follows is essentially fragmentary and unsatisfactory, although the information currently available suggests that Irish vessels rarely dominated any branch of the trade – other than the Irish coasting trade – during the sixteenth and seventeenth centuries. In the fifteenth century Irish shipping showed up well: at Bristol 'Irish vessels . . . took a far larger share in the business than did those of Bristol, which concerned themselves mainly with more distant traffic', and in 1479–80 Irish vessels accounted for 40 percent of the arrivals from Ireland, and 52 percent of clearances; similarly, between 1450 and 1480 Irish vessels comprised over half of the vessels entering the Dee from Ireland.[31] Thereafter Irish shipping collapsed in the northern trade: Irish vessels accounted for less than a quarter of the vessels entering the Dee from Ireland in the 1490s and the proportion of Irish vessels rose over 15 percent in only one decade between the 1500s and the 1560s. A low point was reached in the 1550s when there were only eighteen Irish entries out of 938 vessels for which the port of provenance is known.[32] However, Irish vessels returned to the Dee in larger numbers during Elizabeth's reign: in 1576–7 Irish vessels accounted for 41 percent of entrances which rose to 50 percent in 1589, although in six other years in the last two decades of the reign Irish vessels accounted for less than a third of entrances and in three of those years they were less than a quarter. In the return trade Irish vessels featured less prominently – in eight years between 1576–7 and 1602–3 Irish vessels accounted for a peak of just over a third of the clearances in one year, but in three years they were less than 20 percent.[33] Unfortunately the recent study of Bristol's trade is silent on the subject of the ports of provenance of vessels,[34] but Lewis's transcription of the Welsh port books reveals some interesting information for Milford, the most important of the Welsh ports trading with Ireland. In five out of six years towards the end of Elizabeth's reign, starting in 1586–7, more than half of the vessels arriving from Ireland were Irish and they accounted for over 90 percent of entrances in three of those years. In the return trade Irish vessels were less dominant, accounting for a little over 50 percent of clearances in three years and over 40 percent in two years. However, these figures exaggerate the importance of the Irish vessels to some extent since most of them were very small with an average burthen of less than ten tons.[35]

It has been suggested that the shipping of the south Munster ports declined in the later years of Elizabeth's reign; that may be true but the evidence of the Chester and Milford port books shows that Ireland was by no means denuded of shipping. For the seventeenth century, evidence is equally fragmentary. Thirty-one vessels, or slightly less than a third of those arriving in Ireland with wine in 1614–15 were Irish: of the twenty-eight vessels involved (some made two appearances) six were from Waterford and five from Drogheda. But if Irish vessels were not dominant in the import trade they completely swept the board in the coasting trade: sixty-three of the sixty-five vessels recorded in 1614–15 were Irish.[36] Thus, if Irish vessels were as active in other branches of the Irish coasting trade, native shipping interests were greater than appears from the evidence of the English port books. The use of local, native vessels was also a prominent feature of the English coasting trade where Irish vessels rarely featured. The Ulster port books for 1614–15 show that once again Irish vessels made a relatively poor showing in overseas trade: they accounted for 24 percent of the clearances of vessels for which the port of provenance is known and 14 percent of entrances.

Table 3: Vessels Trading with Ulster, 1614–15

	Scotland	Isle of Man	Wales	North-west England	Southern England	Foreign	Ireland	Uncertain	Total
To Ireland	110	2	2	25	13	2	25	34	213
From Ireland	129	2	2	40	11	2	60	19	265

In addition, many of the vessels listed as 'uncertain' in the table were probably Scottish, referred to in the port books as 'small boat'.

In the livestock trades Irish vessels played an important but rarely dominant role. At Chester in 1614–15 and 1634 Irish vessels accounted for about 20 percent of livestock cargoes, although it is clear that all nearby shipping resources were being stretched by the rapid growth of the trade; in 1634 Scottish vessels were needed to carry 48 percent of the livestock cargoes. Five years later Irish vessels made a better showing – the 131 Irish vessels which entered the Dee carried 29 percent of livestock cargoes. In the early 1660s Irish vessels carried nearly a third of the livestock cargoes arriving at Minehead, but they carried only 15 percent of the cargoes arriving at Ilfracombe in 1662, and a mere 3 percent of those entering the Mersey in 1665.[37]

Most of the vessels engaged in the Irish Sea trade were small: vessels trading out of the Dee were generally between 15 and 30 tons burthen, and in 1634 the average carrying capacity of vessels carrying livestock into the estuary was just over 20 tons.[38] In some trades vessels were even smaller. Irish vessels trading with Milford in the later part of Elizabeth's reign had an average burthen of under eight tons whereas the Welsh vessels averaged 15 tons. As a result, Irish vessels carried an average cargo of just under fifty barrels of coal to Ireland, compared with the 107 barrels carried by the Welsh vessels.[39] Many of the very small Irish vessels were from Wexford where the harbour bar was said to preclude entry by large vessels, although the Welsh port books record a few Wexford ships of more than 20 tons.[40] Some Irish vessels were much larger: three Waterford vessels arrived home in 1615 carrying 136 tons of sack; the *Francis* of Galway carried 103 tons of sack; and the *Peter* of Derry – a vessel of 70 tons – was recorded in the same year.[41] However most of the vessels in the Irish Sea trades were like that which carried Sir William Brereton to Ireland in 1635: he crossed from Port Patrick 'in a bark of about fifteen ton' which was 'a good sailing vessel' although the master took on too many horses and passengers so that 'we had not every man his own length allowed to lie in at ease'. The weather turned very nasty as the vessel approached Ireland so that the passengers suffered 'a wet cold lodging' lying out 'in this open boat'. A fair wind allowed vessels to cross the Irish Sea in a day or so; Brereton believed that Wexford 'is about twenty-four hours' sail from Bristol' and he enjoyed 'a quick, pleasant, and dainty passage' on his return from Ireland – 'within twenty-six hours after we parted with Ireland, the utmost point I mean of Irish shore, we were landed at Minehead in Somersetshire'.[42]

Despite such speedy crossings, the pace of commerce in the Irish Sea trades – as in most contemporary trades – remained slow. Vessels spent long periods in port, hanging around for the cargo to be discharged or sold off, waiting to accumulate a return cargo, or simply hoping for an improvement in weather conditions. As a result, many vessels made only a few crossings each year.[43] The operation of pirates and the possibility of shipwreck built further uncertainties into the system. For much of the period the Irish Sea was the haunt of pirates from the four countries, who were frequently joined by continental marauders, and raids by 'Turkish galleys' were not unknown in southern Ireland. In 1630 it was claimed that 'Egypt was never more infested with caterpillars than the Land's End with Biscayners',[44] although Strafford's exertions against pirates in the 1630s probably had beneficial results, if only temporarily. Many vessels were also 'dashed all in pieces' in foul weather,[45] but these problems were not as serious as we may imagine and the great majority of vessels arrived safely at their destinations with their cargoes intact.

It has been suggested here that, although Irish merchants frequently played a dominant rôle in the Irish Sea trades, Irish shipping usually took a back seat. These conclusions – especially that relating to the provision of shipping – are tentative, based as they are on fragmentary evidence, and clearly there is scope for much more work in both of these areas. A start has been made by Walton's study of the Waterford merchants, but most ships remain all at sea, waiting to be spied by willing historians. However, if these conclusions are correct,we need to ask why Irish shipping so often played a minor rôle in the bilateral Irish Sea trades. Did conditions in Ireland render investment in shipping unattractive to her merchants or did other factors preclude a more diffused investment in shipping?

In England wealthy merchants frequently owned, or part-owned, the vessels which carried their goods to and from the continent, but smaller vessels, such as those that predominated in the Irish Sea trades, were frequently owned – at least in part – by the men who took them to sea. This phenomenon has been studied in depth only for the Dee estuary: there in the later sixteenth and early seventeenth centuries a fleet of some two dozen vessels, mostly between 15 and 30 tons burthen, crossed and recrossed the Irish Sea. Many of the master-owners of those vessels, who lived on the Wirral, were also farmers, although their investment in vessels – valued at perhaps £80 to £100 or more for a vessel of 20–30 tons – set them apart from their land-based neighbours.[46] Turning to Ireland we may surmise that the merchants of the larger ports invested in the more substantial ships which participated in the longer-distance trades, leaving others to invest in the smaller vessels common in the Irish Sea trades. Townsmen of lesser status and wealth may have been able to aspire to ownership of tiny vessels, like those of the Wexford fleet or perhaps the *Margaret* of Holywood, burthen 9 tons, which in April 1615 sailed from Lecale for Workington with 60 barrels of oats.[47] However, it is problematic whether or not there were men outside the larger towns, living up and down the Irish coast with the resources and willingness to invest in shipping like the men of the Wirral. Possibly there were not, or perhaps investors in shipping were not present in such large numbers as in England, or indeed in Scotland and Wales. If that was the case should the town merchants be blamed for not investing more heavily in shipping? This would be unfair, for, as has been demonstrated, the pace of trade was leisurely, vessels spent long periods in port not earning any profit, and it seems likely that Irish merchants – like their counterparts in England – refused to invest heavily in small vessels because they offered a poor return. Instead they bought the shipping services they needed in the cheapest market available. If that was the case, Irish merchants were acting rationally, although the relatively low levels of investment generally in Irish shipping may have stored up long-term problems for the Irish economy. A further possibility is that the activities of Irish merchants in the land market – as at Waterford – absorbed funds which might otherwise have been invested in shipping.[48]

Although the general picture of the Irish Sea trades during the sixteenth and seventeenth centuries is well established there is plenty of scope for research on related issues. In particular more work needs to be done on the nature of the early Stuart export boom and on commercial development within the Irish economy, together with further investigation of communities and the provision of shipping. Many questions remain to be answered. Did Irish shipping collapse generally in the later fifteenth century as the Chester data suggest? If so, why? Was the partial recovery of Irish shipping seen in the Chester records of the later sixteenth century common throughout the Irish Sea trades? To what extent did Irish merchants invest in shipping? Who owned the small vessels which fill the pages of the English and Welsh port books? How many vessels belonged not only to each Irish port, but also to those on the shores and fringes of the Irish Sea in England, Scotland and Wales?

Shipping at Londonderry, from *The Copper Plate Magazine*, Vol. 1, 1793.

6 Merchants and Mariners, Pirates and Privateers:

an introductory survey of the records of the High Court of Admiralty as a source for regional maritime history, c. 1500–1800

JOHN APPLEBY

I. Background

The origins of the English high court of admiralty are shrouded in obscurity. Although the court was probably established during the fourteenth century to deal with cases of piracy and spoil, its jurisdiction seems to have been limited and its existence intermittent. For most of the fifteenth century its business was trifling, and few records survive of its activities. In the early sixteenth century, however, the court was re-established on a permanent basis: it has continued to sit regularly from the 1530s almost to the present day, though since 1873 it has sat as a division of the high court of justice.[1]

By the sixteenth century the court was also claiming an extensive jurisdiction, if, on occasion, this was only vaguely implemented. Geographically it included the territorial waters of the state, as defined at any particular time, which was extended to cover criminal actions by citizens thereof on the high seas (although in many cases of petty crime, and even on occasion more serious matters such as mutiny, action was often directly taken at sea by the captain and senior officers). For much of its early history the jurisdiction of the high court in London over-lapped with, and was rivalled by, local admiralty courts such as those at Bristol or Southampton; admiralty courts in Ireland and Scotland; and other legal institutions which claimed some right to adjudicate on matters relating to the sea. In the long term the high court of admiralty in London was to eclipse local courts, yet it is evident from the published volumes of the Southampton admiralty court, for example, that local jurisdictions retained their vigour –

47

possibly well into the seventeenth century. The situation is rather more complex in Ireland, where a court of admiralty was established in Dublin during the 1570s, but with limited powers and jurisdiction. Although the Dublin court was certainly active during the later sixteenth and seventeenth centuries, few records survive of its activities, and in many cases Irish merchants and shipowners seem to have preferred using the high court in London. In Scotland a separate court of admiralty survived at least until the early nineteenth century, although little is known of its early history. A recent paper by Eric Graham suggests that before 1672 the business of the court was small and its legal infrastructure unsophisticated. Under the impact of the Dutch wars in the later seventeenth century, however, the court was transformed, especially as an agency for the control and regulation of privateering.[2] The Scottish court, unlike its counterpart in Ireland, continued to function as a prize tribunal until 1809 when its jurisdiction was taken over by the high court in London.

There are, then, a number of overlapping, sometimes competing legal institutions whose surviving records contain much that is of value to the historian of the Irish Sea basin. This paper is concerned with only one such institution, the high court of admiralty in London, which emerged as the pre-eminent court of maritime law within Britain and Ireland during the seventeenth century.

The jurisdiction of the high court is usually sub-divided into two divisions: *Instance* and *Prize*. The *Instance* division covers criminal proceedings, including piracy, murder, theft and other offences committed at sea such as mutiny, rape or sodomy. It also covers 'civil' proceedings, relating to such matters as collision, salvage, wreck or disputes over freight contracts. As its title implies, the *Prize* division concerns the regulation and control of privateering. Although the *Instance* jurisdiction of the court came under increasing attack in the early seventeenth century from common lawyers eager to muscle in on a profitable business, the *Prize* jurisdiction went from strength to strength. By the 1620s, indeed, the high court of admiralty was a prize tribunal of international significance; by the eighteenth century much of its business, as evidenced by its voluminous records, was taken up with prize matters.

The distinction between the *Instance* and *Prize* business of the court was formally recognised in the mid-seventeenth century. It should also be noted that there was a marked difference in procedure between different divisions of the court's jurisdiction. 'Criminal' proceedings were conducted in accordance with the common law – before a judge and jury, with witnesses liable to cross-examination – whereas 'civil' and *Prize* cases were determined according to the civil law, with proctors and advocates presenting written examinations and depositions before the admiralty judge, who presided without a jury.

II. The nature and extent of the records

The records of the high court of admiralty form an enormous archive of material which, since the late 1850s, has been housed in the Public Record Office in Chancery Lane. The archive is sub-divided into more than sixty classifications, spanning the period from the early sixteenth century to the 1950s.[3] The bulk of this material is the surviving sediment of cases heard before the court. Any one case could generate a number of different documents, including: a 'libel', or allegation, setting out the case for the plaintiff in a series of detailed articles; an 'answer', in which the defendant's response is set out; 'depositions', containing the examinations of witnesses on behalf of the parties to a suit; and miscellaneous 'exhibits', including ship's papers, charter parties and letters used as evidence in a case. Action taken by the court is similarly documented in a wide variety of material, including 'sentences', 'warrants', or 'monitions' (ordering the arrest or stay of a vessel, for example).

This documentary evidence survives in a variety of forms – bound volumes, bundles, boxes, parcels and files – and is in varying degrees of preservation. Its accumulation, especially for the period before *c*. 1650, occurred in a rather piecemeal fashion; consequently there is a certain degree of confusion and overlapping between the different classifications. The miscellaneous section (H.C.A. 30), for example, contains a mass of unsorted, uncalendared material which never found its way into the correct file. This includes a number of vice-admiralty accounts for Ireland for the 1620s and 1630s, which cast revealing light on the nature of wreck and other sea perquisites at the time. Nevertheless the classification of the court's records (from H.C.A. 1 to 62) tends to reflect real functional differences, which became clearer during the seventeenth and eighteenth centuries.

The 'depositions' (H.C.A. 13), which form the basis of many of the subsequent examples in this paper, are perhaps the most interesting and accessible of the court's records. They survive in an almost unbroken sequence from 1536 to *c*. 1750. Those taken in court are bound in volumes of ever-increasing size; those taken out of court are loosely kept in bundles or rolls, in boxes. The depositions cover an immense range of cases – from the predictable disputes over freight or vessel ownership to the more esoteric cases of slander or fraud. They form a vast treasure-house of material which sheds light on nearly every aspect of contemporary maritime life and conditions. Moreover, as the depositions were usually taken down from deponents verbatim, they often present a vivid, racy account of events through the eyes of the participants themselves. For this reason, of course, they need to be used with some caution: witnesses giving evidence months (sometimes years) after a voyage had ended, were often muddled or confused in their recall of events. In criminal cases this confusion may have been deliberate. Depositions relating to piratical offences present particularly difficult problems as allegation and counter- allegation, as to who was aboard a pirate ship and who was not, and special pleading by mariners (and others) claiming that they were forced to serve aboard such vessels, thicken the files of the court.

III. Subject material

(a) Fishing

The records of the high court of admiralty contain a variety of cases concerning fishing ventures in the Irish Sea, or on its northern and southern fringes. A lengthy deposition from 1567 presents a very interesting picture of the organisation of the fishery, involving the election of an 'admiral' who was responsible for the regulation of the season's fishing, and of levying fines on offenders.[4] On this occasion a dispute had blown up between the fishermen and local admiralty officials at Aberystwyth, who alleged that the admiral had infringed their authority and jurisdiction. This was resolutely denied by Thomas Beaple of Barnstaple, admiral of the fishermen during the year in question, who claimed that they had a customary right (as old as human memory) to fish at Carlingford, Strangford, the Isle of Man, Workington, Drogheda, Aberdovey and various other places. No doubt Beaple was right, but very little evidence now survives of this prosaic but vitally important activity (at least for the pre-modern period); it is only when a dispute arose, which had to be settled by the high court, that glimpses of the organisation and structure of the fishery can be obtained.

Other depositions point to the international character of the fisheries within the Irish Sea, with French fishermen sailing alongside fishing vessels from Dublin at Carlingford in the 1550s.[5] In general, however, many of the cases before the court tend to be of English fishermen exploiting the coastal waters of Ireland. For example, during December 1578 an English ship was captured by pirates as she was fishing in Waterford harbour. Fifty years later, in October 1628, the *Angel* of Liverpool was likewise taken near Waterford by a French man-of-war. The *Angel* had left Liverpool on 'fishing fare' with fifty-five barrels of salt, fourteen pairs of nets and £12 in cash: she was hardly a rich prize, though to her owners the loss might have been considerable – the more so as many of these small fishing ventures do not seem to have been insured.[6]

Further evidence of the organisation of these ventures is provided by the voyage of the *John* of Plymouth to the coast of Ireland in 1578. The ship was owned by John Langford, who was to have a sixth of the catch; the remainder was to be kept by the master (who had victualled and manned the vessel), and was presumably to be shared out among the crew. The flexibility of these arrangements, however, is revealed by the presence of a servant of Langford's aboard the ship who was to fish for himself.[7]

Of course these are random survivals, reflecting the nature and limitations of the court's records. Yet they provide important pointers to the scale and character of fishing activity within the Irish Sea, indicating some of the main fishing grounds, for a period for which very little other evidence survives.

(b) Trade and shipping

The same point could well be made for trade and shipping, although here the survival of customs accounts for English, Welsh and Scottish ports (and a small number for Irish ports) provides a much fuller and surer guide. While the records of the admiralty court contain numerous references to trade in the Irish Sea, especially between England and Ireland, they do not provide any statistical guide to its scale or extent.

Even so the court's records can be used as an important supplement to the port books and customs accounts; identifying merchants, filling out the pattern of voyaging and shedding light on the character and conduct of trade which is sometimes only partially revealed in port books, whose survival, in any case, is patchy. At the same time they also provide some indication of the disruptions caused to commerce by the depredations of pirates and privateers.

The Irish Sea basin was, at one and the same time, both a focus and highway for commercial activity, though the distinction could often be blurred in individual voyages. During the 1550s, for example, the *Jesus* of London was bound on a voyage thence to Lough Swilly; on the way she put into the Isle of Man to take on more men and a lading of Gascon wine, salt and broadcloth. Approaching Lough Foyle, however, she was seized and carried off to Rathlin Island by a French man-of-war. A more complex pattern of enterprise is revealed by a venture involving the *Henry* of Derry in 1638. The *Henry* was a Flemish-built vessel of 60 tons, owned, and on this occasion chartered, by Henry Finche of Derry for a voyage from London to Bordeaux to lade wines for Dublin and Derry, where, on the vessel's arrival, a cargo of tallow was laded aboard for England. It is a sign of the growing dangers to trade during the 1630s, and perhaps of increasingly sophisticated business techniques, that the cargo was insured in London.[8]

Alongside this increasingly complex commercial pattern, however, cross-channel trade between Britain and Ireland seems to have retained its vigour. Typical of many such ventures was the voyage of a Liverpool bark in 1594, freighted by Patrick Cashel of Dundalk, with a cargo of hops, madder, alum, sugars, spices and mercery wares, including hats, pots and glasses. Most of these goods, incidentally, were carried overland from

London to Liverpool to be shipped for Dundalk.[9] Wider merchant involvement is evident in the *Recovery* of Bristol, bound to Cork in November 1606 with a lading of beer, broadcloth, kersey, frieze, hops, glue, iron ware, knives, stockings, hats and woollen cards, as well as £40 in cash. This miscellaneous parcel of goods, which was valued at £800, was owned by Richard Gould, James Tirry, John Roche, Dominic Creagh, Jaspar Meagh and others of Cork.[10] Occasionally the articles of trade cast interesting and revealing light on contemporary social conditions: among a long list of goods bound to Ireland for the earls of Clanricard and Thomond in 1604 were three fowling pieces, a fiddle, two pairs of virginals and a wolf trap.[11]

Evidence of the character and structure of this short cross-channel trade is sometimes revealed in merchants' instructions to servants or factors. Thus James Welch, a young servant to James Burne, a Dublin merchant, was sent aboard the *Harry* of Padstow, bound to London in May 1625 with a cargo of aquavitae, neat's tongues, cloves and pepper, with instructions 'to sell them by the way comeinge for London, yf he could meete with a good markett for them'. On the way, unfortunately, the *Harry* was seized by Captain Quaile, an English pirate. The surviving evidence for the voyage of the *Mayflower* of Derry, in February 1622, is equally revealing of the conditions of this trade. The ship left Derry on 21 February bound for London with a cargo of beef, tallow and hides. Her company consisted of a crew of eight and one passenger. These included John Sadler of Derry, aged 35, the owner of the vessel; John Betson of Coleraine, mariner, the ship's master; John Knocke of Culmore, mariner, aged about 27; Patrick Ray of Derry, sailor, aged about 26; as well as three other mariners and a boy. The ensuing voyage, however, was a catalogue of disasters. On 24 February a storm blew up which lasted, according to Betson, for nearly two weeks. During the storm the *Mayflower* lost her rudder: with the ship dangerously 'driveing to and froe' Sadler was forced to cast some of the cargo overboard. Three days later they managed to reach Douglas, on the Isle of Man, where the rudder was repaired. Ten days later the *Mayflower* was able to continue her voyage; more foul weather forced her into Holyhead, where another ten days were lost as the crew waited for conditions to improve. When the voyage continued the ship was boarded off the Isle of Wight by a French man-of-war, and plundered of a barrel of beef. By the time Margate was sighted the crew discovered that the rudder was not 'well hanged', and further repairs were necessary to get the ship safely up to London. Overall, the voyage must have taken three to four weeks, during which time part of the lading was either thrown overboard or sold off to pay for repairs and extra provisions. Even short-distance trades were subject to the vagaries of weather and the perils of capture by pirates or privateers.[12]

It will be apparent, even from these brief references, that the records of the court contain much of value on shipping and shipowning. The size and ownership of vessels are usually indicated in the depositions, though with the exception of a Dublin man-of-war of the 1550s, there are very few descriptions of vessels. More interestingly, there are few references to shipbuilding. In Ireland this might possibly be a reflection of the small scale of the industry, and an apparent dependence on the purchase of vessels built elsewhere. The admiralty records contain evidence of the purchase of an English ship at Waterford in 1596, a Flemish-built vessel at Youghal in 1623, and a Dutch-built herring buss at Dunkirk in 1637 for the two Derry merchants Henry Finche and Henry Osborne. The *Mary Providence* of Cork, built near Bristol in 1622, was bought by Daniel Gookin, gentleman, of Carrigaline and Richard Kensam, mariner, of Gatcombe. Each man owned a half share. Not long after this purchase, however, Kensam sold off his interest in the ship to Gookin, who later fitted the vessel out for a Virginia voyage.[13] One of the earliest references to shipbuilding in Ireland among the court's records dates from 1640, and concerns the *Lion* of Fairlie which had been arrested at Portsmouth as a Scottish vessel, but which the master claimed had been built at Belfast, and was owned by Thomas Scott of Ballywalter, county Down.[14]

(c) The maritime community

The admiralty records are a rich, as yet almost totally unexploited, source for a socio-economic survey of the maritime community in general. The examinations of mariners, merchants and shipowners give insights into conditions of life at sea, besides providing evidence of their commercial activities and interests. In particular this neglected resource is a useful basis for establishing profiles of seafaring and merchant communities which fringed the Irish Sea, and about whose structure and character in the post-medieval period all too little is known.[15]

James Macconnell of Groomsport, County Down, was probably typical of many others who made their living on the margin of the Irish Sea. Although he had lived at Groomsport for about thirty years, his background was clearly Scottish. According to his deposition of 1639 he was owner and master of a small bark called the *Katherine*, which was usually employed in trafficking between Ireland and Chester, and other parts of north west England. This regular pattern was occasionally interrupted by voyages to France or, as in 1637, by fishing voyages to the coast of Scotland.

About the same time another case before the court sheds interesting light on the activities of some of the new English merchant community in Carrickfergus. This concerned a commercial venture involving John Parks, a young English merchant, aged about thirty, who came from Gloucestershire but who was now resident in Carrickfergus, and his kinsman Hercules Horseman. In February 1639 these two merchants laded a cargo of hides, tallow, butter and beef aboard the *Gift of God*, a Scottish ship, in Carrickfergus. Cormac Boyland, a local butcher and servant to Parks, was employed in barrelling up the beef, and accompanied his master when the ship sailed for England. In addition to the cargo of Parks and Horseman, the ship also carried one hogshead of linen yarn for the account of Alexander Thompson, a Belfast merchant. Subsequently these goods were sold in Falmouth, Dartmouth and London.[16]

The enduring link between kinship and business enterprise is indicated by the voyage of the *Elizabeth* of Topsham in 1635. The ship was set out by Hugh Crocker, a merchant of Exeter, who owned half of the cargo of 'sack' and salt; the other half was owned by his kinsman, Christopher Crocker, a merchant of Waterford. The ship was bound for Dublin where another kin relation, Edward Crocker of Dungarvan, acted as factor for the two merchants. From Dublin the *Elizabeth* sailed to Youghal where she laded a miscellaneous cargo of goods which is summarised below in Table 1.

The impression conveyed by much of this evidence is, admittedly, often a rather static one, more like a snapshot than a moving picture. A different perspective is provided by three depositions from the early sixteenth century, concerning migration within or across the Irish Sea. They include: William Butler, aged about forty, born in Kinsale, who gave his place of residence in 1537 as Exmouth, where he had lived for fourteen years; Richard Elliott, aged about sixty, born in Waterford, who had resided in London and Fowey before moving to Fareham in Hampshire; and Jerman Kelly, aged about twenty-six, born in Carrickfergus, who had lived in Chester, but who was resident in London at the time of his examination in 1539. Such examples of extensive migration may have been a typical feature of many members within the maritime community though they also provide an interesting contrast with the long-term settlement of Macconnell at Groomsport.[17]

Table 1: The cargo of the *Elizabeth* of Topsham

	Value		
	£	s.	d.
Barrels of butter	328	13	0
214 bundles of frieze	5	7	0
1½ dozen of cloth stockings		13	6
7 casks of tallow	20	2	2
1 hogshead of salmon	4	15	0
15 barrels of tallow	56	2	9
12 barrels of beef	16	0	0
11 hides	4	0	0

Source: Public Record Office, H.C.A. 13/52, ff 350-51ᵛ; 13/54, ff 79ᵛ–80.

The court's records thus provide a wealth of material relating to the interests and activities of merchants and mariners. Of course, any profile of Irish Sea maritime communities can hardly be restricted to the confines of that stretch of water, for merchants and others were usually engaged in a diversity of commercial enterprises which, as in the case of Nicholas Weston, a leading Dublin merchant of the late sixteenth and early seventeenth centuries, might range from cross-channel trade with England or Wales to participation in the transatlantic fishery at Newfoundland.[18] Among the miscellaneous prize papers of the court there survives a letter book of Walter Butler, master and owner of the *Catherine* of Waterford, which was regularly engaged in the Newfoundland fishery from *c.* 1750 to her capture by a French privateer in 1757. Butler bought the *Catherine*, a 'brigg', towards the end of 1750. The following year she was engaged in a venture to Placentia in Newfoundland, sailing thence again in 1752 and 1754. In between these years she was involved in trading voyages to Spain and Portugal.[19] The short career of the *Catherine* raises interesting questions concerning the flexibility of commercial enterprise, and underlines the necessity of trying to relate enterprise both in and beyond the Irish Sea, especially when viewed from a mercantile, or entrepreneurial perspective.

(d) Privateering and piracy

Most of the material presented so far is of an incidental, indirect nature, which arose during the course of a legal dispute before the court. More direct evidence is provided for the subjects of privateering and piracy: indeed the admiralty records are an essential source for any study of privateering based in England, Wales or Ireland. From the early sixteenth to the early nineteenth century, much of the work of the court was devoted to the supervision, regulation and control of privateering. While these controls grew in sophistication over the period, the basic means of regulation were established fairly early on. Thus, during the sixteenth century the licensing of private men-of-war, through the issue of letters of reprisal (or marque) was regularised, together with the formal adjudication of prizes by the judge of the court. The growth of these regulations produced a vast amount of documentation which can be exploited in a number of ways.

Among the more important of such materials are the letter of marque bonds (H.C.A. 25) and the letter of marque declarations (H.C.A. 26). The former run from 1549 to 1815 (in more than 230 bundles) and contain details of ship's name, tonnage, armament and crew size. From 1689 the bonds overlap with the letter of marque declarations, which run until 1808 and contain similar material.

From this raw material it is possible to analyse the scale, incidence and nature of privateering from the sixteenth through to the nineteenth centuries – either nationally, regionally or locally. It has been so used by K. R. Andrews for the Elizabethan period and David Starkey for the eighteenth century, while Louis Cullen has provided lists of privateers operating from Ireland from 1744 to 1746 and 1756 to 1758.[20] In addition, it is also possible to reconstruct the business operations of individual adventurers. Table 2, for example, provides details of privateers set out by Waddell Cunningham, the great merchant magnate of Belfast, from 1777 to 1781 when letters of marque were being issued against France, Spain, the United Provinces and America. Occasionally the declarations also provide a brief description of the vessel: the *Irish Volunteer*, for example, was 'schooner-rigged [and] Irish built'; the *Harlequin* was 'American built'; while the *Peace and Plenty* was 'galley built'.[21]

Belfast and Dublin emerge as the leading privateering ports along the east coast of Ireland during this period, although all along the coast merchants and shipowners hastened to set out privateers. Waterford, Drogheda, Newry, Strangford and Downpatrick were all engaged in this activity, as were ports on the other side of the Irish Sea – most notably Liverpool.[22] While some of these men-of-war may have been active locally, a survey of privateering will take us well beyond the confines of the Irish Sea. Cunningham's man-of-war, *Peace and Plenty*, for example, was bound from Belfast to Halifax in Newfoundland in 1777, laden with a cargo of checks and other 'Manchester' goods, shoes, boots, hats, salt and earthenware.[23] Nevertheless the role of privateering as a form of enterprise, its impact on mercantile investment, its relationship with trade and shipbuilding within the Irish Sea, or the connection (if any) between privateering and freight/insurance rates would be worthy of further investigation.

Alongside such details of the privateering effort it is also possible to analyse the type of prizes taken, and identify their place of capture. From 1589 all vessels taken by privateers had to be adjudicated as lawful by the

Table 2: Privateers set out by Waddell Cunningham, 1777–83

1777:	*Peace and Plenty**	Against America	260 tons
1778:	*Peace and Plenty**	Against France	260 tons
	Amazon[1]	France/America	170 tons
1779:	*Peace and Plenty**	Spain	260 tons
1781:	*Irish Volunteer*[2]	Spain/United Prov.	100 tons
	*Lord Bangor**	United Provinces	150 tons
	Harlequin[3]	United Provinces	70 tons
	Peace and Plenty[4]	United Provinces	170 tons

* Indicates sole owner and promoter of the venture.
1. With John McCracken, George Black, David Tomb and others. (The *Amazon* was commissioned again in 1779 when George Black was given as principal owner).
2. With William Galway (principal owners).
3. With William and John Brown.
4. Waddell Cunningham given as principal owner.
Source: Public Record Office, H.C.A. 26 (letter of marque declarations).

high court of admiralty – at least in theory. The surviving sentences of the court are to be found among the libel series (H.C.A. 24) and can be supplemented by the appraisements of prizes (H.C.A. 4), which contain detailed inventories of prize cargoes and ships (although they only run until 1708).

In fact there is an enormous amount of material relating to privateering among the court's records, though obviously by no means all of it is relevant to the Irish Sea. There are problems in exploiting this material, some of which should be touched on here. The survival of the early sixteenth-century records is patchy and uneven – as Andrews' study of Elizabethan privateering makes clear. More important, it is very difficult to estimate the extent of unlicensed, and hence unrecorded, privateering, especially for the sixteenth and early seventeenth centuries when it was fairly common for promoters to ignore the regulations and send out men-of-war without commissions. Finally, while the level of documentary detail becomes much richer for the eighteenth century it is clear, on occasion, that some of this is unreliable. In some cases, for example, the names of crew members of privateers, given in the letter of marque declarations, seem to have been made up on the spot. Thus the leading officers of the *Fame* of Dublin (issued with letters of marque on 31 October 1778) included Edward Blunderbuss, gunner; Thomas Bellow, boatswain; William Wood, carpenter; John Hard-heart, surgeon; and Peter Slush, cook.[24]

There was often a close connection between privateering and piracy: among the criminal records of the court (H.C.A. 1), which run from *c.* 1537 to 1834, there is much relating to the latter activity. The material includes the indictments of persons accused of piracy, and other crimes at sea, on the reverse of which the findings of the jury are usually to be found; and the examinations of accused persons, plaintiffs and witnesses. Although this material has been variously used by C. E. Hughes, Clive Senior and D. G. Hurd, a long-term integrated study of piracy in the Irish Sea is still awaited.[25] Yet it is clear, even from a brief survey of the examinations, that this was an important activity whose impact might have been far-reaching. Indeed there were few years during the sixteenth and seventeenth centuries when the Irish Sea was free of pirates and rovers. All too often government measures to combat the menace were half-hearted and ineffective. In 1633, as the depositions relate, a Dutch vessel was seized in Bullock harbour by a 'Biscayner', within sight of one of the king's ships. About the same time another Dutch vessel was seized in Dublin Bay by an English rover, who carried his prize off to the Isle of Man.[26]

The importance of the phenomenon, of its wider economic impact on trade or urban decline, for example, awaits fuller investigation. The importance of markets for pirate goods – in the Isle of Man, south Wales or elsewhere – needs investigation. And, most crucially, the rhythm of pirate enterprise, and of its eventual decline (or transmutation into smuggling activity?) needs to be established. Such a survey would also take account of the more complex problem of social attitudes and control, and in particular of the changing attitude of gentry and merchants to pirates. The records of the high court of admiralty provide an almost unique range of evidence which could be used to tackle these and other questions covering piracy as well as privateering.

(e) Wreck

One of the more prosaic functions of the court was to deal with the business of wreck and salvage. There are numerous references among the depositions to wrecks, or vessels in difficulty, in the Irish Sea either through negligence or stormy weather. In 1535, for example, a ship was cast away near Holyhead, and two years later a vessel was lost while sailing the short distance from Dalkey to Dublin through, it was claimed, the negligence of the pilot. In 1570 a great Flemish hulk, of 700 or 800 tons, was wrecked in the same area, between Dalkey and the head of Bray. Early in 1620 the *St Justina*, a Venetian vessel, came aground and perished near Waterford, breaking up within days. The Venetian ambassador in London subsequently employed Jacob Johnson, a diver, to salvage the vessel's ordnance. Although he managed to recover five cast iron pieces from the hold of the wreck, at least two others were hidden by sand, 'and so lay covered eight or nine months afterwards until by foule weather the sands were washed awaye'.[27]

None of the foregoing should be taken as a prescriptive summary on how to use the records of the court; rather, the intention has been to provide a survey and introduction to the type of material found among these records. Of course there are problems in their exploitation, some of which have been touched on. Most notably, however, it should be emphasised that they are legal records, usually the result of a voyage or venture which went wrong. As such they need to be balanced, and compared, with other evidence (where this survives) to test the typicality of the picture they represent. Nevertheless there are few other sources which provide such a mass and variety of evidence relating to maritime activity and enterprise. While it would be foolish to claim that maritime history can be written solely from this material, it would be true to claim that thematic studies of the period would be marvellously enriched by their use.

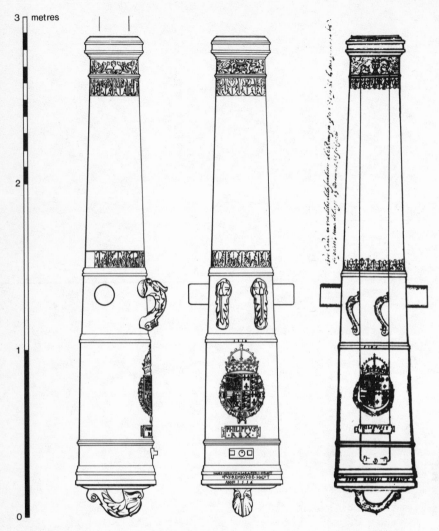

Author's drawings centre and left; the 5316 'canon de batir' recovered from *La Trinidad Valencera*; right, 1587 drawing of the 5186 piece, reduced to the same scale.

7 The Spanish Armada Wreck *La Trinidad Valencera* in Kinnagoe Bay, County Donegal:

a case study in the integration of historical and archaeological techniques

COLIN MARTIN

Introduction

On 20 February 1971 two members of the City of Derry Sub-Aqua Club, Archie Jack and Paddy Stewart, came upon a number of bronze guns lying at a depth of 10 metres some 200 metres offshore towards the western end of Kinnagoe Bay, County Donegal. A search of the surrounding area revealed iron anchors, parts of massive spoked wooden wheels, and various associated small finds. It was immediately apparent that the wreck was almost certainly that of *La Trinidad Valencera*, a major ship of the Spanish Armada which was known to have foundered somewhere in the bay on 16 September 1588. Later study unequivocally confirmed this identification. From the outset the club was determined to ensure that the obvious historical importance of the find should not go by default; a resolve which was not subsequently shaken by heavy collective (and in some cases personal) costs. The satisfactory conclusion of a major underwater excavation to good archaeological standards, the subsequent programme of conservation and research, and the final deposition of the recovered evidence in a major museum, is entirely a result of this unselfish and far-sighted attitude.

It was my good fortune, shortly after the discovery, to be invited to take over the archaeological direction of the project. With the club's support a full pre-disturbance survey was completed in 1971, and in 1973 I was joined by my colleagues from the Institute of Maritime Archaeology at the University of St Andrews, which was formed in that year. Excavation seasons were carried out by the institute in conjunction with the club during

61

1973, 1974, 1976, 1978, 1980, and 1983. Summaries of the work have been published, and a full report is in preparation.[1]

At an early stage the resources of the Ulster Museum, and in particular its expertise and facilities in the field of archaeological conservation, were brought to bear through the good offices of its keeper of antiquities, Mr Laurence Flanagan. Without this essential back-up the project could not have been continued responsibly, and it is satisfying to record that the material is now permanently in the museum's care, along with its sister collection from the *Girona*. The co-operation and goodwill of the Irish Republic in helping to bring this about, and especially the efforts of the officials concerned, cannot be emphasised too strongly. Warm thanks are due also to Professor Geoffrey Parker for placing at my disposal the fruits of his extensive documentary researches at Simancas and elsewhere. Full acknowledgement of the many other individuals and organisations who have helped in various ways has already been made,[2] and their omission here in no way detracts from the value of their contributions.

The aim of this paper is to discuss some of the wider issues raised by the discovery of historic shipwrecks, and in particular to demonstrate how this type of archaeological evidence can be integrated with historical sources to the benefit of both disciplines. It is frequently said that a shipwreck is a time capsule and, though perhaps over-used, the metaphor is an apposite one. But a time capsule can be regarded in more than one way. On the one hand, the varied and often confused jumble of evidence which survives on the sea bed will relate directly to a single dramatic – but probably relatively minor – historical event. On the other hand this same material is likely to provide a series of microcosms relating to more general aspects of the society which created, assembled, and ultimately lost it. Information about technical achievement and operational management will be embodied in the surviving remains of the ship and its fittings; it may be possible to reconstruct elements of social history from the possessions and equipment of its crew; and finally, there will almost certainly be evidence about the specialised activity – whether resource gathering, exploration, commerce, or war – for which the vessel was equipped and manned when lost. Should documentary sources concerning the ship and its background also exist, these can often be combined with the archaeological evidence to focus the very different capabilities of each discipline on common problems.

Work on the *Trinidad Valencera*, both under water and during post-excavation research, has provided practical illustrations of these points. It is hoped that the examples set out below, in addition to whatever interest they may have in their own right, will be regarded as case studies which may be of application whenever similar opportunities of relating the archaeological and historical potential of shipwreck discoveries present themselves.

Local history

The unexpected arrival on the Irish coast of dispersed elements of the
Armada during the autumn of 1588 generated a flurry of activity, at times
verging on panic, on the part of the English crown's officials and agents. At
first it was not clear whether these ships were fleeing survivors of the
débâcle in the English Channel, or new forces sent from Spain. In either
event the large bodies of troops aboard represented a clear threat to
England's tenuous hold on the island's western and northern territories,
and the lord deputy's natural if draconian reaction was to nip these
incursions ruthlessly in the bud, before the troops had time to regain their
health ashore or make alliances with local malcontents. This fear gave rise
to numerous reports and assessments, at first based on minimal information but in time crystallising, as prisoners were taken and interrogated, into
accurate and often highly detailed accounts of the events which were
unfolding. These are summarised extensively, though not exhaustively, in
the *Calendar of State Papers, Ireland*.[3] To these should be added the accounts
of Spanish survivors who eventually reached home, of which the best
known is the remarkable narrative of Francisco de Cuellar, who was
wrecked on Streedagh Strand, County Sligo, on 25 September 1588, and
reached Antwerp more than a year later after a harrowing and eventful
journey via Scotland.[4] Quite apart from their relevance to the Armada story
per se, these sources open a brief window on Irish affairs – political,
military, and social – at a time when clear historical illumination is
otherwise all too rare.

The sources which relate to the wrecking of the *Trinidad Valencera*, and the
fates of her survivors, are especially full. Both Don Alonso de Luzon,
commander of the Neapolitan *tercio* and senior officer aboard the ship, and
his sergeant-major, Baltasar Lopez del Arbol, were subsequently captured
and interrogated.[5] Don Alonso's account is well known, having been
published by Laughton and subsequently much quoted.[6] The unpublished
interrogation of his second in command, however, is (as anyone with
service experience will appreciate) much fuller and better-informed. Del
Arbol's account of the wrecking itself (in which the spelling has been
modernised) is particularly vivid:

> . . . the ship wherein they were took a great leak forty leagues from the coast of Ireland,
> whereupon they made with Ireland as the next land they knew, and coming on the shore in
> O'Doherty's country they took to land in an old boat of their own and some did swim to
> land, and their own boat being broken they gave 100 ducats in money and above 100 ducats
> in apparel, rings and jewels to a boat of the country to help them to land, which being also
> broken there came a third boat which they offered [asked] to have for their help, but the
> owners of the boat would not yield thereto, but went for spoil to the ship, and on the sinking
> of the ship, being entered into her, sank with her. He saith that as they came near the land,
> he saw some 20 of the savage people standing on a rock and in their landing about 4 or 5 of
> them came and did help them out of the boat and used them courteously until the rest of the

wild people that stood on the rock, and more with them to the number of 40, came together
at which time they took from them in money, gold buttons, rapiers and apparel to the value
of 7,300 ducats or thereabouts.

It is not often that we have supporting comment from the lower deck, but
the case of the *Trinidad Valencera* is an exception. Juan de Nova and
Francisco de Borja were two soldiers from the ship who eventually escaped
from Ireland and were interrogated by the Spanish authorities on their
home-coming.[7] Of events leading up to the shipwreck they had this to say:

> They lost sight of the Armada on the night of 12 September, during a tempest. The same
> night their ship sprang a great leak forward, and for the next two days and nights they were
> at the pumps. On the 14th they brought up on the coast of Ireland, towards Blasket [sic],
> and all the soldiers, except 40 who remained in the ship and were afterwards drowned when
> she foundered, were put on shore, with their arms, with a little boat.

De Nova and de Borja also provide us with the fullest (and, as they had
nothing to gain from prevarication, probably the least biased) account of
the survivors' experiences up to their capture by the English. Drawing on
this, and on complementary English sources, we are able to follow their
misfortunes in some detail.[8] After gathering his men together Don Alonso
struck inland, hoping to reach the west coast and the chance of ships to
Spain. They were still a formidable, if somewhat dispirited, military force.
Sustained by horsemeat and butter obtained by local barter they covered
the 20 miles to Illagh Castle, seat of Sir John O'Doherty, in whose territory
they had landed. Negotiations with an Irish bishop apparently in charge of
the castle drew an equivocal response. The Spaniards were requested to
make a show of force, so that the bishop might surrender to them and give
assistance without compromising himself. Though unfamiliar with local
politics, Don Alonso viewed the offer with some suspicion. His doubts were
confirmed when a signal shot was fired from the castle to alert the nearby
English garrisons. The Spaniards withdrew, crossed a bog, and took up
defensive positions in a nearby ruin.

Through his ignorance of local geography, Don Alonso was unaware of
the trap that was being sprung. The peninsula of Inishowen, on whose
northern shore he had landed, was bounded at its narrow southern neck by
two parallel strips of boggy ground running between the sea-loughs of Foyle
and Swilly. Illagh commanded the crossing of the northern bog; that on the
south was guarded by the stronger castle of Burt, garrisoned by English and
'affected' Irish troops under Major John Kelly and the brothers Richard
and Henry Hovenden. The Spaniards had been lured into a killing ground
from which there was no escape.[9]

The Burt garrison surrounded the Spanish position, and a parley was
arranged. Kelly insisted that Don Alonso and his men should surrender as
prisoners of war: the Spaniards refused to do so, and returned to their

trenches. A day later after some skirmishing, negotiations were resumed and Don Alonso, seeing his position to be hopeless, agreed to surrender on fair terms. This he came to regret. After plundering the Spaniards of their clothing and possessions, Kelly's men separated the common soldiers and seamen from those of ransomable status. The former were taken into a field and gunned down, though a number escaped in the confusion and of these a handful eventually reached Flanders via Scotland. The fate of those preserved for ransom was only marginally better. After a nightmare 100-mile march to Drogheda with little food and, for many of them, without adequate clothing or footwear, the survivors were incarcerated while haggling over their maintenance and ransoms dragged on interminably. Many died in the process although some, including Don Alonso and del Arbol, were eventually repatriated.

Naval and military technology

The Venetian merchant ship *La Trinidad Valencera* (a Spanish corruption of her Italian name *Balanzara*) was requisitioned early in 1587 by Spanish authorities in Sicily to convey troops and war materials to Spain, where they were required for the projected Armada.[10] Together with five similar vessels she arrived at Cartagena in May 1587, and by 18 June the *Valencera* was at San Lucar, where she was listed with an armament of twenty-eight bronze guns of unspecified type and size.[11] After reaching Lisbon she was embargoed to take part in the Armada itself, a task which she fulfilled with some distinction before her eventual loss in Kinnagoe Bay.[12]

La Trinidad Valencera was allocated to Martin de Bertendona's Levant squadron, which was made up of big Mediterranean-built grain ships. In a letter to Philip II on 27 February 1588 Bertendona states why he thinks his big Levanters will be so effective in the forthcoming campaign.[13] While he admitted that their *grandeza* – a word which implies overbearing magnificence as well as sheer size – may carry considerable risks, it would give them, thought Bertendona, an overwhelming tactical advantage when it came to close-quarter battle. He envisaged, along with most of his compatriots, capital ships which were, in effect, mobile fortifications filled with troops and their equipment – a Mediterranean concept of warfare diametrically opposite to the 'weapons platform' strategy which events were to show had been adopted with devastating success by the well-gunned and manoeuvreable front-line ships of Elizabeth's navy royal.

In fact, the Levantine ships were invasion transports rather than true warships, and between them they carried the bulk of the heavy siege train which was intended to support the duke of Parma's *blitzkrieg* assault on London once the Army of Flanders, supported by the Armada, had secured a beach-head in Kent. *La Trinidad Valencera* carried three of these big guns, together with all their associated equipment, in addition to her own armament of twenty-eight pieces and a large Turkish gun given to her at Lisbon. With a war-rating of 1100 tons, a crew of seventy-nine seamen and a contingent of 281 troops from Don Alonso de Luzon's Neapolitan *tercio*, the *Valencera* was the fourth- largest unit in the fleet, and her wreck may therefore be seen as a fundamental source of evidence for understanding the Armada as a whole.[14]

Very little of the ship's structural remains has survived on the wreck site: as discussed below, the hull appears to have disintegrated completely, with only isolated components becoming buried and so preserved. Nevertheless there is sufficient evidence for us to postulate that the *Trinidad Valencera* was entirely built of oak. Thirteen mm diameter iron fastenings with 25 mm heads had been used throughout. The countersunk fastening holes were set in regular lines along the top and bottom edges of the planks, each pair some 20 cm apart. The exclusive use of iron is of considerable interest. By the late sixteenth century iron fastenings were generally used in large ships only at points where particular strength was required, notably at keel or frame joints and at the butt-ends of planks. All the other fastenings were made with treenails, long oak dowels whose heads were cross-wedged to ensure a tight fit. While it was a relatively simple matter to drill out and replace rotten treenails, it was almost impossible to do the same to corroded iron bolts. An iron-fastened ship, though initially stronger and tighter, therefore had a more limited life, for once the bolts began to rust the vessel would have to be scrapped.

Lane has shown that the intensive working life of a Venetian cargo vessel rarely exceeded ten years,[15] while Romano has pointed out that the highly industrialised processes of Venetian shipbuilding relied on remarkably sophisticated concepts of assembly-line operation.[16] It is not unreasonable to see in the *Trinidad Valencera's* distinctive construction, so well suited to the efficient use of low-skilled labour and to a short, hard-working, and maintenance-free life, a practical response to the technical and economic demands of late sixteenth-century commercial enterprise within the Mediterranean. Evidence from the wrecks of two other big Armada vessels with Mediterranean origins suggests a similar method of construction. The 800-ton *San Juan de Sicila*, which came originally from Ragusa (Dubrovnik), blew up and sank in Tobermory Bay, Argyll.[17] In 1677 the ninth earl of Argyle, in a memorandum concerning the possible salvage of the wreck, noted that the hull was 'fastened together with iron bolts, which are so rusted and worn that if any attempt were made to raise the hull, it would all fall to pieces'.[18] My own brief examination of a recently-discovered Armada wreck off Streedagh Strand, County Sligo, now positively identified by gun-weight concordance as that of the Sicilian *Juliana* of 860 tons, indicated a similar constructional technique.

This conclusion may help to explain why the ships of the Levant squadron suffered a higher proportional loss than any other group of ships within the Armada – 80 percent against about 35 percent for the fleet as a whole.[19] Bulk cargo carriers were conceived on strictly economic grounds, and stressed to accommodate the thrust of loads within their bellies. Their design criteria did not envisage participation in close range artillery battles. The stresses to which a hull might be subjected during sustained artillery action included not only the obvious one of enemy bombardment, but also the strains imposed by the working of its own guns. Just how destructive the latter forces could be is emphasised by the curious case of the Portuguese galleon *San Mateo* which, according to a Spanish witness, 'pulled herself apart with her *own* artillery' (my italics) during the battle of Gravelines.[20]

Several of *La Trinidad Valencera's* armament of 32 bronze guns, together with parts of their carriages and working equipment, have been recovered from the wreck. These include four Venetian pieces, presumably part of the relatively light complement she carried to counter the threat of small-scale piracy in the Adriatic. They range from a medium-length fourteen-pounder weighing about 1400 kg to a small breechloading swivel piece compositely built of bronze and wrought iron. Documentary sources show that four much bigger guns were added to the ship at Lisbon: one was a heavy Turkish piece (perhaps a trophy from Lepanto), while the other three were matching *cãnones de batir* from the royal siege train destined to support Parma's advance on London. Two of these have been recovered and their weight marks (established by formal weighing shortly after casting and chiselled onto the gun barrel to the nearest Castilian *libra* of 460 gm, and so almost certainly unique to individual guns) of 5260 and 5316 tally with the figures given for two of the *cãnones* issued to *La Trinidad Valencera*, thus establishing the wreck's identity beyond any doubt.[21] By a remarkable coincidence the third *cãnon*, which has not yet been found (there are some grounds for thinking that ordnance was recovered from the wreck in the early seventeenth century),[22] was actually drawn to scale as part of a technical memorandum submitted to Philip II in 1587, as the common weight-tally of 5186 suggests.[23] This particular gun is fully described in the *Trinidad Valencera* inventory (the other two – which, it was noted, were identical in all practical respects – are recorded only by weight):

One cast-bronze *cãnon de batir* from the Flemish foundry which bears on top of the first reinforce a shield with the royal arms and an inscription which reads 'Felipus Rex' and behind the vent three inscriptions of which one reads 'Juanze Manrrique Alara ficunt curavit' [sic] and another '1556'. It weighs fifty one *quintales* and eighty six *libras*. It fires a cast-iron ball weighing 40 *libras*.

The concordance between the description of this gun, the contemporary illustration which appears to represent it, and the modern rendering of its identical sister may be examined on page 60. The minor discrepancies which exist between the wording and decoration on the 5316 gun and those shown in the Spanish written and pictorial records of the 5186 piece are probably errors on the part of the clerk and draftsman concerned, for the guns are clearly part of a matching set.

Something of the complexity of a heavy artillery train can be gauged from the multiplicity of stores and equipment which went with it. The Spanish inventory includes such items as a gun-hoist, tents for the ammunition, wedges and handspikes, and an assemblage of specialised tools. Some of these have been identified on the wreck. Another document records that each of the three guns was supplied with three complete mountings: two dismantled field carriages for assembly and use ashore, and the solid-wheeled carriage on which it was mounted aboard ship.[24] These guns were probably too heavy, and too inexpertly worked, for effective deployment afloat.[25]

The find of instruments connected with the calibration of guns and shot has thrown light on what may have been one of the major reasons for the Armada's poor showing in terms of gunnery – its total lack of standardisation. With a diverse hotch-potch of guns originating from the Baltic to the Adriatic, the Armada planners faced a bewildering variety of weight standards in attempting to match the guns aboard individual ships with the allocation of suitably-sized shot for them. In solving this apparently simple equation they clearly failed, and the abysmal standard of arithmetic which the *Trinidad Valencera* calibration instruments display – ranging from grossly inaccurate to totally spurious – perhaps demonstrates one of the root causes.

Archaeology

In interpreting the archaeological evidence of a shipwreck, an attempt must be made to understand the process of wrecking and the subsequent deposition of material within the natural environment. Only in the light of such understanding will it be possible to work backwards through that process and so develop a theoretical model of the ship before it became a wreck. At one extreme the ship may remain substantially intact, with its contents scarcely displaced: such was the case with Sweden's *Wasa*, and to a lesser extent with England's *Mary Rose*. In archaeological terms wrecks of this kind are relatively easy to interpret, for little change to their original organised state has taken place. At the other end of the scale a ship may be so broken up, dispersed, and reduced by natural forces that it effectively ceases to exist. Most wrecks, however, lie somewhere between these two extremes.

La Trinidad Valencera is one such. As already observed, no coherent remains of the hull have survived, apparently because the rusting of its iron bolts, exacerbated by wave and current action, brought about its total disintegration in a relatively short time. As the hull was breaking up, however, it created a massive anomaly on an otherwise extremely stable sandy seabed, temporarily forming a series of scour pits as natural water movements accommodated themselves to the intrusion. Waterlogged organic debris from the ship accumulated in these pits: debris consisting of splinters and sometimes major components from the disintegrating hull together with a whole range of other material – objects of wood, leather, textile, and bone. Mixed among this debris, but also scattered more widely across the site, were artifacts of metal, stone, and pottery.

When the hull collapsed the natural stability of the seabed reasserted itself, and sand covered the scour pits, sealing their contents and so preserving them from mechanical, biological, and to some extent chemical degradation. Systematic excavation of the site, and the recording of its distributions and stratigraphy, has now revealed in broad terms how the ship broke up and how its various contents were dispersed. In the process a wide sampling of its fragile but often miraculously preserved contents have been recovered. From this varied evidence, and in conjunction with documentary sources of the kind outlined above, there has emerged a fuller picture of *La Trinidad Valencera,* her people, their equipment and possessions, and the great historical events of which they all were a part.

Greenock and Belfast

PACKET.

THE Public are respectfully informed, that the elegant Smack SALLY, fitted up in a most superior Style, for the comfort, pleasure, and accommodation of Passengers, sails regularly once a-week, between Greenock and Belfast.—— Particular care is taken that the Beds and Bedding are kept clean and wholesome.

Rates in British Money.—To be paid before sailing.

GENTLEMEN's CABIN, £1. 1. 0. and to find themselves, or £1. 11. 0. to be found.
LADIES' CABIN, £1. 1. 0d.............ditto............or £1 11s. 0d......ditto.
FORECASTLE, 5s. and Passengers to find themselves.
Children—Half Price.
Steward, 2s.
Dogs—*per Head,* 4s.

Each Passenger in the Cabin to be allowed one Trunk; whatever exceeds that, to Pay 5s. each Parcel.—All Luggage is subject to be taken to the Customhouse, by the proper Officers: the Proprietors are therefore not accountable for its delivery.

RULES

I. No Passengers to take any thing on board the Packet but Luggage; every thing else is liable to seizure: and if any contraband Goods are found, a prosecution will be commenced against them by the Proprietors; and the owners of such Goods are also liable to the penalties, as by law established.

II. To preserve the neatness and cleanliness necessary in the Cabins, Dogs are not to be brought in, nor any person to lay in the Beds with boots or shoes on; penalty for each offence, 10s. 6d.—No smoking in the Cabin on any account.—As good clean sheets are provided, any person wishing to sleep in them in preference to sleeping in blankets, are requested to undress otherwise they will not be allowed.

No Passenger can secure a Bed, unless he has previously secured a Ticket.

Further information may be had of Mr. John Park, Tontine ; Mr. Mac-Nair's Office, opposite the Tar Pots, here ;—or, Edward Brush, Belfast.

Greenock—April, 1817.

Notice re Greenock and Belfast sailing packet *Sally*, 1817. Public Record Office of Northern Ireland D2015/4/2.

8 Davy Jones's Locker:

maritime records in the Public Record Office of Northern Ireland

TREVOR PARKHILL

And why is England now ramified by thousands of miles of railway and Ireland with only three or four short lines of railway not extending . . . over more than seventy miles? Because the sea intervenes and railways cannot be made across the sea and British capital stops at the sea and will not cross the channel till from its redundancy profitable investment becomes a matter of difficulty . . .[1]

William Sharman Crawford would have done well, as he penned this argument in an essay in the 1840s on the case for Ireland to be economically independent of England, to have considered the full extent of the value of the Irish Sea economy to Ireland as a whole and the north of the island in particular. Indeed, his family's mercantile connections should have informed him of the extent to which Ulster merchants had, throughout the eighteenth and nineteenth centuries, played an innovative role in establishing and developing markets via the Irish Sea with Dublin, Glasgow, Whitehaven, Bristol, London and beyond, to Bordeaux, Rouen, Riga, the West Indies and ports on the eastern coast of America – Newcastle, New York, Savannah, Philadelphia and others. This trading complex, and the central role of its shipping network, has been outlined in the recent published research of J. V. Beckett, L. M. Cullen and Laura Cochrane[2] and is, in any case, only one of the many aspects of a consideration of the Irish Sea but it is as well to remind ourselves of the longevity of the economic tradition of merchants in Ulster and the maintenance of their markets by a network of maritime routes. As far as the documentary evidence which remains is concerned – the letter books, ledgers, account books, bills of lading and bills of exchange etc. – it does not recommend itself at first glance to be considered in the category of maritime records. They do, however, provide considerable details on a number of merchants, entre-preneurs, insurers and underwriters operating in, and out of Belfast, Newry and Derry. Among them are the papers of Isaac Macartney, Daniel

71

Mussenden, Peter Galen and Robert Thompson, Gilbert McIlveen and Thomas Greer.

This essay surveys the range of primary documentary sources which relate to the maritime history of the north of Ireland. In addition to these merchants' business records, attention will be drawn to the records of ships and shipping; of sailors in both the merchant and naval fleets; of shipbuilding; and of the passengers who, as emigrants or travellers, recorded their experiences, often as they stared into what they were sure was eternity. The scope will not be confined to the Irish Sea for, although the nature of the shipping routes in the sailing era meant there was a concentration on the near-coastal routes, Irishmen and Irish ships travelled the world.

Among the fields to which particular attention will be paid are the extant records of shipping companies. The growth in size and importance of Belfast as a commercial and passenger port in the steamship age is well evidenced in the archives of the Belfast Steamship Company from the 1850s and G. Heyn and Son (the Head Line Company) from the 1870s. Although the development of Belfast shipbuilding from the mid-nineteenth century is not described here, it is worth pointing out that the records of Harland & Wolff were not wholly destroyed, as had been believed, during the air-raids on Belfast in 1941. The considerable quantity which did survive has been gradually accessioned by P.R.O.N.I. throughout the 1980s. Alternative evidence relating to shipbuilding to be found in government records, particularly files relating to the loans voted by the new Northern Ireland parliament to Harland & Wolff in the interwar period, has to some extent compensated for gaps in the company's archive.

The people who sailed in ships entering and leaving Ulster ports must also feature in a survey of sources. One of the most substantial series of maritime records – both in Belfast and to wherever else they have been dispersed, particularly Newfoundland – are the crew lists and agreements which, from 1863, record names and other details of crew members on coastal and deep sea shipping. Other sailors' records include log books and testimonials of merchant sailors' 'dairies of ships' surgeons from the late eighteenth century, besides lists of emigrants on ships bound for North America in the era of direct sailing. As for recreational seafaring, the records of the Royal Ulster Yacht Club give important insights into the commercial and landed parvenus of nineteenth century Ulster society, who regarded membership as a means of parading social acceptability.

The value of merchants' records in studies of maritime history is exemplified in the letter books of Isaac Macartney 1704–7,[3] which not only chart the routes of trade with Bristol – for linen, tobacco, timber – and Liverpool, Dublin, Aberdeen, London, but also advert to the trouble caused by the presence of French privateers in the Irish Sea in the early years of the eighteenth century, including an eye-witness account of the capture of one French vessel off the County Down coast and its being put ashore at Dundrum. The trade network of Daniel Mussenden, whose business archive of some 1100 items covers the period from 1734 to the late 1760s,[4] portrays in close detail the more sophisticated – relative to that apparent in the Macartney records – trading nexus of which Belfast was an intrinsic link by the mid-eighteenth century. Robert Black, writing from Douglas in the Isle of Man in 1765, after the establishment there of English law which effectively put paid to its smuggling trade, is content to have Belfast as an alternative base for business: 'the late act having effectually shut up every avenue to trade in this place . . . I am resolved to fix myself at Belfast as soon as I can settle my affairs here'.[5] The preoccupation with the central role of the Irish Sea in accommodating effective trade between the north of Ireland and Great Britain throughout the nineteenth century is evident in the letter books of the Belfast Chamber of Commerce.[6] The construction of time signals, clearly visible beacons, lights and buoys and, above all, the expeditious transport of mails and cargo between the British mainland and the eastern Irish coast (as well as between Cork and the United States) form a repetitive and insistent agenda for their communications with the Post Office, the Treasury and railway companies. In fact, complaints were registered about everything except the Irish Sea, but it is clearly the difficulties posed by its presence that were at the root of the Chamber of Commerce's strident lobbying.

However it was not only Belfast which featured in the Irish Sea trade; indeed it may have been that Newry was pre-eminent until the last decade of the eighteenth century, and of course the port of Derry continued to serve as the distributive centre for the entire northwest of Ireland. For Newry the account books of James McClenaghan and J. & J. Lyle, 1797–1858[7], show the wide geographical range of goods, principally flaxseed, timber and sugar, imported direct to Newry from Newfoundland, Holland, Riga and the West Indies, and the series of ports to which exports of provisions – notably butter and pork – were directed, including Leith, Glasgow, Preston, Liverpool, Dublin and London. The two volumes of letter books of Andrew Ferguson for the period 1775–80[8] relate to the commercial traffic of the port of Derry. In particular they record the increasingly sophisticated range of ironmongery goods imported from England by Ferguson. Newry and Derry served as distributive centres for large inland regions so their Irish sea trade, as recorded in the documents of merchants such as Ferguson and McClenaghan, linked much of the north of Ireland with the world's main trade and commerce routes.

The introduction of steamships sailing to and from Ulster ports in the first quarter of the nineteenth century increased Irish Sea traffic. A number of steam packet companies began operating on routes out of the main ports of Belfast, Newry and Derry and a record survives of the first steamship

service, between Belfast and Greenock in 1818.[9] Other strategically situated ports, small though they were, were able to avail of the steam packet
services, at least in the early years. The marquis of Downshire was involved
in the establishment of a packet service operating out of Donaghadee
1823–6[10] (Donaghadee's proximity to Portpatrick on the Galloway coast
had for long given it a role – in postal communication especially – in North
Channel crossings). The spread of local coastal steam packet companies is
represented by some of the records of the Portaferry and Strangford
Steamboat Company.[11] It was the development of harbour improvement in
the late 1840s, and the establishment of the Belfast Harbour Commissioners in 1847 and the Belfast Marine Board – whose minute book and
copy out-letter book for the period 1850–58, after it had been established by
act of parliament, contain detailed accounts of this crucial period – which
enabled the port of Belfast to take commercial advantage of its better
berthing facilities and the general transport revolution for which steam was
responsible on land and sea.[12]

Foremost among the steamship companies operating from Belfast was
the Belfast Steamship Company, established in 1852 with a capital of
£25000, which had, by 1910 when it became a registered company, risen to
some £200000 and included among its directors Thomas and James
Gallaher, tobacco barons, John Sinclair and James Mackie. The extensive
archive of this passenger service and cargo includes the original deed of
partnership which avows the company's aim to be 'the owning and working
of one or more vessels propelled by steam or other motive power, for the
carriage of passengers, cattle and goods between ports in Great Britain or
Ireland'.[13] The establishment of the Belfast Steamship Company heralded
an even greater proliferation of steam passenger services across the Irish
Sea, some of which – among them the Belfast and Liverpool Steamship
Company, whose records are incorporated in the Belfast Steamship Company collection – were in due course absorbed by the senior business. By the
1890s the company was advertising direct sailings daily between Belfast
and Liverpool and three times weekly between Glasgow and Derry.

Belfast was also the home of the Ulster Steamship Company, an example
of the base which Irish Sea passenger trade created for a more extensive and
ultimately world-wide, shipping business. Gustavus Heyn, a native of
Prussia, had initially undertaken steamship sailing out of Belfast in the late
1820s and by 1850 Heyn had a widely based sea-going commercial role as
merchant, shipping agent and consulate office for Russia, Prussia and
Holland.[14] It was not until 1877 that there is a record of the Ulster
Steamship Company, operating with the 631-ton iron screw steamer
Bickley, and in 1879 the company came under the direct management of G.
Heyn & Sons. Henceforth, more and larger ships were used by the firm,
beginning with the 1175 ton steamer *Fair Head*, which began the company's

practice of naming its ships after Irish headlands, and gave the company its popular title the 'Head Line'. In 1916 the Ulster Steamship Company Ltd acquired the Irish Shipowners Company Ltd of Belfast, popularly known as the Lord Line (also from the style of naming its ships) which had been managed by Thomas Dixon & Sons Ltd. When this transfer was made, the Lord Line consisted of six steamers ranging from 3200 to 4800 tons; this brought the number of ships of the Ulster Steamship Company to seventeen, but such were the losses suffered during the first world war that twelve of these were sunk by November 1918.

The extensive archive, which dates from 1870 and allows this brief summary to be pieced together, should be seen as a shipping archive of some significance.[15] In addition to the cargo and continuous crew records, there is a very good photograph collection not just of launches and other ceremonial events but, for a number of the ships before and after the second world war, containing fine shots of interiors and some interesting views of camouflaged ships in both the first and second world wars, besides ice-surrounded ships in the early spring trade to Canadian ports.[16]

At the other end of the scale from the Ulster Steamship Company Ltd are the records of a clutch of much smaller cargo lines such as the Frontier Town Steamship Company, the Newry and Kilkeel Steamship Company, the Mercantile Steamship Company all of which were engaged in the coal trade from the western shores of northern England and from Wales principally to Newry or Bangor, County Down, for the coal importing business of James Fisher & Company whose records, from the 1890s, testify to the predominance of the coal trade, and Northern Ireland dependence on it, in the coastal shipping of the Irish Sea.[17]

The development of passenger services to Liverpool, Glasgow and other ports had the additional feature of allowing intending emigrants from Ulster to sail to the United States or, from the 1850s, to Australia. From the early eighteenth century and indeed until the mid-1860s from the port of Derry, there were thousands of emigrant ships directly sailing from Ulster ports to Savannah, Charleston, Delaware, New York and, in the post-Napoleonic period, for Quebec and the Canadian maritime provinces as well as New York and Philadelphia. From a strictly maritime point of view, it is the diaries kept by emigrants on board their sometimes long and tedious journeys – particularly to Australia – which have greater interest than, for instance, the letters written on arrival containing retrospective descriptions of the voyage. The diaries kept of the trans-Atlantic passenger voyage, on board the *Glasgow*, sailing out of Liverpool in 1834[18], and the journey Alex McCurry made to Australia 1879–80,[19] are perhaps the best examples of this type of record, which can often be as monotonous as the voyages they describe.

The best records of the direct emigrant passenger trade relate to the port of Derry. The passenger books of J. & J. Cooke, shipping agents in Derry, cover the period February 1847 to July 1867 in three volumes and list the names of passengers taken on ships owned or chartered by Cooke to Philadelphia, St John, New Brunswick and Quebec.[20] In addition to the names, the townland or parish of origin of the intending emigrant is, more often than not, given so that the full catchment area served by the port of Derry can be built up. There is also a passenger book giving a list of passengers engaged at Philadelphia by Messrs Robert Taylor & Company, which is a record of the pre-paid passage system which operated between shipping agents in Derry and Philadelphia: the money for the passage was paid in to Taylor in Philadelphia by emigrants, usually sons or husbands who had travelled singly with the intention of earning sufficient money to pay for the passage of their family.[21] Taylor then notified the shipping agents in Derry that the money had been received and 'booked', as it were, the passage of the named individuals on a ship. This system had been operating long in advance of the time period covered by the records: William Smyth, writing in 1837 to his family home in Moycraig, County Antrim, described the procedure in clear detail to his nephew Robert, whose passage he was arranging.

> You wish to come to this country, and say that your mother thinks you too young. But if you want to come you are old enough. The sooner the better. You are not coming to strangers . . . you will come to the best home you ever had and if you are coming I wish you to come in the first vessel that will sail from Derry belonging to James Corscadden as I have paid your passage and sent you two pounds for pocket money which James Corscadden will pay you on presenting this letter to him.[22]

The last entry in the volume of payments made to Robert Taylor in Philadelphia for similarly arranged passages was made in 1871. But the shipping business of William McCorkell and then J. & J. Cooke had, from the evidence of the business's records, been more concerned with the north Atlantic timber and flax trades in the 1820s and 1830s before graduating to the attractions of the increasing emigrant trade, especially to Canada, which was very much their trade route. In his study of the north Atlantic economy[23] Ralph Davis has pointed to the dramatic shift in the source for the provision of Britain's timber requirements from the Baltic shores to the forests of Canada, as a result, initially, of the war in Europe and then, in the post-Napoleonic period, of preferential tariffs in favour of the British territory. The eastward flow of timber and the return journey of the hastily fitted-up ships carrying emigrants created a profitable commercial nexus for Derry merchants. The Cooke business archive, principally the voluminous letter books, narrates the extent of the trade between the port and St John, New Brunswick and Quebec. The letter books, in addition to relating the chartering of ships to effect the transport of timber for sale in Ireland and Britain, also describe the commissioning by the Cooke brothers of the

300 ton barque, *Londonderry*, to be built at St John, following their specifications.[24] Constructed within eight months, the ship was in service,
carrying timber to Derry and, on its first return voyage at least, pre-paid
passengers for New Brunswick. It served in the Cooke fleet until it was sold
to Shearer and Company of Ardrossan in the early 1850s.[25]

With regard to the shipbuilding industry in Derry, there is a small
collection of documents which relate to the first world war activities of the
Foyle shipyard.[26] Other shipyards for which P.R.O.N.I. has scattered
documentation include the small late nineteenth-century establishment of
Paul Rogers at Carrickfergus[27] and a yard at Warrenpoint.[28]

The triangle of academic-archivist-businessman in the deposit and long
term preservation of records has been well demonstrated in the case of the
Harland & Wolff shipbuilding archive.[29] Since interest was initiated by
academic enquiries, P.R.O.N.I. has received some 250 boxes of material,
although it is very much an unknown quantity from the research point of
view. However, the considered view of the National Maritime Museum and
the author of the Business Archives Council's *Shipbuilding records survey* (a
survey which in 1979 was invited by Harland & Wolff to undertake the first
survey of the archive) is that the records relating to the shipbuilders' cartel,
the Shipbuilders and Repairers National Association, are not likely to be
preserved so fully elsewhere, so on that basis at least the archive has a
unique value. The papers reveal the increasingly complex process of
negotiating for, as well as constructing, ships in the twentieth century.
There are specifications for the construction of the hulls, electrical systems,
etc., of a sizeable proportion of the ships built in the yard since the second
world war. These contrast with the examples of early rigging plans and
general arrangement drawings deposited primarily for conservation purposes. For the middle years of the century, particularly just before and
during the second world war, there is a fairly complete set of detailed
annual reports of the work carried out in Harland & Wolff's yards at
Govan, Liverpool and Southampton. Other documents include an interesting series of trade union files, 1911–30, together with papers relating to the
Shipbuilders Employers Federation, 1914–40.[30]

Of the other main Belfast shipbuilding firm, Workman Clark, there is
little surviving constructive research material. Recently, the high court
transferred to P.R.O.N.I. a series of shareholders' volumes which are well
indexed, carefully detailed and give a thorough picture of the sort of
investor which Workman Clark attracted.[31]

A consideration of the subject of sources for the study of ship building in
the twentieth century should bear in mind the increasing role which central
government took, particularly in the protection of Harland & Wolff as a
major employer. The establishment of a devolved system of government in
Northern Ireland in 1921 coincided with the post-first world war shipbuild-

ing slump. There does not appear to be much on this in the Harland & Wolff archive on deposit in P.R.O.N.I. so the government records of the period have a more than complementary role in sketching in the policy of the Northern Ireland government with regard to intervention to support the firm, and then the practicalities of the assistance rendered. Even in view of the seriousness of the economic crisis, and the fact that Harland & Wolff might well have been assumed to have been something of a sacred cow not for sacrificing, the cabinet conclusions of the Northern Ireland government suggest that initial financial support for the company was as much at the insistence of the British government as it was the collective decision of the Northern Ireland cabinet. The government's response to the national shipbuilding slump, and the extension of its policy to Northern Ireland, may well deserve closer study in regard to the working out of the relations between Westminster and Stormont in the immediate post-partition era. As it was, the conditions of the loan guarantee act as they had applied in Great Britain were applied to Harland & Wolff and the files of the Department of Finance contain the details of this particular aspect of government intervention.[32]

The records relating to shipbuilding and shipping are, of necessity, largely concerned with matters of finance, trade and building cycles, construction details and so on. It is worthwhile, therefore, ending this section of the study on a more humane note. One of the heroes and central figures in the construction and loss of the *Titanic* was Thomas Andrews, one of its designers and a managing director of Harland & Wolff. There is in P.R.O.N.I. a small collection of material collected over a number of years by a member of his family,[33] though it does not amount to very much as far as primary source material is concerned. However when one reads the description of Andrews's exemplary behaviour during the last few minutes of the *Titanic* – with his intimate knowledge of its structure, he must have known before anyone of the inevitability of the ship's fate – it is a case of a little meaning a lot.[34]

One other main area of the history of ships and shipping which deserves some acknowledgement are the records that exist relating to seafarers. There are some deposits in P.R.O.N.I. of personal log books and records of time spent on board ships in the merchant fleet. One of these small collections is the records of Captain William Mitchell who sailed out of the port of Derry in the mid-nineteenth century and whose letters to his wife reveal something of the life of a nineteenth-century mariner and his family (who sometimes travelled with him) on near-coastal journeys, voyages across the Irish Sea as well as on longer trips to the West Indies.[35] Writing from New Orleans in February 1849, Mitchell told his wife: 'The first night we got here most of the crew ran away . . . they got into the hands of these man catchers and made them groggy and got their clothes away before I or the captain knew they had any intention of running'. And it was from the West Indies that the following series of correspondence shows how truly demanding the life of a nineteenth century mariner was. Writing from Bahia in March 1855, Mitchell confesses to his wife: 'I wish I had never come on this voyage. The fever is very rife . . . and there is not a vessel except our vessel has had the fever more or less. We have escaped without any sickness as yet and I hope to be out of the harbour tomorrow evening . . .'. In June there is a letter from his son informing another member of the family that his father had died of yellow fever and this is confirmed in a letter from William Mawhinney, of Islandmagee, to Mrs Mitchell.

> When Capt Mitchell and I parted he had no thought but that he would be better in a few days. I went to see him twice and the next time I went the doctors would not allow me to see him for fear of it relapsing on me. The last conversation your husband and I had was concerning the vessel. I never hear him mention anything particular about home. I am very sorry for the loss of Capt Mitchell as him and I was always good friends and he was always very kind to me.

From the point of view of the ordinary seaman, there is a selection of records including copy books, mensuration instructions etc. which Henry Murphy collected and kept during his training as a seaman.[36] There is also a small cache of personal attendance records of William Russell on board a variety of British merchant vessels from 1919: Russell was a young Belfast shipyard apprentice who joined the merchant navy at the end of the first world war and served in it until the late 1940s.[37] For the eighteenth century there are the letter books of Captain P. Cosby on H.M.S. *Centaur* and H.M.S. *Robust* 1778–97,[38] and of Capt. W. Wolsely on H.M.S. *Terrible* 1796–1801.[39] The diary of Robert Shaw, employed in a more manual capacity on the S.S. *City of London* between Liverpool and New York 1872–4,[40] and the log books of some twenty vessels sailing from Belfast 1860–1911[41] represent the range of ships crewed by Ulstermen. The most comprehensive series of sailors' records, however, are the ships' agreements and crew lists, of which there are literally thousands in P.R.O.N.I., beginning in 1863.[42]

Under the 1835 and subsequent merchant shipping acts the master of a British registered vessel of above a specified tonnage had a statutory obligation to enter into agreement with his crew before sailing. The agreements were registered on a variety of standardised forms, and all the forms record essentially the same information – the name and registered number of the vessel, its port of registration, ports of departure and destination, details of the owner (or manager) and the master of the vessel, together with, in respect of each crew member, the name, age, place of birth, home address, next of kin, previous ship, date and place of joining ship, capacity, date and place and cause of leaving ship, rate of pay and advances. A study of the crew lists shows, by the number of desertions recorded, the rapid turnover of crews and suggests the journeys of many should be regarded as the working passages of migrants. There are also occasional official log books, which should not be confused with the ship's log proper. The former do not contain a complete chronicle of the ship's voyage, but only a record of certain categories of incident, such as deaths or disturbances on board, which the master was obliged to report to the registrar of shipping. In most cases the official log books were destroyed under the terms of Public Record Office destruction schedules but some, which recorded deaths, have survived and will be found in this collection.

The main ports which feature as being the place of registration for the ships in this series include, of course, Ulster ports large and small – Belfast, Newry, Coleraine, Strangford, Derry, – but these are liberally interspersed with ships from Dublin, Stranraer, Liverpool, London, Scarborough, Maryport, Carnarvon, West Hartlepool, Wexford to name but a few. The 'notable' merchant ships whose returns have been retained by the Public Record Office in London, include the *Great Eastern, Oceanic, Mauretania, Lusitania, Empress of Ireland,* and the *Titanic.* The ports that are listed in the crew lists and agreements serves to remind the maritime history researcher of the number of harbours in Ulster and for which there are records, often on a considerable scale, in P.R.O.N.I. The most extensive is the archive of the Londonderry Port and Harbour Authority, established in 1854–5 and accessioned by P.R.O.N.I. during the 1970s.[43] There are extensive loading records, plans, correspondence, data relating to cargo; of major interest, however, certainly as a continuous record of the activities of a busy port, are the correspondence books of the secretary of the authority from 1855,[44] and the registers of arrivals of vessels from 1 January 1869 to 1953.[45] For Belfast, there are many maps, plans and drawings of which the earliest original material includes plans and sections of a graving dock to be built, presumably by William Ritchie in the 1790s and in the period 1812–14, plans and sections of what were to be Clarendon graving docks. Thereafter, there is a wide variety of maps, including many marked-up copies of the ordnance survey maps which were available from the early 1830s showing plans for dock development schemes, improvement for the channel, land reclamation, floating docks and so on, with contributions from Thomas Telford, James McCleary *et al.*[46] There is also a nineteenth-century copy of a customs register of ships entering the port of Belfast between 1682, including the names of the ships and details of cargoes. It was probably copied by the secretary of the Belfast harbour commissioners from a customs record.[47]

The Larne Harbour records contain material relating to the pre-1891 period when it was privately owned by the enterprising William Chaine, and between 1891 and 1912 when it had Chaine as its chairman.[48] After 1912 the 'new' company replaced the 'old', including Chaine, and it is from that period that minute books, setting out the policy of the company, and a series of records including manifests of freight carried by ships using the harbour (which in fact begin in 1889 and run to 1939) are available. The records of Coleraine harbour commissioners are even more continuous, including minute books from 1879; letter books from 1897 to 1946; registers of vessels from 1864 to 1969; harbour master's reports etc., in addition to plans and drawings, many relating to the Bann navigation and soundings at the mouth of the river Bann.[49]

The records of harbours should certainly contribute to a quantification of the import and export trade. In this regard, they can be supplemented by appropriate sections of the inestimable quantity of Ulster Transport Authority records which relate to the distribution of goods from the harbours. The U.T.A. archive also contains papers of the traffic and livestock conferences 1867–1947.[50] For the pre-railway era, there is a series of Belfast mercantile newspapers from the early years of the nineteenth century to the 1830s which have already shown their research value in estimating the export from Ulster of pre-famine agricultural products.[51]

Professor Buchanan's introductory essay describes the role and development of small fishing villages and ports on the County Down coast, specifically Killough. About two miles from Killough is the harbour of Ardglass whose development in the 1820s and 1830s as a harbour, and more particularly as a resort, was the dream of William Ogilvie. Very much on his own initiative and with his own money, Ogilvie engaged Sir John Rennie to compile a report presented in 1809 to parliament for a grant in aid of the harbour development;[52] then Ogilvie undertook to provide Ardglass with facilities very much in line with those being developed in coastal resorts in England, such as bathing houses, a coaching inn and so on. It was an ambitious investment which is to some extent detailed in the papers of the Downshire family with whom Ogilvie maintained contact, especially when he needed money.[53] The harbour work instigated by Ogilvie was of more long-lasting value, and Marmion noted in 1855 that it was the most extensive fishing station on the coast, employing nearly 4000 tons of shipping and 2500 men and boys.[54] In spite of his endeavours to improve harbour accommodation at Ardglass, Ogilvie died in 1832 a disappointed man. However his dismissal of his own efforts is perhaps more an acknowledgement of the might of the Irish Sea than a fitting epitaph for his work: 'I am sorry I undertook it at so late a period in my life: it distresses me in every way . . . I wed a beautiful duchess, the noble daughter of a duke, but I have failed to tame the waves on the beach of Ardglass'.[55]

The topic of maritime history is so wide-ranging, and the records available so extensive and originating in so many different sources, that no survey could be complete without a 'miscellaneous' section, and a select miscellany at that. Such items include the two manuscript journals of H.M.S. *Furnace*, March 1740–October 1742, under the command of Christopher Middleton, in the voyage of discovery of a passage through Hudson's Bay to the South Seas; [56] the log book of the *Empress of Russia*,[57] and registration certificate and log books of the *Clyde Valley*, famous for its gun-running role in the campaign against home rule 1912–14. In the personal collection compiled by Captain R. H. Davis, is a series of typescript copies of talks broadcast by Davis on Belfast sailing ships 1936–55;[58] there are cabinet and prime ministerial papers about the visit of the British fleet to the County Down coast in 1927;[59] and the archive of the Royal Ulster Yacht Club from 1870, whose minute books record the names of the members and, just as interesting, the names and recommendations of those applying for membership of this prestigious club, entrance to which betokened the social status symbol many of Belfast's merchants were seeking.[60]

Any selection is bound to leave out aspects which will be regarded by some as glaring omissions. No mention has been made of records relating to the fishing industry nor to those of shipwrecks and groundings, which for years formed part of the black economy for many on the shores of Antrim and Down. The development of lighthouses has been omitted and there is scope for profitable research on the long tradition of ships' surgeons of Ulster origin, exemplified by John White of County Fermanagh, the principal surgeon of the first fleet which landed the first convicts at Botany Bay in January 1788, and whose journal was first published in 1790.[61] Nevertheless the subjects that have been covered – the role of the Irish Sea in trade from the late seventeenth century; the development of passenger services across the Irish Sea; the establishment of shipbuilding; the developing of harbours; the experiences of seamen and passengers sailing from Ulster ports have illustrated the range of primary sources that are available in P.R.O.N.I. where the secrets of Davy Jones's locker may eventually be revealed.

Schooner-rigged, wherry, Skerries, County Dublin, from Wallop Brabazon, *The deep sea and coast fisheries of Ireland* (Dublin, 1848).

9 Smugglers in the Irish Sea in the Eighteenth Century

L. M. CULLEN

Smuggling in Irish waters in the eighteenth century was extensive.[1] However, that fact in itself was not exceptional for the age: such illegal activity was commonplace in any part of Europe where duties were high, and where they ranged widely, as in Ireland, over goods such as tobacco or spirits which were already staple necessities or tea which bore a prohibitive weight of taxation. Nevertheless, in an age in which smuggling activities in Europe reached historic benchmarks, the volume of activity in the Irish Sea was by comparative standards very high. This was a consequence of two factors. Firstly, the northern reaches of the Irish Sea were surrounded by rich hinterlands. Dublin was easily the second largest city of the British Isles; Liverpool handled the traffic of the populous Lancashire region, and both the Ayrshire and the Antrim–Down coastlines were points of supply for the burgeoning hinterlands of the ports of Glasgow and Belfast respectively. Apart from London, served in contraband from the Suffolk and Kent coasts, no compact maritime region in western Europe could remotely rival the northern reaches of the Irish Sea in scale and wealth. Secondly, the Irish Sea and the North Channel between Scotland and Ireland could both be supplied from the Isle of Man.[2] The island was in effect a vast warehouse whose immunities left it totally free of any direct interference from the revenue authorities of three jurisdictions: England, Scotland and Ireland. Revenue vessels could call into the ports of the island, but they were powerless to take any action. Hence the traffic grew to extraordinary heights; it first became an object of prime concern in the 1720s; the turnover of the island doubled between the mid-1740s and the mid-1750s, and doubled again by 1761.[3] Such a state of affairs could not be tolerated indefinitely; the island's indemnities were purchased in 1765 for what was in effect the discounted future income from the island's low duties on goods in transit. No such action was taken then or in the future against Guernsey whose constitutional position was not dissimilar. More remote from populous markets, it never held, even when favoured by the closing of the Isle of Man, quite the same position in the supply of contraband.

The significance of the Irish dimension in this activity was not simply that Dublin was the largest single market in this region, but that much of the operational expertise in handling contraband on both sides of the Irish Sea was possessed by the smugglers and sailors of Rush. The reasons for Rush's prominence was in part its proximity to the largest city in the Irish Sea region: Rush sailors and fishermen provided the city's needs in both contraband and fish. Other factors contributed as well: the Irish parliament's subsidies for the fisheries supported the build-up of a smuggling fleet,[4] and the smugglers of Rush both learned their skills in the distant ling fisheries of the Shetlands and the herring fishery off the Rosses, while drawing on the subsidies to develop the smuggling fleet.

Perhaps more importantly still, the configuration of the northern Irish Sea helped as well. The separate customs jurisdictions of Scotland and Ireland were divided by as little as fourteen miles of water and goods, especially tobacco, shipped from Liverpool and Glasgow to smugglers in Ireland, could be readily trans-shipped from Ireland to Scotland. After 1765 Ireland served as a substitute for the Isle of Man. The reason that Ireland played this role to Scotland to a greater extent than Scotland to Ireland was operational: given westerly winds, vessels from the west had the benefit of the sea in the face of Scottish revenue vessels sailing to meet them, and the manoeuvrability they enjoyed in consequence made it possible for smugglers both to outsail revenue vessels and to choose locations for landing at short notice.

The fisheries, involving a long voyage to Donegal, disguised involvements in smuggling in the northeast of Ireland and the neighbouring Scottish coast,[5] though locations on the Antrim and Down coasts opposite Scotland were the prime focus of activity. Red Bay, north of Glenarm on the east Antrim coast and facing into the huge Firth of Clyde, was a centre for smuggling vessels as early as 1768; it was to become notorious because of a battle at sea there between the smugglers and the revenue men in 1772.[6] The full importance of Red Bay emerged later when the Brackenridges (Breckenridges) of Ayrshire set up there, and used it as a transit point for goods for Scotland.[7] In the late 1760s and the 1770s, Mourne, meaning the coast line from Rostrevor to Newcastle, was the main location of activity in the more northern reaches of the Irish Sea. The organising genius in the traffic seems to have been Arthur Hughes of Greencastle near Newry, described by no less a person than Luke Mercer, head of the Irish revenue vessels, as 'the greatest smuggler in the kingdom'.[8] Hughes seems to have operated in tandem with Jeremiah Atkinson or Acheson of Glassdrumman at Annalong and was involved in the running of rum into Ireland. He also smuggled goods into Roberts Burn in Scotland; one vessel belonging to Hughes and Acheson, whose master claimed that he was in the region simply to call at Newry on his homeward voyage for instructions, was held on suspicion of an ultimate Scottish smuggling destination.[9] In 1771 two vessels were reported to have been dispatched to the Welsh coast to take goods destined for Annalong off a vessel owned by Hughes.[10] Mourne was the focal point for goods for Belfast and its hinterland; tea for Belfast was carried 'on horseback and in turf sacks'.[11] However the importance of the district was greatly enhanced by the Scottish business; vessels either landed goods there, or lay off Dundrum Bay, waiting for a favourable opportunity and a westerly wind to run their cargoes ashore in Scotland. While Rush smugglers crop up in reports on the trade elsewhere, Mourne is the most frequently mentioned location for the voyages of Rush men in these years. One reason for the enhanced importance of the region was that the reduced duties on tea in Ireland in 1767 – it fell from 1s. 9d. to 6d. and 4d. a lb. and the drawback on legal tea exports to Ireland from Britain was enlarged – made the Irish market less attractive to the smuggler. Indeed the revenue commissioners seem to have been misled into believing that the smuggling trade would decline in consequence in the Irish Sea.[12] However what resulted was increased involvement by Irish vessels in the Scottish market where no comparable easement of the tax burden had taken place. The Rush smugglers were intimately involved in the business at Mourne, in one instance to the point that Atkinson and the Rush smuggler Christopher Farran were both owners of a cargo.[13]

The combined consequences of Dublin's large domestic market, the impetus that the Isle of Man had given to business at large, the narrow waters of the North Channel and the advantage that westerly winds gave to vessels sailing from Irish staging points, were that Rush vessels and seamen dominated the smuggling trade in this region more particularly after 1765. Various debt cases in the Isle of Man chancery court in the 1750s and 1760s bring to light a host of Rush names: Hore, Sweetman, Doyle, Connor, Field, Knight, Kane, Dunn, Harford, Grumley, Rickard, Farran, Rigg, Russel, Stanley, Oram and Murphy. No less that fifty vessels were said on one occasion to be owned in Rush; in fact eleven distinct vessels under north county Dublin masters can be identified as sailing from a single port (Lorient) in a single year (1787).[14] Given the problematic division between fishing and smuggling, the size of the smuggling fleet is really impossible to measure. The Customs Commissioners in Edinburgh reported in December 1768 the sailing of nine vessels from Rush in the expectation that when laden they would run their cargoes on the Ayrshire and Galloway coasts; five vessels which had sailed outwards from Rush were anticipated in May 1776 on the Ayrshire and Galloway coasts.[15] This type of report could be multiplied. A group of Rush smugglers who pioneered the movement into bigger vessels and broader markets can be identified in the 1760s and early 1770s: the Connors, Fields, Farrans along with John Creenan, Thomas Knight, Christopher Stanley and Stephen Rickard were the key figures. They are in essence a well-identified generation of smugglers whose presence did not outlive the mid-1770s. Another generation of Rush men is associated with the smuggling in the late 1770s and 1780s. The war of 1778–83 led many of them into privateering either on Irish vessels or on French vessels fitted out under American or French colours in France. Indeed, one vessel fitted out under British letters of marque seems to have passed into American colours simply as an act of revenge for its seizure in Dublin on account of a smuggling episode. Of this generation the most celebrated were the privateer masters Luke Ryan, John Kelly and Patrick Dowling.[16] They were a legend in their day, and even afterwards. Patrick Dowling made no less than 185 captures,[17] and the vicissitudes of Luke Ryan were celebrated widely: although captured, he was pardoned because of the French nationality the French court had already given him, though imprisonment for debt then deprived him of his liberty.[18] Those who entered French service rather significantly represented only part, perhaps not even the more solidly propertied part of Rush business and navigational talent: privateering under home colours and smuggling remained their forte. Their association with Dublin businessmen and their investment in hulls under Irish colours makes it too improbable that they would have relished a hand in the systematic destruction of trade in the Irish Sea attempted by privateers manned by other Rush men under American or French colours.[19] Some divide seems probable between the central Rush interest and the more marginal or daring spirits in Rush who had little to lose personally and who in war time, facing a decline in smuggling at home and abroad had the prospect of serving on privateers fitted out in Dublin. Moreover, if they remained in home waters they ran the risk of impressment for the navy. Letters of marque frequently were simply a convenient cover for regular trade – or even smuggling – with the prospect of an occasional prize; many vessels under letters of marque, and certainly most of the Irish vessels did not entail full-blown privateering cruises. Significantly Luke Ryan had started as a privateer in 1778 under English letters of marque, and had resorted to American colours when his vessel under English letters of marque had been seized at Rush for smuggling and had then been forcibly rescued by him after it had been taken by the revenue officers to the Liffey: at his trial Ryan claimed that he had been ill-used by his king.[20] These years, 1778–82, represent something of a second generation of smuggler.

A very definite third generation can be detected for the 1790s, 1800s and 1810s when names not particularly prominent in the past were now the best-known of the Rush men. John Doyle and John Murphy are two celebrated names of the 1790s. Doyle was a household name, member of a family well-known in the business in Rush. Murphy, whose exploits were recorded both in the poetry of Mayo and in the French records of the Killala expedition seems to have been a regular visitor to Mayo, but was a Rush man.[21] Morris, equally famous, may also have been a Rush man: a petition to the revenue commissioners in 1771 by a Nicholas Morris of Skerries was presented on his behalf by the Dublin merchants Hugh and Val O'Connor who had close connections with the smuggling world.[22] Most famous of all was Captain Mathews. A James Mathews, a Roman Catholic, was a member of the crew of the Rush vessel, *Happy Return*, seized off the Scottish coast in 1768.[23] There is a memorial tablet to a Mathews, gentleman, in the now ruined catholic graveyard at Kenure, It seems likely that Mathews also was a Rush man. He was lost off the coast of Donegal during a storm in an October voyage in 1820; he, like Murphy, lingered in the folk poetry of Mayo;[24] Maxwell in his *Wild sports of the West* has a memorable description of meeting him aboard his vessel, the *Jane*, off the Mayo coast on the voyage which preceded his fatal last trip.[25] George O'Malley the Mayo smuggler recalled him as 'the bravest and best of them all – poor Captain Mathews, who would stand to his guns and wouldn't flinch from an armed frigate'.[26]

The Rush smugglers, even if dependent on the alliance of Dublin (and Drogheda) merchants, were by no means without resources of their own. Among them were some merchants, and these men in war time fitted out privateers on their own account or in conjunction with Dublin merchant houses. The two Rush merchant houses fitting out vessels were the Sheridans and the McCabes. They can be identified as involved in financing privateers in 1778–82, and Richard Sheridan was master of a vessel fitted out by the O'Connors as late as 1793.[27] A report in the *Freeman's Journal* of 23 February 1779 stated that 'we find the little fishing village of Rush has already fitted out four vessels, one of them is now at Rogerson's Quay, ready to sail, being completely armed and manned, carrying 14 carriage guns and 60 of as brave hands as any in Europe'.[28] The Rush families enjoyed close ties with Dublin merchant houses, though these links by prominent Dublin merchant houses, being discreet, cannot be teased out very directly. The O'Connors were the most notable of these houses: their links with the Rush interests are the most clear-cut, and also the longest-lasting. The O'Connors originally had a business in the Isle of Man, and settled in Dublin after 1765.[29] It is likely that the other Dublin business houses who, like the O'Connors, took an interest in letters of marque also enjoyed links with Rush. Certainly, in 1778–82 most of the Dublin houses interested in privateering vessels seemed to come from the milieu of radical merchants, catholic and non-conformist especially, who were opposed in business interests and politics to Dublin's dominant anglican business establishment. In some cases Dublin ownership may simply be a cover for Rush investment, in which case the Rush initiative is in fact quite substantial. Luke Ryan, the future privateer, served his apprenticeship under a boatbuilder named King, possibly Henry King of Ringsend, a specialist in fast sailing craft. It has been speculated that King was a Rush man,[30] and the likelihood that he was seems to be borne out in the fact that several Kings at Rush can be traced as recipients of fishing bounties: indeed a Henry King was owner of several Rush vessels in 1771–73.[31]

In a wider context, Belfast and Scottish business interests also had some hand in the background to the smuggling trade. Some direct tie between Rush interest and the Achesons at Annalong, one of the pivotal interests in this traffic, seem probable. The contraband trade involved Rush men at all levels, from the lowly seaman up to Rush merchants respectable enough to have a solid business connection with big business in Dublin. Some smugglers were minute operators like Phelix Doran, whose outlay, according to his petition, that 'of a poor old man', amounted to a mere £19 sterling.[32] Other Rush men were however regularly incurring debts of up to £150 in the Isle of Man. Some of these intermediate-level figures had real substance at their modest level. John Creenan (Crenane) was both master and owner of the *India* of Rush, taking a cargo worth £1000 in 1762,[33] while in a dispute between William Rigg and John Russell in the same year, John Russell was represented as having 'both certain effects, cash, bills and notes remaining in the hands, power and custody of several persons within this isle'.[34] Another Rush man, John Hore, at the time of his decease was indebted to several persons in the island for £200 and was 'possessed of considerable effects within this island and elsewhere' including a share in the wherry *Peggy and Mary* of Rush.[35] Significantly, some of the smuggling families provided the parish priests of Rush: Barnaby Farren (Farran) was parish priest in 1756, Thomas Murphy in 1785, and William Murphy in 1795.[36] Modest in scale though individual Rush operators often were, they frequently worked on their own account. Small operators, with restricted access to merchant credit, often paid cash brought with them on their outward voyage for their contraband. This can be seen in the mid-1780s when trade in Cognac brandy enjoyed a short-lived revival, and some Rush masters made an unaccustomed appearance in Charente or Bordeaux.[37] In one instance, the Irish brandy merchant, John Saule, in Cognac made the error of giving credit for a cargo to a plausible and well-spoken Rush man, John White. The subsequent protracted saga of the attempted recovery of the debt brings out the murky side of Fingall business life: no process-server would serve a writ in the district, and the story was a long and frustrating one. John White himself went off to Norfolk, Virginia after the sale of his cargo.[38]

The Rush men were owners in 1765 of a substantial fleet of wherries. The masters and owners can all be identified in the details in the *Commons Journals* of subsidies to the fishing industry. After 1765 some of these vessels were lengthened and decked for the longer voyages to the continent now necessary. The initiative in taking this step was immediate, and if the capital involved was their own, as was conceivably the case, the investment in a short period was by no means inconsiderable. The Connors came to the fore at this stage of the story. They were no relations to the O'Connors of Dublin. At this stage they seem to have been partners or associates of the Farrans, a family well-established in Rush's business, and of John Creenan. Three of the Farrans had been involved as early as 1758 in a gratuitously violent incident when they with others were charged with 'a certain assault and riot made upon certain officers and mariners of H.M. cutters now lying in Douglas'.[39] This episode may identify them as the leaders of what was to emerge as a desperate gang within Rush's business and marine circles. There are not many references in the chancery court in the Isle of Man to the Connors and they appear relatively late. Michael Connor is first mentioned (along with Richard Connor) on 9 September 1763, and his name recurs five times between March and May 1765; John Connor's name occurs only in April 1765, and one of the three references in that month refers to an assault on an officer.[40] The fact that a family not widely associated with Rush's activity came so quickly to the fore in the 1760s emphasises the likelihood of a new breed among its seamen. The later biographical account of John Connor represents Thomas Field as his partner when he set out his first vessel, with Field soon setting out a second vessel which accompanied Connor's on his expeditions. In fact, this group of Rush men, embracing the Connors, Field, Christopher Farran, John Creenan, and a few others seems to have pioneered the movement of Rush men into direct voyages to the continent on larger vessels, and more positively still the novel tactic of sailing in fleets. The Connors appear in Europe very quickly after April 1765. The only shipping records which cover their movements appear to be those of Nantes, then about to lose its position as one of the prime sources of supply of tea to the contraband trade in 1760s. No other relevant port has good records of shipping movements for these years. John and Michael Connor first appeared in Nantes toward the end of 1765; they both made trips again in February 1766 and in February 1767. In the interval Christopher Farran and George Russell took cargoes abroad in April 1766. Most of the vessels appear to have been consigned to Andrew Gallwey (Galwey) who had supplied contraband to the island in pre-1765 days, but one of the vessels was handled by Park who had been clerk to an Irish partnership in the Isle of Man.[41] By 1766–7 as we know from other evidence Andrew Galwey was supplying tea to smugglers at Lorient, and the Parks had opened up business in Roscoff. Nantes itself was not henceforth important to the Rush smugglers, but the visits between late 1765 and the outset of 1767, solely by members of the gang, must have had an exploratory significance which went beyond routine purchasing.

The tactic of sailing in fleets is most closely associated with this group, and broadly speaking it did not outlive them. As early as 27 March 1767 Luke Mercer detailed the expected return of ten Rush vessels which each had sailed from their home port on various dates between 1 January and 21 March.[42] In June Sir Randal O'Neal, coast officer for Rush, reported the sailing of six Rush vessels for Gottenburg, being Creenan's, Fields's, the two Connors' vessels, Stanley and Farran's, and the 'Scotch wherry' (which was probably a vessel of John Kane's).[43] On 18 February 1769 the Riding surveyor at Strangford wrote on 'undoubted authority that John Connor alias the Batchelor and one Carr intend to land two cargoes of tobacco and spirits at Mourne, that they are to be convoyed by Michael Connor who has a cargo in from Wales, and that they are not to part company until they have all landed their cargoes'.[44] An object of these tactics was to overawe the revenue vessels, often smaller, slower and less well-armed. A proposal from George Vernon for a preventive wherry to be stationed in Dublin Bay was turned down by the revenue commissioners with Mercer 'having reported that smugglers on the coasts of this kingdom are becoming so formidable not only by using large decked wherries and cutters, but sailing together in fleets, that pretending to annoy them with a small vessel would be ridiculous'.[45] In intimidating or holding off the revenue vessels the tactic of course also permitted some of the smugglers to land their cargoes. If the smugglers had the wind, as they would normally have against Scottish cruisers, then their flexibility was enormous. An interesting account survives of manoeuvres at sea in which the wind blew from the east, giving the Scottish vessels the advantage. Hugh Campbell, tide surveyor at Donaghadee, reported in November 1767 that

> being on a cruise on Friday, he fell in with the Connors, Field's cutter, and a cutter belonging to Air [sic], on the west coast of Scotland, that the sternmost put about thinking to cut him off the land, but that he bore away for Loughryon and acquainted the collector there with what he saw, who had the army sent to guard the landing places, that the wind being east he sailed for the Irish shore but at half channel saw the vessels drawn up in a line taking in about four miles, that the smugglers kept between him and the Irish shore, that at sun set he bore away as far as Larne, and that evening all the said smugglers came within gun shot of Donaghadee, that they have all increased their force, and are masters of the sea there, that they have been three weeks on the coast of Scotland, but cannot land, the coast being guarded but that the four boats intend to land there, and to keep by each other.[46]

Other captains emerged to play similar roles to the Connors and their early associates, notably individuals such as Thomas Knight and Joseph Grumley.

After the notorious August 1767 episode by the Connor band (which will be shortly described), the revenue commissioners sought 'most particular' descriptions of John Connor, Richard Connor, Thomas Field, Patrick Baun, Nicholas Kane, Luke Rooney, James Rooney, Stephen Connor,

Patrick Farran, George Coppage, James Sweetman and Patrick Croghan.[47] Admiralty warrants were issued for their arrest, and advertisements offered a reward for their capture.[48] John Connor was the most famous of the band, at least in the sense that contemporaries and later legend both seem to have singled him out. He became the hero subsequently of a book entitled *The life and adventures of John Connor commonly called Jack the bachelor the famous Irish bucker.* The second edition is dated 1821, price 1s. 8d., but an earlier undated edition, described as a new edition for 1s. 0d., also exists, omitting a poem and the reference in the title to 'the famous Irish bucker'.[49] Thus it seems likely that there was a still earlier edition, and given the style of the work, it is conceivable that it was composed prior to 1800. It is a partly biographical account in which the hero's life becomes the vehicle to relate three amorous adventures suggested by the title 'bachelor' (frequently spelled batchelor in contemporary accounts). In reality, Connor was no bachelor, and the epitaph recording the existence of a wife and five children points to a long married life. The nick-name 'bachelor' was perhaps made necessary by the fact that there were two John Connors in Rush, both smuggling masters, the other being known as Shan Baun (Sean Bán).[50]

The book is something of a rags to riches story, but is in the tradition of the picaresque tale, and is not necessarily to be taken literally. According to the biography, John Connor was taken for his first trip to the Isle of Man when he was thirteen, by a man with the initials 'S.F.' It is plausible to assume that this would have been a Farran rather than a Field, the former being better established in the business; subsequently he traded on his own account on the vessel of 'Capt S', who could have been a Stanley, but as Stanley was a contemporary of Connor, it is more probable that the letters stand for a member of the well-established Sweetman family. Many of the facts in the biography relating to Connor are accurate. For instance, it states his age as thirty-six and year of death as 1772. This is borne out by the epitaph in Kenure church which mentions his age as thirty-seven, and the date of decease as 16 June 1772. His father, aged seventy-two, according to the tablet, had preceded him on 9 March of the same year, and in the context the reference to Connor's wife and five children could, though not necessarily so, suggest that they had preceded him also. Some verse follows on the tablet:

> Alas he's gone the generous and the brave
> Whose bounteous hand to every object gave.
> Friend to the stranger and the distressed
> These most he honoured and he most possess'd.
> To paint his many virtues all must say
> Requires the pen of Milton, Pope or Gay
> But these like him are fall'n away to dust.

This verse recalls the lines affixed to the gravestone of Arthur O'Leary in County Cork and suggest a wish to see him in a heroic mould. The biography states variously that he had two and three brothers. Apart from Michael described as his elder brother, a Richard and Stephen Connor were participants in his exploits and could be brothers. Connor was not a common Rush name, and the biography states that he was born in County Wexford in 1736, and that his parents settled in Rush when he was in his twelfth year. The account mentions an apparently curious episode to seize Connor in Rush while at the height of his success: 'Sir E' obviously Sir Edward Newenham, collector for County Dublin, entered Rush disguised as a beggar, and enquired from some children whether Connor was then in town. Tall though the tale sounds, it had some basis in fact in that Newenham, a member of parliament, resident at Belcamp in north County Dublin, seems to have taken not only a close but an obsessive interest in Connor. In December 1767 the revenue commissioners informed the surveyors of the revenue at Skerries and Baldoyle that as soon as they heard of Field's or Connor's boats on the coast or at sea 'they are immediately to send an express to Sir Edward Newenham in Granby Row, whether it be night or day'.[51] In late August 1769 Newenham in person informed the commissioners that Connor was expected back by 24 or 25 September from his current voyage, following a course via the Saltee Islands.[52] On 2 April 1772, in a remarkable letter to the chief secretary, Newenham suggested a pardon for Connor who would return to a peaceful life of fishing.[53] Was this letter prompted by direct contact between Newenham and Connor, as Connor died in June of the same year? Was the contact prompted by a wish, in the knowledge of ill-health, to have his outlawry cancelled so that he could spend his remaining days at home? We can only speculate. His death marked the end of an era: his contemporaries do not seem to have greatly outlived him: death even from natural causes came early to Rush men, and a whole new generation achieved notoriety over the next decade.

Connor and his contemporaries had, however, transformed Rush's business from a relatively narrow base, confined to the northern reaches of the Irish Sea and the fisheries off the Rosses and the Shetland Islands, into one which reached over the next twenty years to as far afield as Gottenburg and Bordeaux. They fitted out and manned a new generation of fast cutter. The refrain 'new' comes up repeatedly in the revenue correspondence. Quite apart from Connor's own vessel, Farran's and Field's 'new cutters' are mentioned in March 1767; more vividly still Field's 'famous new cutter' in July, and John Creenan's 'new cutter' are mentioned in June 1767, and Stanley's 'new cutter' in January 1771.[54] The vessels became larger and faster: the tonnage roughly doubled, and could reach fifty tons. Stephen Rickard's vessel in 1771 was quite novel: a French-built lugger, crew half Rush-men, half English, carrying three masts, fourteen brass guns and described as 'one of the fastest going vessels in the smuggling trade'.[55] In 1774 at Gottenburg, an Irish vessel, 'rigged as a schooner, burthen about

120 tons, square stern'd, clinker built, about thirty men, all Irish, was going to load teas which were then putting up for him and the master said was intended for this coast [Whitby] or Scotland'.[56]

The weakness of the smugglers' tactics of sailing in larger vessels and in fleets was that the revenue could respond in kind. Interestingly the revenue commmissioners at first underestimated the threat. They thought that the combination of the closure of the Isle of Man in 1765 and the reduction of tea duties would lead to a fall-off in smuggling in the Irish Sea, and consequently recommended proposals to Mercer for a shift in the emphasis of revenue cruiser strength to western and southern waters.[57] However, in the face of the challenge from the smugglers, the revenue commissioners had already sought from William Harrington, a boatbuilder in Cork, a plan for a vessel of 100 tons to cope with the smugglers 'who are now grown so formidable'.[58] Hitherto the revenue had relied on barges, slow sailing and manned by small crews. In May 1768 the revenue authorities decided to accept from Harrington, who was minuted as having the reputation 'of building fast-sailing vessels' and as being 'the best shipwright in Cork', an estimate of £960 for the construction of a cruiser of 55 foot keel and 20 foot beam, proper dimensions for a prime sailor.[59] The Malahide barge which, under its master Arthur Luske, had distinguished itself in a battle with the smugglers in August 1767 was lengthened, renamed the *Revenge*, and nineteen men were put aboard under the same captain.[60] At this stage two vessels were on the stocks in Cork for the revenue, being built by William Harrington and Edward Allen.[61] Carrying larger crews and a more formidable armament, these vessels put the revenue more or less on a par with the smugglers. Other tactics were resorted to as well. A determined effort seems to have been made to have the revenue officers (coast officers and coast surveyors) actually reside at Rush, and for the countryside to be 'rummaged' if goods were landed there.[62] The use of the army supplemented revenue resources. In 1772 the collector at Newry proposed the use of the army in Annalong and in Mourne,[63] and by 1775 the army was used in Rush on occasion to support the revenue officers.[64]

However, the most effective of all tactics in response to the smuggling fleets was for the revenue cruisers to operate in conjunction with one another, at times also with Scottish cruisers; as the revenue commissioners maintained contact with the Scottish commissioners of customs in these years. At the end of July 1768 Luske on the *Revenge* and another vessel, the Carlingford cutter, were instructed to sail under orders to keep at sea until they fell in with the Connors' and Field's vessels 'which are expected hourly'.[65] In 1771 Causer, one of the revenue captains, was instructed to put himself and his vessel under the command of Luske, captain of the *Revenge*, cruising between Dublin and Mourne.[66]

The resort to these tactics began early, ahead even of the arrival of new vessels, and before sailing practices had been standardised. In fact, the clash at sea between revenue men and smugglers in August 1767 showed that by such methods the revenue had prospects, even with the inferior vessels they had at that stage, of matching the smugglers on equal terms. In July 1767 Robert Thompson, surveyor of the Strangford barge, informed the commissioners in Dublin that he had 'positive information that John and Michael Connor's two boats and also Thomas Field's famous new cutter are now at Gottenburg loaded with teas', and that they were expected on the coast between Annalong and Newcastle, 'determined to come in company and fight their way, that each of the said boats have upwards of twenty men on board, and carry four guns on each of their decks, besides swivels and small arms'. The board agreed to dispatch the Dunleary, Malahide and Carlingford barges to meet him at Ardglass. The Larne barge was instructed to act as look out, as they were expected through the North Channel, and, following Thompson's instructions, 'if she should see them, dog them into the bay'. The vessels were instructed to prepare for a three week cruise, and to take extra hands as necessary who could be depended on for 'activity and spirit'.[67] The redoubtable Arthur Luske, surveyor of the Malahide barge, wrote on 8 August, describing the action which began late on the night of Thursday 6 August:

> That on the sixth at half an hour after eleven o'clock at night being at anchor in the bay of Dundrum off Newcastle in company with the Killough barge which lay a little distance from him the watch acquainted him, they saw two wherries and a cutter standing into the bay, upon which taking them to be smugglers, and believing that Mr Wheeler surveyor of the Killough barge did not see them, he sent his boat and four men to acquaint him thereof, but by the time the boat got alongside him, three vessels were up with him, and all three fired into him, by which one of his [Luske's] men was shot dead, that Wheeler having so short notice was not prepared for them, that he [Luske] immediately got ready for action and stood for them, and engaged them, which prevented the Killough barge from being destroyed (as appears by a letter from Mr Wheeler), that three all fired at him [Luske] and he returned the fire to each and again amongst them, and continued the engagement until two in the morning in the hopes of having assistance, but the Killough barge was so disabled from the first fire, that she could not give him any, that he continued a running fight, and they continued firing at him until four o'clock, by which time all his sails and rigging were torn to pieces, that two of the vessels then boarded him, one on his quarter, and the other on his bow, that the largest came on his quarter, and tore down the barge almost to the water, by which they thought she must sink immediately, that he and his crew were obliged to retreat to the cabin with their small arms, so that when the smugglers came on board, they were afraid to go down, and their stay was short, as they were sure the barge must sink; that when they were gone he threw the ballast overboard and lightened her so as to keep her above water, that he saw a running fight afterwards between the Strangford and Killough barges, and the smugglers, but the Strangford barge fired a gun and quit the chase, that Wheeler took him and his crew into Carlingford, that the Malahide barge has also been towed into Carlingford in a shattered condition, that three of his men are wounded, two of who he fears cannot recover, and that he has employed a doctor to take care of them, and it also appears from Wheeler's letter that Mr Luske is slightly wounded himself.[68]

Mercer subsequently reported on his own examination of the barge, 'greatly damaged and shattered, that she has many marks of shot through different parts of her hull, and that her sails and rigging are shot to pieces, that he has had carpenters on board consulting and contriving how to make her equal to any smuggling cutter, and as she is a fine molded [sic] boat, a prime sailor and of sufficient breadth', he recommended decking and lengthening her. This was agreed to without an estimate.[69]

The action also led to some questions such as the failure to shadow the smuggling vessels on their route and to giving news of their being sighted, and the early abandonment of action by the Strangford barge, but the basic tactic was sound, and the barges cruising between Dublin and County Down were supplemented.[70] Revenue vessels from both Scotland and Ireland now patrolled in the North Channel and its approaches. The results showed quickly. On their return from the continent in November 1767, the Connors and Fields were held off the Scottish coast for three weeks by the manoeuvres of the revenue vessels, and were unable to land their cargoes during that period.[71] In January 1768 the customs commissioners of Edinburgh communicated details of the seizure of a cutter by Captain Edward Thompson of the Scottish vessel *Tartuffe* aided by an Irish revenue vessel.[72] The seizure of another Rush vessel, inappropriately named *The Happy Return* with its crew of thirteen 'dissolute dangerous persons' soon followed.[73] In August 1769 the Scottish revenue vessel *King George*, sighting Thomas Hore's wherry, made signals, and was joined by the Larne barge, the Carlingford cutter, and Luske's *Revenge*. Outsailed by the Carlingford cutter, Hore was boarded and brought into Carlingford port.[74] A few days before, the *Revenge* and the Carlingford barge had a still bigger catch. Though a chase had not prevented Christopher Farran's cutter from landing her cargo, Luske seized the vessel. For want of proof, she had to be released. However the outcome illustrated the changed circumstances at sea and that the odds had now evened.[75] In February 1771 the surveyor at Ballycastle reported that after a fight with Scottish cruisers, the smugglers had left two injured men at a public house in Ballycastle, intimating that they would return for them later: one had his hands shot off, the other was wounded by a musket ball in the back.[76] One of the craft involved in this action was Christopher Stanley's vessel. She and her cargo were seized in a long chase off Lambay by Luske a month later.[77] By May, Knight's vessel, the *Fly*, also believed to have been involved in the battle with the Scottish cruisers was under arrest in Dublin.[78] In the meantime, Jack the Batchelor's vessel, which had run aground near Dundalk as the culmination of a chase by Luske, was condemned and subsequently purchased at an auction for the revenue service.[79] In October 1771 John Creenan's vessel was taken by two Scottish revenue cruisers.[80] Worse was to follow for the smugglers. The bloody fight in the North Channel with the Scottish cruisers was repeated, when in January 1772 two smuggling vessels had the worst of a battle off Red Bay with the Irish revenue vessel *Lurcher*. According to the report of her master, Captain Walter Long, 'several of the smugglers were killed and particularly the brother of Jack the Batchelor as he is informed who has been buried near Glenarm and requesting to know whether his body is to be taken up in order that he may receive the reward offered by the advertisement of the 18th May 1770'.[81] This was Michael Connor, and his burial at Glenarm explains why though he predeceased his brother Jack, his name does not occur on the tablet in Kenure church. Through 1772 and 1773 the Scottish revenue officers continued to make an impressive run of seizures of Irish vessels.[82]

The accumulated losses of the preceding years along with the deaths of John and Michael Connor marked the end of an era. During these years the smugglers responded by still larger crews and more guns. In 1769 Knight had only four 4-pounder guns,[83] and by August 1770 Field and Knight both carried eight carriage guns, while John Connor and John Creenan had six, apart from swivel guns and small arms.[84] The smugglers' tactics also changed, as sailing in fleets seems to have been abandoned. Moreover, with a quicker and more effective response by the revenue, goods could no longer be warehoused so boldly as in the past. Hence very large numbers of men were assembled not simply to take the cargo ashore but to disperse it across as wide a hinterland as possible. This method of dispersal by many hands was by no means unknown in the past – there is a good description of the practice near Larne in 1733[85] – but it now became the general norm in the trade.[86] In turn, revenue officers, often arrogant and high-handed in their methods affected a wide range of the inhabitants of their districts by the zealous performance of their duties and helped strengthen rather than weaken the bond of silence and conspiracy on which the smuggler depended.

Despite improvement in the revenue service, smugglers frequently continued to outsail the revenue cruisers and indeed if seized, more often than not they had already landed their cargo or part of it. They could still on occasion outgun individual revenue cruisers. For example, in 1770 the Connor gang attacked the *Pelham* in Beaumaris Bay, plundered her and ran her aground.[87] As late as 1774 an Irish cutter had chased a revenue cutter into the port of Falmouth.[88] Although the abandonment of fleet tactics by the smugglers meant, in effect, a victory for the revenue, it was victory in a battle, not in a war. The shift to larger, faster and more heavily armed and manned vessels, sailing individually, meant that much of the initiative could again be exercised by the smugglers. Nevertheless smugglers' losses were numerous, and they relied on the high profits of successfully-landed cargoes to compensate for the losses occasioned by the frequent seizures that they had to bear. As always the real enemy of the revenue was the high duties which they had to administer and which meant that even a high rate of attrition left the business remunerative for the smugglers. Lowered duties in the 1780s and early 1790s successively reduced activity in tea and tobacco smuggling; while increased duties during the long revolutionary and Napoleonic wars, from 1793 to 1815, sent the level of activity soaring on the return of peace in 1815.

Opening of the Victoria Channel, Belfast, 10 July 1849, from D. J. Owen, *A short history of the port of Belfast* (Belfast, 1917).

10 The Development of Belfast Harbour

ROBIN SWEETNAM

Belfast harbour is today the largest port in Ireland and a shipbuilding centre of international repute. The growth of the port owes much to its geographical position as the natural gateway to the fertile Lagan valley and the lowlands beyond. It is comparatively close to the coalfields and industrial centres of Britain and, unlike the other sea loughs on the Ulster coast, Belfast Lough has a wide, deep opening giving easy access to shipping, particularly vessels under sail. Some credit for its growth, however, must be given to the industrious nature of the Ulster population and to the merchant members of the independent harbour authority, who for 200 years have encouraged the industrial development of the port by providing shipbuilding and repairing facilities and by making land available by reclamation for port-related industry.

The site of Belfast at the lowest ford across the river Lagan, at its confluence with the rivers Blackstaff and Farset, was a natural landing place for many centuries. However, Belfast's development as a port is usually dated from 1613 when the lord of the castle, Sir Arthur Chichester obtained a charter incorporating the town as a borough with power to erect a quay. This first quay was built, not on the Lagan, but on the south bank of the Farset near the site of St George's church at the foot of the High Street.

The seaborne trade through Ulster's ports at that time was minute by modern standards. In 1614–15, shipping, including that entering Carrickfergus, then the principal port in Belfast Lough and within whose customs jurisdiction Belfast was situated, numbered only some seventy vessels, totalling less than 1000 tons burden. Belfast's share would have been but a small proportion of Carrickfergus's trade, valued that year at £3423, but it would, almost certainly, have included the 41000 pipe and barrel staves exported and valued at £147. By 1637 trade had risen dramatically and the annual value of Carrickfergus's customs revenue, £183 in 1614–15, had increased more than tenfold, prompting the lord deputy, Lord Strafford, to buy out, on behalf of the crown, Carrickfergus's existing privilege of retaining for the town's use one third of the customs collected. Deprived of this advantage, and lacking adequate sheltered anchorage, Carrickfergus's share of the rising trade fell and Belfast rose rapidly in importance.

By 1685 when Captain Thomas Philips made a survey of the garrison towns of Ireland for the crown, he reported that 'Belfast was now third in the kingdom for trade'. The tonnage of shipping entering the port that year exceeded 7000 tons and Belfast merchants, whose ventures ranged from the Baltic to Spain, to the West Indies and America, owned at least forty ships totalling more than 2100 tons burden.

Despite the impressive volume of trade, the port suffered severely from the shallowness of the tortuous channel up to the quay. At low water the head of the lough virtually dried out and the river Lagan, less than two feet deep in front of the town, wound its way between sand and mud banks to deep water at the pool of Garmoyle three miles downstream. This made the landing of freight a slow and expensive business, as only small ships could come up to the quay without first discharging all or part of the cargo into lighters.

An attempt to improve conditions was made in 1729 when, by an act of parliament, control of the port was transferred from the lord of the castle to the town corporation, though with little apparent success. To cope with the steady rise in trade more quays were built privately by the leading merchants, but no deepening of the river was achieved. Eventually, in 1785, following the repeal of the English acts restricting Irish trade, the newly-formed chamber of commerce petitioned the Irish parliament requesting a straight grant of £2000 towards the cost of making a straight canal from the quays down to Garmoyle. Parliament refused a grant, but gave instead what was to prove even more important, the transfer of responsibility for the control of the harbour from the town corporation to the merchant community, which had a direct interest in its efficient management and development. By an act of 1785 a new body was formed, the Corporation for Preserving and Improving the Port of Belfast, commonly called the ballast board. It is from this date that complete minute books and statistical information regarding shipping are available. Belfast's population now numbered more than 15000; over 700 ships totalling over 30000 tons were arriving annually and trade was rising as the industrial revolution made its mark.

The first objectives of the new board were the improvement of the channel up to the town and the acquisition of ground where a wharf to store ballast could be built and ship repair facilities established. The provision of commercial quays was considered to be beyond their financial resources as the board's income was limited to that which could be derived from tonnage dues on vessels, from their monopoly on the supply of ballast and from pilotage, which, in view of the state of the channel, was made compulsory on all ships of more than 4 feet draught coming up to the town.

By 1795 the worst of the shoals had been removed, either by hand spading at low water or by use of the primitive 'bag and spoon' method, improving the minimum depth of the channel by 2 feet, but its course, as shown in the chart prepared in 1789 by the haven master, Lieutenant James Lawson, was still as tortuous as that indicated on a chart drawn by Greenville Collins a century earlier. In 1795, after protracted negotiations, the board also obtained 10 acres of foreshore from the marquis of Donegall, the lord of the castle; this was reclaimed and a dry dock 'capable of containing at one time three vessels of 200 tons each' constructed. The contractor for the work was William Ritchie, a shipbuilder from Ayr, whom the board had encouraged in 1791 to set up a shipbuilding and repairing yard in Belfast. This dry dock, opened in 1800, is still in use today.

Despite the war with France the economic outlook at the beginning of the nineteenth century was not unfavourable and the trade through the port began to double and redouble every sixteen years (Figure 1). The fundamental problem of improving the approach to the port had yet to be tackled for, in spite of the board's efforts to deepen the channel, all but the smaller vessels still had to lighten ship at Garmoyle, involving the merchants in heavy extra handling charges and seriously inconveniencing the customs

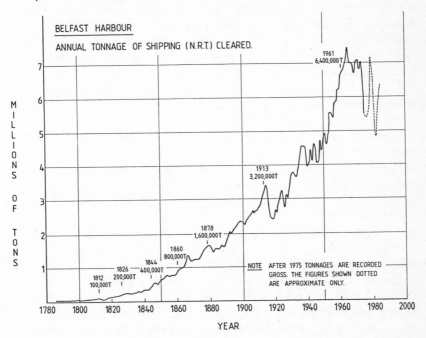

Figure 1.

officials who had to supervise all the handling of goods between ship and shore in an effort to ensure that no revenue duty was lost due to 'pillage'.

In 1814, with the prospect of peace with France in sight and with customs revenue at the port approaching £400000 a year, both the ballast board and the commissioners of customs decided independently to seek engineering advice on how best to improve the port; renewed hostilities caused the proposals received to be shelved and it was not until 1819 that the search for a solution was resumed. Reports were obtained from many of the eminent engineers of the day, including John Rennie and his son, Sir John Rennie, and from Thomas Telford. All agreed that the best solution to the problem was the construction of one or more floating docks – enclosed basins behind lock gates where vessels could be kept afloat at all states of the tide – with access by a ship canal; their plans varied only as to the extent and location of the proposed docks and the routes of the canals. The use of a tidal approach channel was dismissed as being impractical, although marginally cheaper in cost. Each scheme in turn was rejected both by the government, which refused to pay for the work, and by the merchants who found the proposals 'objectionable' as involving too great an initial outlay.

It was not until 1830, when steam power had made dredging, particularly maintenance dredging, a more practical proposition, that an eminent London engineer, James Walker, suggested that a straightened tidal channel leading up to a deepened river in front of the town would now be economically feasible, and that the work could be carried out in stages as need arose and financial resources allowed. Walker's step by step ideas were very much in line with the thinking of the merchant community and were welcomed by the board. A bill promoted by the community to secure powers to carry out the work and to buy out the private quays was, however, bitterly opposed by local landed interests and it was not until 1837 that a compromise was eventually reached and an act obtained.

Belfast was now the first town for trade in Ireland; the population had risen to 70000, shipping at 300000 tons was treble that in 1814 and the value of exports continued to exceed substantially the value of imports. The board now tried to obtained a loan from the government to carry out the work but had great difficulty in obtaining even £25000, half of the minimum sum required. Fortunately the Belfast Bank agreed to advance the balance and, early in 1839, William Dargan, the foremost contractor in Ireland, was engaged to form a cut across the first bend in the river below the town. The excavation was carried out by hand inside tipped banks and the spoil deposited on the east side of the cut forming a 17 acre island which, as Queen's Island, was later to become world famous for its shipyards. The cut was completed early in 1841, providing a 9 feet deep channel up to the river in front of the town where deepening by dredging had been carried out in the meanwhile.

The board's next step, the purchase of all privately owned quays, was complete by 1845. The provision of deeper berths for the larger ships, which could now come up the channel, was met first by building alternative accommodation on the County Down side of the river and then, in 1847, by the construction of a continuous line of quays out in the river across the front of all the old County Antrim docks and quays, which were incapable of being deepened.

Despite the famine and the general depression, shipping through the port had risen to more than 0.5 million tons – half of the tonnage representing steamers – and the board, anxious to provide relief work to the numerous unemployed, brought forward their plans for the formation of the second cut to complete Walker's channel down to Garmoyle. Once again the contract was awarded to William Dargan.

The board was now the owner of extensive lands and quays, with greatly increased responsibility, and it was felt that greater powers were required if the progressive improvement of the port was to be maintained. A bill was promoted in parliament, and on 21 June 1847, a new act was given royal assent repealing all former acts and constituting a new body, the Belfast Harbour Commissioners, with wide ranging authority.

The second cut was completed in 1849 and, on 10 July, the Victoria Channel was officially opened providing at last the straight deep channel between Garmoyle and the quays so long sought by the merchant community. The improved access to the port, together with the completion of railways to Ballymena, Armagh, Holywood and Comber confirmed Belfast's position as the first town for trade in Ireland.

The increase in trade brought with it the need for improved office accommodation for both the customs and the harbour commissioners. A suggestion that the two authorities should share accommodation in a new building was not pursued and in 1851 the harbour board proceeded to build a new office close to the first dry dock. The office, designed by their own engineer, George Smith, was opened in 1854. The old office at the foot of High Street was demolished to make way for a new custom house completed in 1857.

Parliamentary authority was obtained in 1854 for the further development of extensive reclamation, dock, timber storage and shipbuilding facilities on the County Down side of the harbour where, at the south end of Queen's Island, a 1000 ton capacity patent slip and a timber shipbuilding yard had already been established by the board. Work on the reclamation of the remainder of the proposals was halted at the start of the Crimean war. The depression caused by the conflict, followed by the severe monetary crisis of 1857, further delayed the planned improvements and it was not until 1863 that contracts were let for a vast floating dock, 17 acres in extent, on the County Antrim side and for a large tidal basin and dry dock on the

County Down side. The dry dock was urgently needed to service the increasingly large ships being built by Edward Harland, who had taken over an iron shipbuilding yard established near the patent slip on Queen's Island in 1853. The County Down facilities were opened in 1867 but those on the Antrim side, where the design had been altered to a mainly tidal system, were not completed until 1872.

Prior to the opening of the new Antrim docks in 1870, increased trade had been matched in large measure by an increase in the number of ships entering the port. After 1870 the increasing volume of trade was met to a considerable extent by the use of ships of larger carrying capacity without any significant increase in number. The main thrust of the board in the period between 1870 and 1890 was therefore directed mainly towards the reconstruction of the earlier and shallower facilities to suit the new deeper-draughted ships.

Deepening of the river and of the Victoria Channel to provide a minimum depth of 11 feet at low water had been carried out between 1858 and 1861, but in 1886 a programme of dredging was started to provide a straight channel 17 feet deep at low water between the quays and the open sea off Cultra. The work involved the formation of a new cut nearly 4 miles long through the west and Holywood Banks and was not completed until 1891.

Meanwhile iron shipbuilding was expanding rapidly. New yards were built by Harland & Wolff and by two new firms, Workman, Clark and MacIlwaine & Lewis. Tonnage content reached 23000 tons gross in 1881, rose to 80000 tons in 1890 and nearly 140000 tons by the turn of the century. To provide adequate facilities for the long narrow ships now being built, the board built another dry dock in 1885, the largest of its time, and also erected a 100 ton capacity crane for fitting out purposes.

By 1892 Belfast was the third port in the United Kingdom for customs revenue, being exceeded only by London and Liverpool. Shipping entering the port had risen to over 2 million tons and was continuing to increase. To meet the demand for more accommodation another tidal dock was completed on the Antrim side in 1897, but by now all the available land bordering the Victoria Channel had been put to use for commercial docks or for shipbuilding. The board decided, therefore, that a new channel should be constructed on the County Down side of the harbour to provide for future expansion of facilities. The new channel, the Musgrave Channel, was completed in 1903 and the spoil raised was used to reclaim 140 acres of foreshore for future industrial purposes.

The shipbuilding yards at Belfast were now producing the largest vessels in the world. To provide for their fitting out and putting to sea the board built four new deep water fitting out berths and deepened the Victoria channel by three feet in 1900, and again by the same amount in 1911. Another dry dock, once again the largest in the world at the time, was completed in the same year, the first vessel to be docked being the 45000 ton *Olympic,* sister ship of the *Titanic.*

By 1914 Belfast, the largest port in Ireland, led the world as a shipbuilding centre of unrivalled excellence. Trade had risen to some 3.4 million tons and its continuing upward trend seemed assured.

The war years, 1914–18, saw trade reduced to essential traffic only and tonnage through the port dropped by 1 million tons. Shortage of materials restricted harbour work to essential maintenance, but the shipbuilding yards, after initial uncertainty, worked to capacity. The demand for new ships to replace those lost through enemy action occasioned both Harland & Wolff and Workman, Clark (which had taken over MacIlwaine's yard in 1893) to expand their capacity in 1917; then and for several years after the war, shipbuilding remained at a high level, but trade in general remained depressed. It was not until 1929 that the tonnage of shipping once again approached the 1914 record.

The war years had seen a great increase in the use of oil and oil products and, although a small oil tank farm had been established in 1889 at the side of the Victoria channel, there was now a demand for improved bulk storage. This was met by leasing newly reclaimed ground to the major oil companies where new tank farms were established and linked by pipelines to a purpose-built bulk oil jetty at Musgrave Channel, opened in 1923.

In 1929, when congestion at deep water berths was once again becoming a problem, the board decided to construct a new channel on the County Antrim side of the harbour to provide accommodation both for general cargo and for new facilities for the bulk handling of grain. The new channel, the Herdman Channel, was completed in 1933 and the 0.5 million tons of dredged material from the scheme was pumped inside pre-formed banks on the County Down foreshore, adding to the area of reclaimed ground near Sydenham, where the board had constructed an aerodrome. The foresight of the Commissioners in developing the aerodrome was rewarded in 1936 when Short & Harlands established an aircraft factory on harbour ground nearby, bring much needed alternative employment to the area. It played an even more vital role in the war which was to break out three years later.

The war years 1939–45 saw the harbour facilities once more working to full capacity, with cargoes handled reaching new records. The establishment of a naval base in the harbour added to the congestion at the berths and necessitated the construction of additional deep water berthage for general cargo and specialised naval accommodation.

The end of the war saw a brief decline in trade. A start was made in tackling the accumulated backlog of repairs and by 1947 most of the essential work had been completed despite chronic shortages of materials. With trade once more at record levels, plans for major redevelopment and improvement began to be formulated.

A significant change in cargo handling was beginning to emerge which, as it developed, was to affect the whole port industry. This was the concept of transporting goods in large unit loads and in forms requiring minimum handling. As early as 1947 plans were put forward to the board for a roll-on/roll-off service based on wartime tank landing craft and using a link-span to join ship to shore. The necessary facilities for this new concept were put into operation in 1950.

The use of standardised containers also began to gather momentum, and at the same time the average tonnage of ships, both coastal and foreign-going, increased rapidly. To meet these changes and the surge in trade, which rose from 5 million tons in 1953 to 7.5 million tons in 1965, a vast programme of new works was undertaken.

Between 1955 and 1965 over 6000 feet of new deep water berthage was constructed; some 4000 feet of existing coal quays reconstructed, a 200 ton capacity crane erected and an oil terminal built for a new oil refinery. In addition the Victoria Channel was widened and deepened in two stages from 300 to 500 feet in width and from 23 to 32 feet in depth at low water, and extended 2.5 miles seaward, to handle both the new generation of oil tankers arriving at the harbour and the very large vessels which Harland & Wolff were planning to build. The spoil from the dredging was used to reclaim some 140 acres, mainly on the Antrim side of the channel.

The next few years saw a continuing rise in unit loads. New berths with roll-on/roll-off and lift-on/lift-off facilities were built, not only for cargo traffic but also for the new passenger ships coming into service. Between 1953 and 1973 unit load traffic rose from 100000 tons to a peak of 2.5 million tons with a comparable decline at the old break-bulk berths, some of which were filled in to provide additional marshalling space for the refurbished berths.

Other improvements were the construction of another dry dock, the largest in the United Kingdom, capable of accommodating 200000 ton bulk carriers. Opened in 1968, it was named Belfast Dry Dock. In the same year Harland & Wolff commenced the construction of a giant building dock at what had been the south end of the Musgrave Channel with the capacity to accommodate a 1 million ton bulk carrier. Completed in 1970 it has already been used for the construction of 333000 ton ships.

Goods traffic reached a record figure in 1973 when 7.7 million tons were handled. The impact of huge increases in the price of oil that year had a serious impact on trade, and industry and tonnage declined. Tonnage of shipping was further adversely affected when, 1975–6, the Heysham and Ardrossan passenger services were withdrawn in the face of competition from air transport and the drop in tourist traffic caused by the Northern Ireland 'troubles'.

By 1982 goods traffic had fallen to 5.5 million tons, but in recent years, trade through the port is increasing again. This upturn is largely due to strong marketing, a resumption in passenger services and continuing upgrading of facilities. It has also been helped in part by the development of a government-promoted enterprise zone in the reclamation area on the County Antrim side of the harbour estate.

In 1979 the constitution of the harbour board was amended and the commissioners, previously elected by the ratepayers of Belfast, became a government-appointed body, representative of all sections of those interested in the working of the port. The objectives set by the board 200 years earlier of improving port facilities and the encouraging of local industry still hold good today.

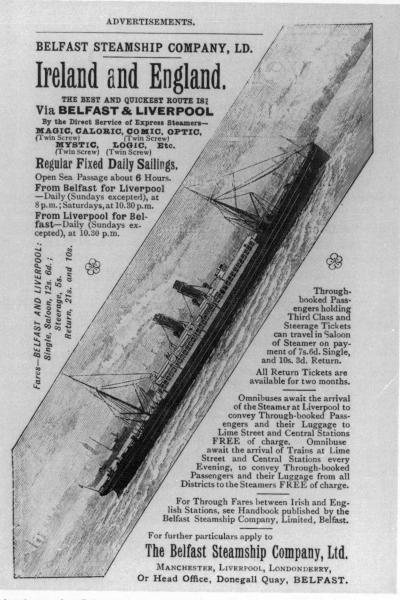
Advertisement from Robert Lloyd Praeger, *Official guide to County Down and the Mourne Mountains* (Belfast, 1898).

11   Steam in the Irish Sea

A. W. H. PEARSALL

A number of phases can be discerned without much difficulty in the development of Irish Sea steamship services. The 'early' period lasted from 1820 or so until about 1840, being followed by the 'first railway' period thence until about 1880. The 'high railway' period, continuing to 1914, was probably the apogee of steamer services in number and variety, for in the inter-war phase which followed, progress in some directions was associated with recession elsewhere. Since 1945 there has been a transitional period up to about 1965, culminating in the present 'car ferry' era. It is not my intention to deal with any of these in detail but to present the general characteristics of each of these phases, and to show how one merged into the next.[1]

Shipping has always been a conservative occupation, so that the new motive power was at first largely taken up by the existing owners of sailing vessels whose business lay in conveying people and goods across the Irish Sea. The smacks employed in these trades were supplemented and finally displaced by the early paddle steamer, often run by the same owner, such as Langtry's of Belfast, or by a pooling of resources in a local company, to take advantage of the greater reliability and speed of the steamer, although in these early days breakdowns and even boiler explosions were liable to occur. As a result of these origins, the routes offered were those between the principal accepted ports, namely Glasgow or Greenock, Ayr, Whitehaven and Liverpool with Bristol and south Welsh ports on the eastern shore of the Irish Sea, and Derry, Belfast, Newry, Dundalk, Drogheda, Dublin, Waterford and Cork on the western shore. Usually the individual businesses were quite small, and it was noticeable that it was the out-ports which sought communication with the great ports like Liverpool, whose enterprise seemed to be directed further afield. Glasgow was an exception to this rule, for many of the early steamers were built, engined and owned there. An exception to private ownership was the Irish Mail service from

Holyhead to Howth, where the advantages of steam were rapidly appreci-
ated by the Post Office, which provided two steamers on the route as early
as 1820.

The steamers of this period were built of wood and driven by paddle
engines with very low pressure boilers. They were rarely of more than 200
tons, had their best accommodation aft with 'fore cabin' as the equivalent of
second-class, and, owing to the size and midships position of the engines
and boilers, had limited cargo space. Their speed was rarely above 10
knots, more often six to eight. However, as time went on, ships became
larger and faster, rising to 500 tons with improved accommodation.

There were considerable variations in frequency of sailing: the mail route
was daily, while others varied from weekly up to thrice-weekly. Most
sailings at this time, and for long afterwards, were governed by tides, which
in the Irish Sea imposed very severe restrictions upon access to ports. In the
early period there was already an extensive network of cross-channel and
coastal steamers operating in the Irish Sea, even before the widespread
development of railways in Britain and Ireland.

Advent of the railways

While some short railway lines had been constructed during the early
period of steamship innovation, large-scale railway construction only set in
during the later 1830s and it was not until the mid or late 1840s that railway
influence became strongly evident. It was also combined, in the case of the
Irish Sea, with a minor boom in building new British ports, apparently in
response to the alleged profits to be had from the Irish trade, not only in
passengers and cargo, but also in coal. The latter branch of trade was
particularly important because of its connection with the rise of many early
railways. For example, it was part of the purpose of the Maryport &
Carlisle railway to bring coal into the Irish market, while the ports of
Fleetwood, Morecambe and Ardrossan and, rather later, Silloth and
Barrow, developed to serve the Irish trade. For similar reasons improvements were made to existing ports like Preston, Troon and Whitehaven.
While some of these places never entered the general cross-channel trade,
most did, and indeed, Fleetwood, the pioneer example dating from about
1840, was more strongly biased in that direction than others. In all cases,
these ports depended on railway communications to bring coal and other
traffic in quantity from inland locations.

However difficulties could arise. While general shipowners were quite
ready to take cargoes like coal, for which the business was steady and
negotiated as a 'once-only' transaction, the prospects of offering a regular
service from an entirely new port were more daunting. Many of the new
ports were in isolated locations and as operators of regular services had

established businesses, based on some already prosperous ports, there was reluctance to change from the known to the unknown. Occasionally an operator who was established on another non-competitive route was prepared to extend his operations, but even then the expense of extra vessels circumscribed his activities. Moreover, railway companies were statutory companies, unable to own and run undertakings of any kind without parliamentary powers, which at this time were rarely granted owing to shipowners' opposition. Thus, many railways found some difficulty in organising steamship connections with their lines. The Chester & Holyhead railway was fortunate; it obtained parliamentary powers, it seems by an oversight, and was able to run its own ships from Holyhead to Dublin. At Fleetwood, however, a separate steamship company was set up by the promoters of the port, but at Morecambe there was much bargaining, and, it is to be feared, surreptitious contributions from the railway company. Ardrossan too seems to have had a service supported by the owner of the place, the earl of Eglinton. The rail service from Holyhead, which was always a law unto itself, was run until 1848 by the admiralty, and then by contract with the City of Dublin Steam Packet Company. Its political importance ensured that the contract was always generous enough to run the service, at this period and later, at a standard of speed and comfort above almost anything else in the world, and certainly far above anything on the English Channel at that time. Thus, by 1855, there were railway services, or railway-connected services running from the four ports of Holyhead, Fleetwood, Morecambe and Ardrossan to places in Ireland, mostly Belfast and Dublin, and to these four, Silloth and Neyland were soon added.

This was also a period in which ship design underwent great changes with the advent of iron for hulls and the adoption of the screw propeller to drive ships. Iron provided a much stronger hull, with less space taken up by structure, while also reinforcing a change towards narrower and longer hull shapes. Screw propulsion gave a great advantage in that the engines could take up less space in the hull, and so provide more room for cargo. In the early days, however, low pressure boilers and slow running engines driving one screw, the propeller was necessarily large, and to obtain full immersion the ship had often to be of quite deep draft by coastal standards. Hence paddle steamers continued in use for many years on cross-channel routes where vessels with high power, fairly shallow draft and manoeuvrability were needed. Screw vessels were first used on the routes where economic conditions required ships with moderate speed combined with passenger, cattle and cargo carrying capacity. In short, they were confined largely to the less prosperous services such as those to the smaller ports of Newry and Sligo, where passengers were fewer. Later, however, the private owners increasingly used screw vessels of the coastal type, while the mail service and the busier passenger routes remained the preserve of paddle steamers, although sometimes a slower separate service was maintained for cargo and cattle.

The pattern of traffic in these years was one of steady increase punctuated by occasional slack periods. In addition to the impulses encouraging travel, such as the rise of the annual holiday and the great exhibitions from 1851 onwards, steamship operators derived much business from Irish emigrants heading to Liverpool to board transatlantic ships and the seasonal migrations of Irish agricultural workers to England and Scotland. Furthermore the growing demand of industrial towns for food supplies stimulated an increase in the cattle trade, while the shipping of general goods reflected the growth and spread of manufacturing industry.

Heyday of the Railways

During the 1870s and 1880s great improvements took place in steamship services. However, the railways found drawbacks to private operators making use of their ports. Partly this was due to the general disregard of the shipping world for anything but tides, whereas railway companies were concerned with precise timetables, and the idea of weekly or even twice-weekly services did not go well with an organisation running its trains every day. When a railway wanted to improve its service, of course, it found either that the shipowner had no ships or was unable or unwilling to provide additional vessels for financial reasons. To a railway company the cost of a ship was something like a mile of line, and consequently small in total value; but to a shipowner the same amount might represent a very large sum. The result was that more and more railway money was put into their associated companies to finance improved services. In the late 1860s, parliament began to view railway ownership of steamers more favourably, and the companies began to take over the services directly. Moreover, as competition between routes increased there was a general trend to improve facilities. As demand increased for fixed timetable services, sailings dependent on tides were regarded as inadequate. Money had therefore to be spent in dredging channels or on new quays, while better interchange facilities from train to ship were also required. The railways were prepared to make these provisions, while private companies, running from large, separately owned dock systems were not. In addition to these new works, the railways made improvements in operating methods, and with an emphasis on journey speed introduced new ships which were both faster and provided with better accommodation.

Until 1872 the only fixed-timetable services from England to Ireland were those from Holyhead. In that year the Stranraer and Larne service started from a new rail-connected pier at the former port to a new quay next to the station at the latter. Barrow, to which the Morecambe service was transferred in 1867, together with Fleetwood steamers managed to sail 'at or after' a fixed hour, but the great tides of Morecambe Bay still caused frequent delays. At Liverpool the Belfast steamer had to lock out of the docks at variable times. Matters were better in Scotland, though it was often preferable to board or leave the ship at Greenock rather than Glasgow. After 1872, however, a series of improvements were made with the construction of a new harbour at Holyhead in 1880, the new Ramsden Dock station at Barrow in 1881 and a new station at Fleetwood in 1883. A new route to Belfast from Holyhead was provided in 1873 by the opening of a harbour at Greenore, which was the first purpose-built railway port in Ireland. In the south the Great Western took over the service from Neyland in Milford Haven to Waterford. Apart from the Clyde services, where the railways were content to connect with the steamers of G. & J. Burns, the private owners were outpaced. As a result of these faster trains and steamers, the overnight service now became the rule, by which the traveller could leave London, Leeds or Manchester after 4 p.m. and reach Belfast or Dublin next morning.

Although no comparative statistics seem to survive, there can be little doubt that traffic in general remained buoyant, as the rate of building new ships and the provision of improved facilities continued up to 1914. Two of the biggest improvements, Heysham Harbour and the Fishguard and Rosslare project, were initiated in the 1890s and carried through by 1904 and 1906 respectively. As harbours improved, new ships became larger and faster with better accommodation. Paddle propulsion finally gave way to twin screws, while triple and quadruple-expansion engines and then turbines were introduced. The old practice of having all the passenger accommodation within the hull was supplemented by superstructure above it, with many more cabins. The cargo business is less easy to judge, as older ships were often kept in service for long periods but such indicators as there are do show similar trends, even to the improvement of accommodation for cattle, as required by legislation.

The Situation Before 1914

Prior to the first world war two principal private companies, G. & J. Burns and the Laird Line, operated the routes between Scotland and Ireland. Both characteristically were Scottish-based. G. & J. Burns provided the services, of all types, between Glasgow and Ardrossan to Belfast, and also controlled a company which provided a good passenger service between Glasgow and Dublin. It also, incidentally, ran one of two services from Glasgow and Liverpool. The Laird Line's main service was from Glasgow to Derry, but it also sent ships to the west coast of Ireland, and, by becoming concerned in its early days with the port of Morecambe, the line still ran from there to Derry and Dublin, and from Liverpool to Westport. Most of these services, however, were relatively minor. Both companies had also opened daylight passenger sailings from Scotland to Ireland with special fast cross-channel ships akin to the railway steamers – from Ardrossan to Belfast and from Ardrossan to Portrush respectively, with railway connections to Glasgow. However, most of their vessels were slower than the railway steamers and they also carried cargo and cattle.

The railway services, working southwards, began with the Stranraer to Larne route. This was operated by a company whose shares were held by the several railway companies involved, and which included the London & North Western and the Midland. Because of the short crossing, the fast turbine steamers were 'day' vessels with no extensive sleeping accommodation. In contrast the three competing companies working out of More-cambe Bay all operated overnight sailings to Belfast with night vessels having many berths. The former Furness railway and Midland railway route from Barrow still ran, though now outclassed by the Midland railway's new Heysham route, while the third, and probably most used of the three, was the Fleetwood service of the joint London & North Western and Lancashire & Yorkshire railways. The sailing from Holyhead com-pleted the railway services in the northern Irish Sea and at this port a complex series of routes existed. The Irish Mail service was still in the hands of the City of Dublin Steam Packet Company, while the London & North Western railway had developed several routes to provide equally good facilities. Thus the railway provided two daily fast services to Dublin, North Wall, competing with the two rail services of the City of Dublin to Kingstown (later Dun Laoghaire). The L.& N.W.R. also ran two or three fast cargo ships every day to North Wall, and it had a separate service for northern Ireland every night to Greenore. (The City of Dublin had its own cargo and passenger service from Liverpool to Dublin). All of these numerous services were provided by a series of extremely fine vessels representing the highest development of the cross-channel steamers.

Routes between Ireland and Liverpool were primarily operated by private owners, although, as always, they were mostly based at the Irish end, comprising many 'port' companies. The City of Dublin and the Belfast Steamship companies were the most important and were complemented by the Newry, Dundalk and the Drogheda companies working the northern ports, and the Waterford and Cork companies working to the south. The Belfast and Dublin services were daily, but most of the others were only once, twice or thrice weekly. The Drogheda company, however, had been purchased by the Lancashire & Yorkshire railway, and this was the only railway intrusion into the Mersey steamer services. Nevertheless several of the companies had through booking arrangements with railways, though mostly those without direct interests in the Irish Sea. Secondary routes comprised those from Whitehaven and Silloth to Dublin, calling at the Isle of Man. In addition the Isle of Man Steam Packet Company operated regular and seasonal sailings from Douglas and Ramsey to Liverpool, Fleetwood, Dublin, Belfast and Ardrossan, with several of their steamers being of the highest class.

At the southern end of the Irish Sea, the Bristol Steam Navigation Company and the Cork and Waterford companies ran services of the coastal type between those ports and to some of the south Wales ports. The Great Western railway had now transferred its operations from Neyland to Fishguard, whence it ran two fast services daily to the new Irish port of Rosslare, and its old service, now mainly cargo and cattle, to Waterford. The City of Cork Company provided a good passenger service from Fishguard to Cork, and shared with the Belfast Steamship Company the reputation of operating the best private service, with vessels of the overnight cross-channel type. Finally there were other interesting services by the Clyde Shipping Company of Glasgow, which ran vessels of the coastal variety from Glasgow and Belfast to the southern Irish ports, as well as round Land's End to English channel ports and London. Sloan's of Glasgow ran services thence to Belfast and to south Wales as well as operating in the coastal route market.

Between the Wars

The 1914–18 war badly disrupted services and in the post-war period steamship owners were faced with harsh new economic conditions. The political troubles in Ireland were followed by the introduction of customs on the southern routes, while general economic difficulties culminated in the slump of 1929–31. In addition, there was an acceleration of the trend towards the cessation of passenger services on the less busy routes, owing to more stringent legal requirements for passenger ships, and the more exacting needs of the public for comfort. The decade 1920–30 thus became one of rationalisation with rival companies undergoing reorganisation. The railways were formed into the four groups which remained in being until nationalisation in 1948. As the London & North Western railway with the Midland and Lancashire & Yorkshire became part of the London Midland & Scottish railway (or L.M.S.), all the northern routes came under single control with only the Great Western services remaining independent on the southern routes. At much the same time Sir Alfred Read was building up his Coast Lines group which took over all the private companies except the Clyde and Sloan's. Moreover, the new group was itself part of Lord Kylsant's shipping empire. Although the shipping lines were now effectively organised in two opposing combines, economic realities were recognised and unnecessary competition was avoided. Moreover, most of the ships were by now at least semi-obsolescent or at best war-worn.

The L.M.S. had a very severe problem as it fell heir to so many competitive routes, few of which were profitable in post-war conditions. However the L. & N.W.R. had at last managed in 1920 to obtain the Irish Mail service, for the City of Dublin Steam Packet Company, after losing two of its vessels during the war, had been unable to compete, and the new vessels then built by the L. & N.W.R. were the only modern ships in the L.M.S. fleet. The Barrow–Belfast service did not survive the war, and after long consideration the L.M.S. decided to concentrate its Northern Ireland services at Heysham with three new ships built in 1928. Sir Josiah Stamp, president of the L.M.S., came to an agreement with Sir Alfred Read for a mutual withdrawal from various routes, by which Coast Lines gave up the Heysham–Dublin service and the L.M.S. the Liverpool–Drogheda route. The North Wall passenger services ended in 1922 and that to Greenore in 1926.

Coast Lines likewise had to make economies. Passengers ceased to be carried on many of their lesser routes, and apart from some new ships completed just after the war there was little new building. However rivalry was not dead, for the arrival of the new and luxurious L.M.S. Heysham steamers led to the construction of three equally fine new ships for the Liverpool–Belfast service. Following Kylsant group practice, the new vessels were not steamships, but were propelled by diesel engines. The previous ships on the Liverpool–Belfast service were transferred to the Liverpool–Dublin route, much to the latter's benefit.

After the worst of the slump some modest improvements began and by 1935 the Northern Ireland services were again busy. The L.M.S. built two new ships for the Larne–Stranraer route in order to extend its scope to the traffic from Scotland to Ireland which hitherto had received little encouragement. Coast Lines replied with a reorganisation of their Ardrossan and Glasgow to Belfast overnight service using two new motorships. They continued by building two more such ships for the Liverpool–Dublin service. The L.M.S. provided a fourth steamer for the Heysham service in 1935, and a special cargo steamer in the next year, together with some new cargo vessels for Holyhead, where the mail steamers were refitted in 1932–3. The Great Western replaced its old ships on the southern crossings and in 1939 the first car ferry on the Irish Sea was introduced to the Stranraer–Larne route.

After 1945

The period from 1945 to the early 1960s was in many ways similar to the inter-war years, although economic conditions were hardening against the less prosperous services. The principal routes remained, and allowing for new construction and some reshuffling of ships to replace war losses, they continued much as before. Passenger traffic showed marked peaks in summer, so that, as the letter mails now went by air, the daylight Irish Mail service operated in summer only. Only two new vessels were built to replace the three pre-war ships, while a third was transferred from the Stranraer route. Coast Lines too found the same problems and at first met them by retaining two very old ships as relief vessels, though eventually a single modern ship was built to act as a general relief on all their services. This type of expediency, hitherto unknown, also became evident when the Stranraer–Larne *Princess Victoria* car ferry was lost as a marine casualty in 1953, and the now nationalised railways were forced to adopt strategies to maintain the summer service this ship had provided. New developments were not lacking, however. The railways were using containers more and more for Irish traffic and eventually began a service with specially-built container ships. Coast Lines also ventured into the 'unit load' field while general cargo traffic also remained brisk. In the mid-1950s both operators introduced new and modern passenger ships.

From 1960 onwards ferry operations changed dramatically. The with-drawal of the railways from general goods traffic accentuated the drift to road transport already taking place; what did not go by container now went by lorry while the tourist increasingly took his car. The live cattle trade was increasingly replaced by the carriage of refrigerated meat, while the development of air transport reduced passenger traffic. At the same time, against a background of mounting competition and increasing inflation, the high capital cost of ships compelled high utilisation and the emphasis turned sharply to the short crossings where a ship could make more voyages. Such routes had always been attractive to passengers but now they also became much sought after for vehicular traffic as was evident by the establishment of the Larne–Cairnryan service and by the British and Irish Company's anxiety to obtain access to Holyhead and Rosslare. Meanwhile former important crossings like Glasgow and Heysham to Belfast and Fishguard–Cork disappeared. All new vessels were built with high car decks to accommodate lorries, and usually with both bow and stern loading. Although the railway interest in shipping was much reduced, independent operators began new services such as Garston–Warrenpoint for container traffic. However Coast Lines virtually disappeared, the group being taken over by the major shipping group P. & O. which closed its main routes but established new ones for lorries from Fleetwood to Dublin and Belfast.

The railways had redrawn the map of commerce from the 1850s onwards but in the 1960s the motor-lorry created a fresh revolution in ship design and operation. Modern ferry services reflect the traffic requirements and patterns of distribution of contemporary economy and society and in this respect they differ little from those which have operated on the Irish Sea over the past one hundred and sixty eight years.

Kilkeel harbour, County Down with William Paynter's boatyard in background, *c.* 1876.
Ulster Folk and Transport Museum photograph collection L1741/5–6.

Enlarged view of section of above photograph.

12 Dandys, Luggers, Herring and Mackerel:

a local study in the context of the Irish Sea fisheries in the nineteenth century

MICHAEL McCAUGHAN

... Within the last ten years large sums have been expended upon Kilkeel, which is now an important fishery station. During the season fifty luggers are constantly employed, eighteen or twenty of the boats belonging to the immediate neighbourhood. When it is recollected that the victualling of each lugger amounts to about £4 a week, it will be perceived how great is the advantage reaped by the traders of Kilkeel.

Mr Donald Stewart, of Newry, has opened a herring curing establishment in the town, and his enterprise promises to be not only of much advantage to himself, but will also greatly promote the interests of the fishermen. We may also add that Mr Painter, a Cornishman, contemplates the establishment of a boat or shipbuilding yard at Kilkeel...
Downpatrick Recorder, 18 September 1875.

This contemporary account of an improving fishing economy in the County Down market town of Kilkeel conveniently illustrates the central theme of this essay. Essentially it considers aspects of small-scale entrepreneurship, during the second half of the nineteenth century in this locality, through investment in, and exploitation of the offshore herring and mackerel fisheries of the Irish Sea region. Numerical and technical changes in the first class fishing fleets of Kilkeel and neighbouring Annalong are identified and related to a wider maritime economy, based on the supply of fresh herring and mackerel to cross-channel British markets. Between 1870 and 1896 west Cornish luggers and their Manx derivatives entirely replaced the hitherto predominant boat type in the offshore fleets of Kilkeel and Annalong. The technical and economic factors favouring innovation of the west Cornish model are examined in the context of similar adoptions elsewhere, notably in the Isle of Man and Campbeltown in Argyll. In particular, the business and marketing strategies of William Paynter, a St Ives boatbuilder who established a yard in Kilkeel for the construction of

121

west Cornish luggers, are deduced and the success of his entrepreneurship assessed within the limitations of available evidence and absence of business records.

For much of the nineteenth century, the Irish fisheries, considered as a whole, presented a gloomy picture to contemporary observers. From the abandonment of a system of government bounties in 1830 until direct government intervention in the economy of the west of Ireland in the 1890s, the Irish fisheries were perceived as a rich national resource for food and employment, which was neglected and underdeveloped especially by government. Decline was reflected in the falling national figures for numbers of men and boats engaged in the sea fisheries. For example, in 1874 the inspectors of Irish fisheries reported that the number of fishing boats were reduced to nearly a third of what they had been in 1846 and the crews diminished to less than a quarter.[1] Various reasons were advanced for this enormous decline, but they can be summarised as a dramatic fall in the population resulting from famine and emigration, coupled with deprivation and lack of government loans to impoverished fishermen for the repair and purchase of boats and equipment. However these allegedly causal factors have yet to be tested by economic historians, for modern scholarship has largely bypassed the investigation of the nineteenth century Irish fisheries, in both national and regional forms.

Certainly the depressing national statistics disguised important regional exceptions; specifically these were the Irish Sea summer herring fishery centred on the east coast of Ireland, and after 1862, the offshore spring mackerel fishery based initially on the County Cork harbour of Kinsale on the south coast. The scale of exploitation, and prosperity generated by these seasonal pelagic fisheries was considerable. In 1870 their combined value over 250 miles of coastline was almost £300000, and represented two thirds of the value of all fish taken over a total Irish indented coastline of 2250 miles.[2] Of course the working and wealth of these valuable fisheries was not confined to Irish vessels. Indeed for much of the period under review Irish fishing boats were outnumbered by the sum of fleets from the Isle of Man, Cornwall and Scotland. For example, in 1877 at the peak of the east coast herring fishery, a total of 876 boats worked out of Howth, north of Dublin and then the most important landing station. Of these 876 boats, 26 percent were Irish-owned, 20 percent Manx-owned, 26 percent Scottish-owned and 28 percent Cornish-owned.[3]

Characteristically the east coast herring and south coast mackerel fisheries were offshore activities, requiring both harbour facilities and capital investment in nets and boats of the best description. Ideally these offshore boats provided relatively stable working platforms combined with good sea-keeping qualities and, increasingly, a capacity for fast sailing as the fisheries became more competitive. In addition they had to accommodate nets, fish, sails and a seven or eight man crew. Herring and mackerel are migratory fish which arrive in large shoals off the Irish coast, to feed and spawn, at reasonably predictable times of the year; hence the summer herring fishery on the east coast and the spring mackerel fishery on the south coast. Both species of fish were caught in drift nets, although mackerel nets were bigger and coarser in the mesh than herring nets. Drift nets were so-called because they simply drifted below the surface of the water while suspended from floats, and with the boat secured or driving at one end. Nets were 'shot' just before dusk, so that the herring or mackerel swimming in shoals in the darkness near the surface would easily enmesh themselves in the wall of nets. Numbers of nets carried, together with details of design, differed in time and place, although the trend was for an increase in size and quantity coupled with the replacement of herring nets by cotton nets in the 1850s and 1860s. Boats from Newlyn in Cornwall attending the Irish herring fishery in 1866, for example, carried sixteen or more nets, although the largest boat, the *Colleen Bawn*, 48 foot keel, carried twenty-five nets.[4] In contrast the Cornish-built and Cornish-derived boats owned in and working out of Kilkeel forty years later fished with trains of fifty or sixty nets. At this period each herring net was about 15 fathoms long and 360 one inch meshes in depth. Mackerel nets, in order to catch and hold the bigger fish had a two inch mesh. It generally took from three to four hours hard work hauling the nets using a hand capstan and working with an eight man crew, including a boy who was also the cook.[5]

In the period after 1865 it is possible, through an emergent and widening range of government statistics, to quantify changes in the Irish fisheries in general and the pelagic fisheries in particular.[6] Despite problems of formulation and presentation, fishing activity can be quantified, for example, in form of amounts and values landed, prices obtained, boats engaged and average earnings gained. Statistical evidence structures and corroborates documentary sources which indicate an east coast herring fishery boom lasting roughly twenty years from the early 1860s to about the early 1880s (Table 1). The boom was characterised by rising quantities and values of fish landings, which peaked in 1877. The movements were accomplished by increasing numbers of boats engaged and encouraged by a fluctuating,

Table 1 Ireland: Quantity and value of herrings landed, averaged in five year periods 1865-89.

Years	No. of mease	Value realised	Average price per mease
1865–69	141152	£109092	£0.77
1870–74	160822	£143788	£0.89
1875–79	192143	£226615	£1.17
1880–84	85227	£94142	£1.10
1885–89	90200	£61919	£0.68

though generally upward trend in the average price per mease.[7] After peaking in 1876 the average price gradually declined, and with the exception of two temporary recoveries in the 1880s, the trend continued downward until 1887. Following an overall reduction in the value and quantity of landings in the 1880s, the statistics show an improvement in the 1890s, but these result more from an extension of the herring fisheries on the west coast than from any revival on the east coast. It is important to emphasise that the national herring fishing statistics are the product of statistics relating to local micro-fishing economies, whose prosperity varied in response to internal as well as external factors. In general though, there is a recognisable correlation between herring statistics for most of the individual east coast ports and the national figures.

The overall pattern of rising prices and increasing prosperity in the 1860s and 1870s, followed by decline and economic depression in the 1880s was paralleled by the experience of the Scottish east coast herring fishery, as well as by other sectors of the British and Irish economies.[8] However there was a fundamental difference between the structures of the east Scottish and Irish herring fisheries. Essentially the Scottish industry was confined to Scottish boats and was based on the export of cured and branded herrings to foreign, mainly European markets (but also including Ireland). While a limited amount of commercial curing took place on Ireland's east coast, including Kilkeel and nearby Annalong,[9] the vitality of the Irish herring fisheries depended on a continuing demand for fresh herrings in the British urban markets. This trade in the supply of a perishable product expanded as the development of steam communication on land and sea made possible its large-scale rapid transit from producer to consumer. However as other foods, in particular imported refrigerated meat, began to compete with fresh herrings, in price and choice, resultant gluts in the English markets had an inevitable impact on the Irish Sea herring fishery.[10]

Like the summer herring fishery, the south coast spring mackerel fishery in the 1860s and 1870s was primarily a fresh fish trade for British markets. Initially based at Kinsale it was a valuable and highly profitable fishery which gradually extended westward and northward from the late 1870s. By the late 1880s the mackerel fishery had divided into spring and autumn seasons. The great bulk of the spring-caught fish were exported to England in a fresh state. In contrast the majority of the autumn-captured mackerel were salted, packed in barrels and exported to America, where in 1889 there seemed to be almost unlimited demand.[11] However it was the Kinsale-based spring mackerel fishery in which the Irish east coast boats principally engaged, prior to returning to the Irish Sea for the summer herring fishing. As with the herring fishery, the spring mackerel fishery was not an exclusively Irish activity, but was worked equally by Manx, Scottish, English and Cornish boats, most of which also participated in the herring fishery. In this respect it is useful to consider both of these offshore fisheries in terms of a pan-Irish Sea market economy, as well as a sector of the Irish economy as a whole.

From 1862, when it was pioneered by Manx fishermen, the spring mackerel fishery gradually increased in value and hence in the numbers and nationalities of boats it attracted. In 1864 the developing fishery was graphically described:

> The large boats are now off the south coast mackerel fishing. Four are from Howth, twenty-six from the Isle of Man and twenty-eight from Kinsale. The Manx and Howth nets are worth £170 to £200 a boat; the boats from £200 to £300 each. The season is generally from March to June and the fishing has been very successful. The fish are readily sold to fish buyers who go out in boats to meet the mackerel boats. They pack in ice and send off the best fish to England; the remainder have good demand in Ireland . . . one of the Manx luggers made £167 for the week ending 18th May 1863; she was a boat of fifty-six tons, with a train of eighty-seven pieces of mackerel nets . . .[12]

Ten years later, in 1874, the total value of the mackerel fishery was £93000 and was attended by 287 boats, with average gross earnings per boat of £324. Of the total fleet Irish boats represented 21 percent, Manx boats 68 percent, Cornish boats 10 percent and Scottish boats one percent.[13] In common with the herring fishery, the mackerel fishery was characterised by considerable annual fluctuations in the total value of fish landed. Nevertheless the trend was generally upwards, and unlike the east coast herring fishery there was no significant decline in the 1880s.

This, in brief outline, was the economic environment in which Kilkeel entrepreneurs and fishermen competed in the offshore exploitation of pelagic fish resources in the Irish Sea region in the second half of the nineteenth century.

Unlike the historic County Down harbour of Ardglass, Kilkeel was a newcomer to large-scale fishing activity. Situated at the southern extremity of the county on the coastal plain between the Mourne Mountains and the Irish Sea, the town's commercial life, until the 1860s, was based on the scenery and agriculture of its hinterland. However there was an extensive small boat fishery on the nearby coast and the practice existed of shopkeepers extending credit to fishermen for tackle and gear.[14] During the 1860s the commercial vitality and growing prosperity of Kilkeel and district was reflected in the establishment of a flax market and the opening of a branch of the Belfast Banking Company.[15] The population of the town was relatively small, being 1251 inhabitants in 1861. Despite an ample supply of capital and produce, Kilkeel merchants and shopkeepers were in general discouraged from engaging extensively in maritime trade through the lack of a pier or harbour, although some use was made of nearby Greencastle in Carlingford Lough.[16] The difficulty related to an extensive gravel bar at the mouth of the Kilkeel River about half a mile from the town. In the opinion of the engineer to the Board of Fisheries in 1821, this bar rendered the stream incapable of improvement.[17] Nevertheless by 1864 the commercial desire to invest in and profit from the rapidly expanding east coast herring fishery, by establishing Kilkeel as a fishery station, brought about a solution to the problem. An influential meeting was held, the Board of Works produced a plan, capital was made available largely through public funds, the bar was cut and a pier completed in 1868.[18] Improvements were made in 1872, but by 1880 it was apparent that the harbour was quite inadequate to accommodate the locally owned fishing boats as well as those fleets attracted to Kilkeel because of its proximity to the fishing grounds. At a public meeting in February 1880 Thomas Grills, the harbour master deposed that,

> they had only accommodation for about twenty-one fishing boats in the basin and that was quite insufficient for their fleet during the summer. He had often witnessed boats in stormy weather beating about the channel to the pier, but the harbour was filled up, and the crews, cold and wet, could not get in either to Kilkeel or Carlingford, and they were obliged to go to Ardglass or Howth. If Kilkeel Harbour were enlarged they might have got into Kilkeel as a harbour of safety. They should have accommodation for at least 200 boats. They had as many as 400 boats coming in during the herring fishery. There were very large takes of herring brought into Kilkeel.[19]

Four years later in 1884, it was recognised by government that Kilkeel had developed into one of the most important centres for the herring fishery on the east coast and that the existing harbour did not meet the requirements of the district.[20] Accordingly a major extension and improvement was undertaken by the Board of Works and financed by a combination of government grant and county presentment under the terms of the Sea Fisheries (Ireland) Act 1883. The work was completed in May 1887, a new wharf having been built, together with a jetty. The basin was also deepened and completely walled round some eighteen inches higher.[21] Unfortunately the harbour still could not be entered at all states of the tide as the entrance dried out at low water. This remained the case until further improvements were made in the twentieth century.

Within a period of twenty years a substantial infrastructure, essential for the successful prosecution of the herring fishery, but benefiting also the export trade in granite and potatoes, was developed in Kilkeel. In addition to the harbour structures, largely built at public expense, boat-building and repair facilities had been established and three fish curers were in operation in a small way.[22] Furthermore in 1873 the L.N.W.R. had opened a cross-channel steamship service between Holyhead and Greenore on the County Louth shore of Carlingford Lough. Though the newly-built company harbour at Greenore attracted substantially more herring landings than Kilkeel, until harbour improvements were made there in the 1880s, nevertheless the advantages for Kilkeel's fishing trade were greater than the disadvantages. If to some degree the harbour facilities were provided too late for full advantage to be taken of the 1870s herring boom, they nevertheless contributed to a higher level of landings and earnings than those achieved in either Ardglass or Howth at this later period. As a measure of importance, Kilkeel at its nineteenth century peaks in 1886 and 1890, accounted for 36.5 percent and 35 percent of the total value of herrings landed in Ireland. (Table 2 and graph).

In addition to wealth derived from the landing of herrings, together with victualling and supplying other needs to the large numbers of boats annually congregating at Kilkeel, profits were generated from capital invested in the offshore fleet engaged in the herring and mackerel fisheries. As early as 1866, when the new pier was still under construction, a few local entrepreneurs had purchased large boats and initiated the development of Kilkeel's first class fleet, and thereby improved the employment opportunities for fishermen.

> The herring fishery on this coast has, for the past week fully realised the expectations of those who have, at considerable expense, fitted out a little fleet of luggers, well manned and good seaboats, which will have the effect of securing the hardy-going fishermen's services at home, who had formerly to go to the Scotch coast for fishing purposes. It is expected, when the pier is finished, which is fast progressing, others will invest capital in this remunerative business.[23]

By 1870 ten first class vessels were owned in Kilkeel and a further ten in the neighbouring village of Annalong. First class fishing boats were those over 15 tons burthen registered at Newry Customs House under part II of the sea fisheries act 1868. Although the regulations defined three classes of fishing boats, the registry of first class boats is the most useful means of indexing investment and entrepreneurship in the offshore fisheries. Clearly the first class fleet profiles of Kilkeel and Annalong between 1869 and 1900 reflect the relative profitability of the herring and mackerel fisheries in

Table 2 Kilkeel: Value of herrings landed as a percentage of the total value of Irish herring landings 1871–1900.

Years	Percentage	Years	Percentage	Years	Percentage
1870	–	1880	3.5	1890	35.0
1871	3.5	1881	19.6	1891	19.1
1872	3.7	1882	7.6	1892	9.1
1873	8.2	1883	3.3	1893	12.7
1874	3.3	1884	9.5	1894	10.6
1875	0.6	1885	7.1	1895	7.5
1876	2.8	1886	36.5	1896	3.5
1877	1.5	1887	12.0	1897	2.1
1878	0.7	1888	14.6	1898	2.5
1879	2.7	1889	17.0	1899	1.7
				1900	4.7

which they were both engaged. From 1870 to 1880 the Kilkeel first class fleet increased by 100 percent, with a peak of twenty-four boats in 1877. A plateau was maintained from 1880 to 1890, but a decrease of 60 percent occurred in the decade 1890–1900. Although the Annalong fleet was smaller, a broadly similar pattern of change took place over the same period. Considering the pattern of ownership, of the thirty-five boats initially registered at Kilkeel between 1869 and 1892, twenty-five boats (80 percent) had one owner; four boats (11.4 percent) two owners; two boats (5.7 percent) three owners; and one boat (2.9 percent) had four owners.[24] Significantly the three boats with the larger shareholding were first registered in the early period, when investment was more speculative and it was considered prudent to share the risk capital. Not surprisingly the occupations of the owners and part-owners reflected the commercial life of Kilkeel. Besides sixteen owner/skippers there were seven haberdashers and drapers, six grocer and provision dealers, six spirit dealers, three general merchants, three farmers, two bakers, two gentlemen, one tailor, one boatbuilder and one bank manager.[25] Some of these individuals also owned or held shares in boats other than those of the first class as well as in mainly first class boats working out of Annalong.

An assessment of the financial network underlying such diversity of ownership is problematic because of the paucity of relevant business records. However, the fragmentary accounts that are extant indicate a complex interweaving of kinship and business relationships. For at least one Kilkeel merchant, George Gordon, fishing boat investment formed part of his wider maritime business interests. Besides a quarter share in the first class fishing boat, *Mary* N4, working out of Annalong, he had a three-quarter shareholding in two trading vessels. His rather unorthodox accounting system for the fishing boat is complicated by accounts for the nets, which as was usual, were an investment distinct from the boat. Essentially though, £52 15s. 5d. was paid for a quarter share in the boat. In 1872, each of the four owners received £8 11s. 7d. profit; in 1873, £15 9s. 0d.; and in 1874–5 £4 8s. 7¾d. Clearly generalisations cannot be drawn from these limited figures, but they are a useful indicator of the scale and variable nature of the returns from fishing boat investment in a period of expansion in the fishing trade. Over the three years 1872–1874/5, the invested capital of £52 15s. 5d. for a quarter share in the boat returned a profit of 16 percent, 30 percent and 8 percent which averaged 18 percent per annum for each of the four owners.[26]

Significantly the boat's accounts do not itemise payments to the crew other than the skipper. They would have been paid out of the proceeds of each catch on a share basis. This system varied from place to place in its proportional working, but essentially half the value of the catch was divided amongst the crew, the rest going to the boat and the owners. Fishing of course is a hunting activity, the success of which is dependent on knowledge, skill, equipment and markets, besides an adequate supply of an unseen resource renewable only by nature. It was, and is a speculative business with earnings varying from catch to catch and within cycles of prosperity and recession. In the herring boom of the 1870s, it was possible for crews of some Kilkeel boats to earn from £1 10s. to £4 per share per week.[27] On the basis of Kilkeel's landing figures, fishermen's earnings were buoyant, if not improving, until about 1893, after which earnings decreased. Jobs were also lost as the fleet was in continuous reduction from 1890 until early in the next century.

From the statistics relating to boats engaged and values landed, a notional figure representing annual average gross earnings per boat can be calculated for Kilkeel. This does not take account of earnings made elsewhere, especially at Kinsale. By averaging annual figures over five year periods to even out fluctuations, it can be shown that at Kilkeel from 1880 to 1884, the annual average gross earnings per boat was £73; from 1885 to 1889, £104; from 1890 to 1894, £124 and from 1895 to 1899 it was £44. The latter figure reflects the general depression in the east coast fisheries, which can partly be attributed to a scarcity of fish.[28] The figure also quantifies the incentive that Kilkeel fishermen and owners had for working more productive distant grounds and for extending the fishing season.

Between 1875 and 1889 the first class fleet reached and maintained its maximum size in the nineteenth century. Over the fifteen year period an average of twenty-one boats were in register per annum. Taking the average value of each boat, complete with mackerel and herring nets, at £550,[29] the average annual value of the Kilkeel fleet was £11550. This scale of investment was remarkable for a market town with an average population of 1386 between 1871 and 1891. Significantly a population increase of 8 percent between 1871 and 1881 corresponded with the period of rapid fleet expansion from 1869 to 1877, when the number of boats increased by 83 percent.

In addition to numerical change the Kilkeel first class fleet, together with that of Annalong, underwent structural change by way of a complete replacement of boat types between 1869 and the mid-1890s. Essentially the introduction of the new type, referred to here as a 'lugger', but also known as a 'nickey', was in response to the need for a faster and more close-winded craft, and hence a more competitive fishing boat than the 'dandy' type hitherto employed.

The innovation primarily related to the rising importance of the Kinsale mackerel fishery, which resulted in a widespread demand for luggers of west Cornish build and design. As the mackerel is a fish that deteriorates particularly rapidly, it was essential that catches were landed as quickly as possible to command the highest price. Of course, the need to land fish in as

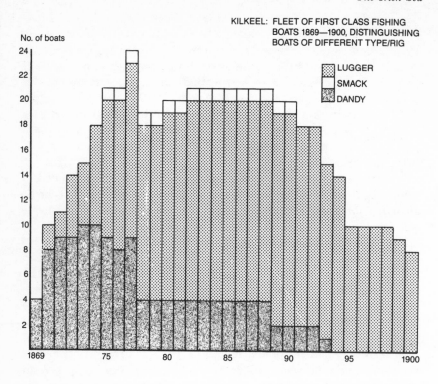

KILKEEL: FLEET OF FIRST CLASS FISHING
BOATS 1869—1900, DISTINGUISHING
BOATS OF DIFFERENT TYPE/RIG

No. of boats

LUGGER
SMACK
DANDY

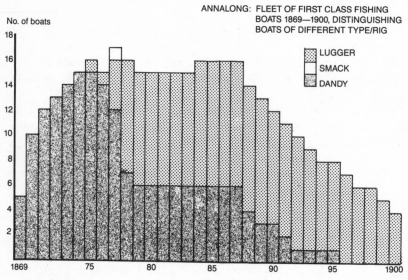

ANNALONG: FLEET OF FIRST CLASS FISHING
BOATS 1869—1900, DISTINGUISHING
BOATS OF DIFFERENT TYPE/RIG

No. of boats

LUGGER
SMACK
DANDY

Profiles of first class fishing fleets, Kilkeel and Annalong 1869–1900.

fresh a state as possible applied equally to the Irish Sea herring fishery, but there fast sailing boats were of less significance, at least in the boom period, as the fishing grounds were generally only 12 to 15 miles offshore, while at the mackerel fishery, boats worked up to 70 miles from the coast. From the late 1860s when fishermen from St Ives and Mount's Bay went to Kinsale in increasing numbers, the fast sailing qualities of the Cornish boats, especially their performance in working to windward, gave these fishermen a marked advantage over their competitors.[30] The incentive to compete was considerable, for in the 1870s the profits to be made at Kinsale were greatly in excess of even the lucrative herring fishery on the east coast. The average annual gross earnings per boat at Kinsale in the five year period 1870–74 was £376, whereas at Howth for the same period it was £181, at Ardglass £124 and at Kilkeel £160. Thus from about 1869 a combination of economic and technical factors created a rising demand for west Cornish luggers by fishing entrepreneurs in the Irish Sea region, including of course Kilkeel. Fundamentally innovation was triggered by the mackerel fishery but was reinforced by the herring fishery. Change continued to occur as old boats needed replacing and as later economic conditions forced the adoption of more efficient boats.

The qualities of west Cornish luggers had been apparent from about 1818 when fishermen from Penzance and St Ives first came to the Irish Sea herring fishery. They were of course mackerel boats designed for the Cornish mackerel fishery, but were equally effective as herring boats. In 1827 a Tynwald committee in the Isle of Man commented on the Cornish boats' superiority of design, build, lug rig and equipment, which together with smaller skilful crews and larger trains of nets, made them more efficient than the large smack-rigged boats used by Manx and many east coast Irish fishermen.[31] During the 1830s and 1840s a new type of Manx fishing boat evolved in response to the advent of the Cornish luggers. Essentially it was a compromise between the existing single-masted smack and the two masted Cornish lugger, as it set a gaff mainsail and a standing lug mizzen. This type of boat became generally known by Manx and Irish fishermen as a lugger, although strictly it was a dandy smack.[32] To avoid confusion through nomenclature it is referred to here as 'dandy', while the Cornish boats, and later Manx-built copies known as 'nickeys', are referred to as 'luggers'. By the 1860s the dandy was the predominant offshore herring boat used in the Irish Sea by Manx and Irish fishermen. It was the type subsequently replaced by Cornish-built luggers and their Manx-built derivatives.

As the Cornish offshore mackerel fishery extended further out into the Atlantic approaches from the 1840s onwards there was a trend towards building boats of a larger size, with finer lines and with improvements in the cut of the sails. Rail communication with Cornwall after 1859 opened up new markets and the need for prompt delivery of mackerel further encouraged the development of yacht-like hulls at the expense of carrying capacity. Nevertheless west Cornish luggers remained fine seaboats and at a meeting of the committee of the International Fisheries Exhibition in 1883, the Mount's Bay fleet was declared the finest in the world.[33]

The basic advantage of the Cornish luggers at the Kinsale mackerel fishery was that they were boats which had evolved for distant offshore mackerel fishing. Indeed they were referred to in Cornwall as 'mackerel drivers'. This was the basis of the unprecedented demand for Cornish boats by Manx, Irish and Scottish fishing communities, beginning in the late 1860s. Although several second-hand Mount's Bay luggers had been sold to Howth interests primarily for herring fishing, as early as 1866,[34] the Cornish export trade in new-built boats did not begin until 1869, when the lugger *Zenith* was built and delivered to owners in the Isle of Man.[35] Further orders followed, and by January 1870, a well known St Ives boatbuilder, William Paynter junior, had completed six boats for Manx owners with two more laid down.[36] The growing prosperity of the two principal Manx fishing harbours of Port St Mary and Peel was firmly based on the success of their fleets at Kinsale. Investment in, and wealth generated by this fishery was considerable. At Port St Mary, for example about seventy boats brought home £14000 from Kinsale, averaging £200 per boat.[37] From 1869 to about 1875 Manx purchases of new and second-hand Cornish luggers were continuous and substantial. Innovation was reflected in the registry of first class fishing boats. In the Castletown district in 1870 five of the nine new boats registered were dandys and four were luggers, whereas in 1872 only one of the eight boats registered was a dandy, while seven were luggers.[38]

It was in anticipation of a continuing demand for new-built Cornish luggers that the remarkable and enterprising boatbuilder, William Paynter, was encouraged to leave St Ives in 1875 and establish a boatyard in Kilkeel.[39] Geographically the developing fishing station was strategically placed to supply the established Manx market, where Paynter already had business contacts. Kilkeel was also well placed to take advantage of an embryonic market in west Scotland based on Campbeltown in Kintyre. From 1872 Campbeltown fishermen had been buying new and second-hand luggers from St Ives and the signs were favourable for an expansion of this market based on the Kinsale mackerel fishery.[40] Above all, Kilkeel was rich in opportunity: the town was thriving; there was a steamship service to Britain from nearby Greenore and in common with their Manx and Scottish counterparts Kilkeel boat owners were already expanding their fleet by the purchase of Cornish luggers. The neighbouring Annalong fleet was also expanding and market potential existed there as the lugger had not yet been introduced. Furthermore repair facilities were always in demand

and a convenient plot of land beside the harbour was available for laying out a boatyard. Accordingly Paynter took a lease on the three quarter acre site and set up business as a boat and ship builder.[41]

It can be deduced from the sparse evidence available that Paynter's venture was not the success he anticipated. His attempt to capitalise on an expanding demand in the Isle of Man largely failed, only building about three boats for island owners. This was a consequence of Manx boat-builders undercutting his market by turning out from 1875 their own 'nickey' version of the Cornish lugger.[42] Subsequently boats of this type were sold new and second hand to Irish fishermen, particularly to those on the southwest coast, where the Manx had a reputation for building both well and cheaply.[43] Furthermore the potential Campbeltown market did not materialise for Paynter, as of the seven luggers that were acquired in 1875 and 1876, six were new-built in St Ives, while the seventh was bought second-hand from Lochranza owners. The difficulty in breaking into this market was compounded in 1876 when a Campbeltown boatbuilder began local production of luggers based on the Cornish model.[44] At Kilkeel, Paynter's initial investment in boatyard plant was substantial, but the whole enterprise was put in jeopardy in November 1876 when a disastrous fire destroyed his enginehouse, workshop and everything they contained, all valued at £1000.[45] Undaunted, Paynter rebuilt his premises and although orders continued to be placed for new luggers by local owners, the number supplied did not reach two figures. Clearly the local market alone could not sustain Paynter's business, especially in a period when the underlying economic trend was towards recession. When it was evident that the Kilkeel and Annalong fleets had expanded to their limits, and that there was no demand for new-built trading vessels, William Paynter sold up and returned to St Ives in 1883.[46]

Herring curing, Ardglass, County Down *c.* 1920. Ulster Folk and Transport Museum photograph collection WAG 783 (detail).

13 Change in the County Down Fisheries in the Twentieth Century

VIVIENNE POLLOCK

Situated in the north east of Ireland, County Down comprises 957 square miles of mostly low-lying farmland. The county measures 49 miles at its longest and only 25 miles at its widest; its area is made up by its winding coastline which stretches for 200 miles from Newry to Belfast. This coastline forms part of the western boundary of the Irish Sea, a shallow, saucer-like depression, whose productivity has not until recent times been affected by pollution and overfishing. In past years, the waters adjacent to County Down were home to an enormous variety of commercially valuable marine life. The rocky, indented shoreline which enclosed most of the region provided a habitat for crabs and lobsters, while fertile oyster, mussel and whelk beds, succoured and scoured by Irish Sea currents, occurred naturally in estuarine areas. Populations of many species of demersal food fishes, ranging from great fish such as cod and ling to smaller round fish such as haddock and whiting and flat-fishes such as plaice, sole and turbot, abounded in nearby fishing grounds. In addition, local inshore waters were regularly visited by huge shoals of herring, a fish which remains the most important of all pelagic species landed in the British commercial sea fisheries.

In County Down, therefore, opportunities existed for several types of fishery enterprise. Diversification of effort was clearly possible and, in fact, the local seafishing industry traditionally existed as a conglomeration of different types and branches of activity which were followed in the region in some or other combination and on a number of different commercial levels. For many fishermen this represented a year filled with a variety of fishing pursuits. Indeed in 1927 the 'mainstay of the scattered coastal population'[1] was described as:

an intermediate class of boat which engages at different times of the year in shellfishing, inshore herring fishing, and whitefishing. Their crews consist of two to four men, and their equipment includes lobster pots, longlines, trammel nets, trawl nets and herring drift nets.[2]

However professional fishermen often supplemented their primary income with earnings from secondary fishery; for example, when oyster fishermen in Carlingford Lough were asked if their main fishery would profit from an extension of the statutory season they replied that they; 'did not care to begin oyster dredging here until 1 November . . . the men here earn £2, £3 and £4 a night herring fishing, and if there was anyone out after the oysters it would be very injurious to the herrings'.[3]

The structural flexibility of the sea fishing industry in County Down also allowed a wide range of fishermen to participate in the one commercial venture. This was perhaps most marked in the local herring fisheries, which were exploited as part of a nation-wide cycle of herring activity but whose seasonality was particularly suitable for exploitation on a purely part-time basis. However, other sectors of the local industry functioned in similar fashion; for example whitefishing was followed as a full-time, or sole, occupation by some fishermen, and by others as an extension of the working year besides a supplement to land-based employment outside seafishing.

This particular organisation indicates an inherent lack of exclusive specialisation among commercial fishermen in County Down. It does not, however, reflect the degeneration of local commercial sea fishing. On the contrary, this diversity represented the relatively efficient maximisation of available resources, both natural and capital, within a framework of independent local activity. As such, it was a strength rather than a weakness, and was of major significance in the modern development of the seafishing industry in this area.

This paper examines some of the changes in the local fisheries which were associated with the mid-twentieth century shift in importance from herring fishing to fishing for whiting. The nineteenth century saw enormous expansion in the commercial herring industry in the region; this was a hugely productive and valuable concern for a fishery in which local commercial activity lasted at the most for only four or five months in the year. According to the official figures, in the period 1863–99 over 200000 tons of herring, valued at more than one million pounds, were brought in to County Down ports. This represented an average for each season of over 5000 tons of herring, landed, and quayside sales of nearly £30000. The prominence of the region is also suggested in the official records, which indicate that from 1875 to 1899 one-third of all the herring landed in Ireland came in through this area.[4] These figures are, however, by no means complete. They take no account of herring caught by boats which fished from County Down harbours but landed their catches elsewhere. More significantly, they ignore the substantial amounts of herrings which were regularly transmitted from fishing boat to central markets by 'buying' boats working from the fishing grounds. The County Down herring fleet reaped a much greater harvest than that officially described in the returns for the area.

Although small quantities of surplus herring were very occasionally cured during the nineteenth century, it was not until the early years of the twentieth century that an export-based herring curing industry began to take shape in this region. In 1908, 300 barrels of herring were cured for export in Ardglass. In 1909, five curing firms worked in the port; in that year 7870 barrels and 2240 half-barrels were sent to Russia. The Russian agents who had organised the trade remarked that they 'were greatly pleased with the quality of the fish and expressed their intention of again visiting the place'[5] In 1911 the crown brand for herring was introduced to fish cured in Ardglass and in Kilkeel. Fish sold with this guarantee of quality fetched 'very satisfactory prices . . . information received from the continent [indicated] that a favourable opinion was generally formed among buyers'.[6] In 1912, just under 30000 barrels of cured herring, with an estimated fresh weight of about 5600 tons, were exported from the region.[7]

The loss of continental European and Russian markets during the first world war was a severe blow to the British curing industry. However, compensating markets were found in America, where Ardglass herring enjoyed 'a very high reputation and [met] with ready sale'.[8] Although the revolution in Russia in 1917 meant the end of the export trade to that country, trade with and through Germany was resumed after the end of hostilities. In 1926 herring cured in Ardglass was 'eagerly bought up on the spot by the U.S.A. and Germany'.[9] In the same year when fourteen curing firms worked in the port where 'all available space . . . was occupied as curing plots'.[10]

The establishment of a major curing industry in County Down did not mean the end of the original fresh fish trade. On the contrary, substantial quantities of herring continued to be sold fresh in British and Irish markets. An assessment of the exact quantities involved in these separate enterprises is somewhat complicated; for example, according to official sources, in 1913 80133 cwt of herring were landed in Ardglass of which 22500 barrels were cured for export, ninety-eight crans were sold fresh locally, and the 'balance' sent to distant markets as fresh fish. A similar jumble of diverse weights, measurements and proportions exists for other years and for other County Down ports. The size of the fresh market for local herring should not, however, be underestimated; in 1923, the Fishery Development Commission were advised that in Ardglass alone, 'twenty tons of herring can be disposed of daily . . . for sale as fresh herrings to Belfast and throughout Ulster, distribution being effected by means of rail and motor lorry and to convenient agricultural communities by means of hawkers' carts'.[11]

The first major signs of weakness in this sector appeared in the 1920s. The immediate post-war period was not a good time for herring fishing in County Down; the end of the war-inflated prices for fresh fish caused a sudden decline in the local value of herring which fell from an average of £1.40 per cwt in 1918 to an average of 43p. in 1923. At the same time, the industry was further reduced in County Down by the government's refusal to extend to Ireland the guaranteed markets it had granted for Scottish and English-caught herring.[12] Of much greater long-term damage, however, was the increasing unpredictability of the local resource base. In 1929 the overall decline in the returns from sea fishing in the area was accounted for solely by the reduction in the quantity and quality of herring landings.[13] These adverse conditions continued throughout the 1930s; in 1934 herring fishing was so bad that the government allowed the introduction in mid-July of an unprecedented scheme of weekly payments to local fisher men 'to enable boats to continue operations in the hope that the situation would improve as the season advanced'.[14] Improvements did not occur and in that year only 6500 cwt of herring were landed in County Down.

Although the failure of local herring grounds and the subsequent deterioration in the fishing obviously affected County Down fishermen, the erosion of the herring industry in the 1920s and 1930s was not as damaging in local terms as might first appear. Herring landings in the region characteristically represented the combined efforts of a largely cosmopolitan fleet; thus a sizeable proportion of income from herring fishing invariably went to fishermen from outside the area. However a considerable part of the drop in herring landings during the years of decline consisted of lost 'foreign' input; as a result, the actual decrease in local earnings was much lower than the recorded decrease in overall values. This is to a certain extent confirmed in Table 1 in which the season of 1926, a relatively good year for herring fishing, is compared with the season of 1931, a relatively poor year. As can be seen, while a decrease of approximately two-thirds occurred in the volume and value of herring landings and in the number of foreign boats which worked from County Down, the average return for each participant boat in terms of both catch and quayside sales fell by less than one-half.

Table 1: Herring landings in the County Down ports in 1926 and 1931.

	Value of Herring Landings £	Volume of Herring Landings cwt	Participant vessels			Average Return £	Average Return cwt
			Local	Foreign	Total		
1926	73838	127000	199	178	377	195	337
1931	25677	41630	157	72	229	114	185
% decrease	65.2	67.2	21.1	59.5	39.2	41.5	45.1

The figures for local vessels offered above include every County Down fishing boat which took part in herring fishing during 1926 and 1931. A wide diversity of capacity and involvement is therefore represented by these inclusive statistics. It is very likely that the earnings of local full-time, first-class herring vessels were higher than the average returns presented here indicated, although the lack of specific quantitative evidence makes this difficult to prove. It is known, however, that a reduction in the overall volume and value of herring fishing did not necessarily result in a reduction in the return to each participant vessel. In 1927 the Northern Ireland fishery inspectors noted that although landings at Ardglass had fallen considerably since the previous year, 'the average catch per boat approximated fairly closely to the average in 1926'.[15] Indeed, closer examination of the relevant statistics for this port reveals that the average financial return to boats working to Ardglass stood at £303 in 1926 but £315 in 1927.[16] In this case, a drop in overall capacity was accompanied by an increase in average individual return.

The existence of two herring industries in the region – one freshing and the other curing – also sheltered County Down fishermen from the worst effects of decline. The brunt of the post-war collapse in commercial herring fishing was borne by the export-based curing industry. But the salient feature of this enterprise in County Down was the extent to which business activity in all sectors was carried on by outsiders. The decline of the local curing industry certainly hit spin-off trades, such as coopering and cartage. But it had little direct consequence for the majority of local workers. Even the fleet which supplied the curers tended to be composed of visitors. For example, in 1928 curing for export in the region was delayed until the first fortnight in August and the arrival of foreign steam drifters from Shetland and north Scottish grounds.[17]

In fact, there were not one but two catching seasons in the local summer herring fishery. The 'early' season lasted from about April to mid-July and was worked only by local boats and directed only at fresh markets. This season was thus of tremendous importance to indigenous fishermen: in 1930 their earnings in this period grossed £6928 giving 'almost £200 a head' on top of what was gained during the remainder of the fishery.[18] The 'main' season, in which curing took place and the local fleet was supplemented by steam and motor drifters from outside the region, started in mid-July and lasted until both the visitors and the fish left. This split in the fishery was accompanied even by a change in the way herrings were counted; until mid-July they were sold by the 'mease' which was an Irish quantitative measurement of 635 fish, but once curing started, they were sold by the 'cran', which was the standard Scottish weight measurement.

There was, however, no compulsion for any fishing boat to sell exclusively either to the fresh market or the cured market. There was thus keen

competition between buyers for freshing and buyers for curing and considerable evidence that the needs of the fresh market were generally served
first. For example, in the dearth year of 1934, there was only 'one day [at
Ardglass] when surplus herrings were available for curing'.[19] This competition greatly inflated the quayside price for herrings when they were in
short supply, thus offering some respite to local fishermen for the reduction
in the amount of herring that they brought in. In 1930 it was recorded that a
decline of over 10000 cwt in the volume of herring returned in County Down
had led to a reduction of only £678 in their total value, 'indicating that
fishermen were proportionally better rewarded by the smaller quantity of
herring landed'.[20] Indeed, during the lean years of the 1920s and 1930s the
average quayside price per cwt of herring sold in County Down was
considerably higher than it had ever been, apart from four years of
artificially high prices during the war.

The local benefits of the expansion of the herring industry were enormous, both in the short and the long term. Part of this value lay in the
revenue raised by fishermen in quayside and boatside sales, and in the
trading profits realised by curers. But the presence of a successful herring
fishery secured a new foundation for local commercial sea fishing as a whole
in the region. On the one hand, capital which accrued from, or was ensured
by, herring fishing was often injected into the general fishing operation –
often in the shape of better-equipped boats, which might be used for
purposes besides herring fishing. On the other hand, demands for harbour
improvements and extra road and rail links, which benefited all classes of
fishermen, were often weighted and met because of the needs of the wider
herring industry.

However the local effects of the contraction of this major industry were
limited. In the first place, much of the loss this represented was sustained
not by local fishermen or businessmen but by outsiders. Although decline in
the 'foreign' curing industry was profound, and some local secondary trade
was affected, it was of little direct relevance for most local enterprise. And
while there was a corresponding decrease in the local demand for herring,
the large quantities that the curing industry required had been supplied by
a mixed local fleet, supplemented by highly efficient travelling drifters from
Scotland and elsewhere. As has been demonstrated, a substantial proportion of the decline in the local volume of the herring industry was related to
a decrease in the local complement of travelling drifters. In addition, it was
possible to match local landings to local demand by restricting the access of
these visitors to County Down ports, In 1936 the use of local harbours by
steam drifters and ring-netters before 12 July was forbidden by statute.[21]
Secondly, the physical manifestations of previous success at herring fishing
survived in the shape of an improved fleet, and restored harbour facilities.
Thirdly, markets for fresh herring, which were largely domestic, remained

viable. Herring fishing was undoubtedly reduced in value after the first world war, but it was not completely moribund.

During the years of overall decline in the local herring industry a new fishery had developed in County Down. This was a winter fishery for whiting, which grew steadily in importance during the 1920s and early 1930s and which by the end of that decade assumed tremendous significance in the region. In 1925 local landings of this fish totalled 1564 cwt; in 1938, they totalled 17061 cwt. From 1938 to 1947, the amount of whiting landed multiplied another eight-fold, while its total value in quayside sales rocketed from £11565 to £209746, and although it remains true that part of this escalation was due to higher war prices and expanding domestic markets for fresh fish, corresponding figures for the herring fishery describe a rise in production of less than 50 percent and a rise in value of less than £37000. The average price of whiting also increased more over the same period than did the average price of herring; at its highest level, whiting fetched three and a half times its pre-war price, while the highest war-time average for herring was only three times higher than in 1938. In 1940 whiting replaced herring as the single most valuable species landed in County Down.

This switch in supremacy signified a number of local changes in fishery activity. Commercial herring fishing in County Down was a summer affair, taking place in the locality from about April to September. Whiting were caught during the winter months, in a season which lasted from about November to March. Methods of capture also differed. Herring are pelagic surface-swimming, shoaling fish, traditionally taken with stationary drift nets, while whiting are demersal, bottom-feeding, slow-moving, solitary fish, caught with the Danish seine net, whose introduction depended on the use of fully motor-powered fishing boats. The two fisheries therefore demanded different organisation, different equipment, different skills and technical knowledge, and a different awareness of resource behaviour. The substitution of one for the other thus opened the possibility of serious upheaval at operational level in the County Down fisheries.

However, the industrial structure of commercial seafishing in the region enabled the transition to whiting fishing to take effect with the minimum of disruption. Of major significance was the prevalence of combination fishing in the region. As we have seen, most County Down fishermen were masters not of one art but of several. Knowledge of white fishing in the area was thus extended to fishermen who were neither primarily nor exclusively involved in this sector of the industry. Nevertheless the traditional local reliance on a diversity of fishing activity was important, not only because it widened the occupational base of the local white fisheries but it also aided the introduction of new forms of whitefishing – in this case, Danish seining.

Danish seining was a comparatively recent innovation. It had been

invented by the Danes after the mid-nineteenth century for use in the North
Sea for fishing plaice and first appeared in the Irish fisheries in the early
years of the twentieth century. Danish seining was an extremely productive
and relatively cheaply-fitted method of catching white fish. However, the
key feature of its early history was its original development as an adjunct to
herring fishing at a time when the herring industry was predominant.
Indeed, the first Irish boat officially described as carrying a Danish seine
was an experimental motor drifter, the *Ovoca*, which was launched in
1907.[22] The first County Down vessel credited with its use was the fishing
boat *Tuskar*, which was registered in the area as a herring drifter, as were the
next Mourne boats to be so fitted, the *Winifred* of Newry and the *Peace and
Plenty* of Kilkeel.[23]

This connection is clearly indicated by the spatial distribution of the
method in County Down. The first local census of fishing activity, which
related to 1926, revealed that the use of the Danish seine was very much
concentrated where herring fishing was strongest. Thus seventeen of
County Down's twenty-one seiners hailed from Portavogie and the
remainder belonged to Newcastle, Annalong and Kilkeel. The relationship
between herring fishing and Danish seining becomes even more pro-
nounced when the whole of Northern Ireland is taken into consideration. In
1930, for example, 157 of the 174 Northern Irish boats which were engaged
in herring fishing belonged to County Down, as did twenty-six of the
twenty-nine Northern Irish seiners.

Various factors contributed to this situation. Commercial sea fishing as a
whole was more important in County Down than it was in the rest of
Northern Ireland. A context for fishery development thus existed in the
region in which investment in new fishing techniques was more likely. This,
however, does not wholly explain the predominance of Danish seining in
herring fishing areas. The answer lies also in the timing of the fishery which
was based on the new method. Danish seining was a winter activity. As
such, it fitted very neatly into the herring fishing year, where local activity
was confined to the summer months.

It was already common for home-based herring fishermen in County
Down to turn to other types of fishing when herrings were not locally
available. It was in this grey area of secondary enterprise that Danish
seining gained its major foothold. Indeed, the first official mention of the
employment of this method in the region was a comment regarding its
increased use by County Down herring boats between herring seasons.[24]
Herring fishermen who fitted for Danish seining did so either as an
additional supplementary pursuit or a substitute for existing supplementary pursuits. However the innovation was not entirely risk-free. For
example, Thomas Cully of Portavogie explained to the Northern Ireland
Fishery Department in 1924 that he had forgone instalments on his loan

because he 'had bought a seine net and outfit which was not a success so I got into a lot of debt'.[25] But it was, arguably, much less risky than fitting the new device to displace a primary fishing enterprise. A herring fisherman who adopted Danish seining was able to keep on herring fishing; a trawl fisherman who turned to Danish seining had first to decide whether to give up trawling itself. And although seining was slowly adopted by north Down white fishermen after 1926, the seemingly inexplicable statement made by the Northern Ireland Fishery Department, that 'on the County Down coast the trawl has been almost completely superseded by the Danish seine . . . the changeover to the more effective type of net is of course proceeding gradually',[26] makes sense only if the introduction of the new device occurred as a stop-gap substitution rather than as a main-method replacement.

In fact, the initial expansion of Danish seining was very much governed by the extent of the local herring fishery. For example, it was reported in 1927 that 'the numbers of seiners that year would have been very much greater had not numbers of Portavogie boats, which normally finish off the year seining . . . not crossed to Scottish waters to continue herring fishing instead'.[27] On the other hand, its establishment undoubtedly helped to compensate for the fluctuating success of herring fishing; in 1929, the Northern Ireland fishery inspectors submitted that 'in view of the great variations to be expected in the returns from summer herring fishing from year to year the comparative stability of the returns from white fishing is gratifying'.[28] And it seems likely that the 'outstanding feature' of 1934, namely, the success which attended nine Kilkeel luggers which went seining rather than being laid up as usual when their main fishery ended, was prompted by that year's disastrous herring season.[29]

The establishment of Danish seining also gave a new and wider prominence to the white fisheries in County Down. By 1938 whiting fishing had 'come to be seen by Portavogie fishermen as their main source of earning a living, even more so than herring fishing'.[30] Even the Kilkeel fleet, which had previously been geared almost exclusively for herring drifting, now included a number of vessels which had been bought specifically for Danish seining.[31] This switch in allegiance is clearly indicated in the local employment statistics: in 1926, when Danish seining was in its infancy in the region, only 2.4 percent of local boats and 10.7 percent of local fishermen engaged in the method. By 1947 this had jumped to 38 percent of boats, and 58 percent of fishermen, with Danish seining being the major fishing method employed in all County Down fishing ports except Kilkeel, where inshore herring fishing continued to attract a substantial part-time following.

In many ways the changeover in County Down from the previous supremacy of herring to the new supremacy of whiting fishing was but a shift in commercial and industrial emphasis. While herring fishing was no longer as important as it had been, it was still commercially exploited in the region. Furthermore the expansion of Danish seining and the subsequent major reliance on white fishing did not emerge 'from scratch' but was occasioned when contraction in the herring industry stimulated the growth of an existing secondary activity. There was thus no great upheaval in either the composition or the constitution of the local fishing industry. There was instead a change in primary function; whereas professional fishermen in the area in the early twentieth century had tended to be herring fishermen first and foremost, after the mid-twentieth century they tended to be Danish seiners first and foremost.

This is not to suggest that no new departures were initiated by this change of direction. Unlike the peripatetic herring industry, whitefishing in the region was a purely local affair. The establishment of a strong, indigenous, primary sector therefore provided a much sounder base for future fishery development than did the previous reliance on local manifestations for foreign enterprise. The expansion of Danish seining in the County Down area corresponded with an increased professionalisation in the industry; in the 1920s, an average of about 50 percent of County Down fishermen gained their sole living from fishing; this fell to about 40 percent in the 1930s. By 1947 it had reached 67 percent. Danish seining certainly contributed to a new vitality in the local fishing population. According to the Irish Commission on Population and Emigration, which reported in 1949, a key feature of the post-war industry in County Down was the number of young men who had been attracted to fishing – in some cases, the owners of the newest seine boats were only twenty-four years old.[32] Only twenty years earlier the Northern Ireland Fishery Development Commission had bemoaned the ageing of Northern Ireland's fishermen, and the great disinclination of young men to follow 'their father's uncertain calling'.[33]

The source of this improvement was undoubtedly Danish seining, credited, rightly, as the first of the modern systems of fishing to appear in County Down.[34] However the prevalence of combination fishing, and the prior contribution of the declining herring industry had been crucial to the initial expansion of this method. The changing aspect of the fisheries in County Down was conditioned both by the past and by the traditional structures which obtained in commercial sea fishing in the region.

Kilkeel fishermen *c.* 1950. Ulster Folk and Transport photograph collection L2978/12.

14   The Social Anthropology of an Irish Sea Fishing Community

Kilkeel, County Down

REGINALD BYRON

This paper discusses some aspects of the contemporary social organisation of fishing in Kilkeel, County Down. Kilkeel today is the most important fishing port in Northern Ireland, having a fleet of about eighty-five trawlers which support nearly 25 percent of the employment in the local area. The way that fishing is organised in Kilkeel shows a number of similarities with other fishing places round the coast of the British Isles, but also exhibits some instructive differences.

Fishing in Kilkeel, as in other places, has in recent years become highly capital-intensive. A new 800 foot boat now costs in the order of £500000 and has monthly expenses of £10000. The management of these boats calls for a good deal of professional expertise if they are not only to cover their costs but to make a profit. Yet in comparison with most other kinds of businesses, fishermen have to contend with a markedly higher degree of unpredictability in the conditions under which they operate. This is because fishermen are basically hunters, who must pursue their quarry over hundreds of square miles of sea. The sea is common to all, and no fisherman is able to assert any territorial claim that is likely to be respected by others. Thus the individual fisherman has no means of husbanding the resource upon which he depends to ensure a continuity of supply from one day to the next. The fish move about according to their own lights, and reproduce themselves in greater or lesser numbers that are determined by a complex interplay of ecological factors quite beyond the fisherman's control. And, as the fish are not uniformly distributed in the sea, but tend to occur in concentrated, highly mobile shoals, not only must the fisherman first locate a shoal of fish before he can begin to try to capture it, he must also compete with other fishermen who are attempting to do the same. Fishing is regarded by the

147

fishermen as a zero-sum game: since all are competing for access to a finite resource, one man's gain is another man's loss. Extreme individualism and rivalry among fishermen, manifested in many ways, is thus a characteristic feature of fishing societies.

In such societies the basic unit of social organisation is that of the crew: the group of men who work together in the same boat, along with their associated wives and children on shore. It is to his crew mates that a fisherman typically owes his primary social obligations, and these loyalties are expected to take precedence over other ties of kinship and neighbour-hood, where such ties are not coterminous with one's membership of a crew; often they are, for crew mates are frequently kinsmen or neighbours or both. The family crew is a commonplace phenomenon in communities all round the North Atlantic region.[1] Family crews are remarkably cohesive social and economic units. That they endure today, it should be emphasised, is not because they are survivals from a peasant past, but because they are very well adapted to the exigencies of modern commercial fishing; in fact, family crews in many places are a comparatively recent development.[2] Apart from kinship, which may or may not be present, other common features of crews which express their solidarity include a high degree of guardedness in their dealings with other crews; and within the crew, a generalised sharing of tasks and favours, corporate decision-making, the division of the proceeds into approximately equal parts, and the joint ownership of the boat by several, if not all the members of the crew. In crews that display these features, the criteria for the recruitment of new members are very exclusive indeed. Rarely will anyone be taken into a crew who is not already well known to its members and who cannot be trusted to be loyal to it. If individualism and rivalry are characteristic of the relations between crews, within the same crew social relationships are characterised by consensus and cooperation. Features of this kind are typical of the social organisation of fishing crews in the British Isles and northern Europe as well as maritime Canada, for example.[3]

In Kilkeel, there are significant departures from this pattern. Perhaps the most striking difference, and one that has an effect on other elements in the social organisation of fishing, is in the way that boats are owned. In most other places, ownership is shared among three to six members of the crew, one of whom is the skipper. But in Kilkeel, ideally it is held that the boat should be owned solely by the skipper. Any other arrangement is con-sidered merely a temporary expedient toward this goal. Sole ownership has many attractions: financial, managerial and social. Financially, the skipper is entitled to keep all the profits for himself, as well as taking a wage. How he spends this money, whether to give himself a higher standard of living, to pay off a mortgage on his boat, or to re-invest in the business is entirely his own affair. Although he may consult his crew in certain matters, he is under no obligation to do so and he has sole authority in his management of the enterprise. By virtue of his proprietorship, he is also boss in the workplace: he has the power to hire and fire at will, and his leadership cannot be disputed by any other member of the crew. As the skipper is both the owner of the boat and leader of the crew, the success of the boat is identified with him personally. If the boat does well, he will be accorded the respect of the community and he and his family will gain in social standing.

Yet few men who aspire to skippership can afford simply to buy a boat outright. Nowadays banks and governmental agencies are prepared to make loans to fishermen, but this was not always so. In the past, and to some extent still today, aspirant skippers have formed partnerships with merchants and businessmen in the town. There is a history of this in Kilkeel that goes back until at least the beginning of this century. Shopkeepers, boatbuilders, engineers, merchants, building contractors and other tradesmen and craftsmen have regularly invested in fishing boats. Until the second world war, it would appear that over half the boats in the preceding fifty years had been purchased with local land-based capital. Some of these boats were owned either solely by a local businessman or jointly by a group of businessmen who employed a skipper to run the boat; other boats were jointly owned by a land-based investor and a skipper. This practice continued after the second world war, when some businessmen gradually built up their boat-owning interests to the point where they depended upon these investments for a major part of their incomes. Within the past twenty years, however, the greater cost of boats and the greater preparedness of banks to lend money to fishermen has caused a decline in the role played by local businessmen in the capitalisation of fishing. Nevertheless, these arrangements are by no means a thing of the past; they are still common, though on a smaller scale than formerly.

The usual pattern in the post-war period has been a form of joint ownership between the land-based investor and the skipper, each holding a variable proportion of the thirty-two shares into which a fishing boat's ownership is customarily divided. The skipper generally begins as a minority shareholder, with the intention of gradually buying out his businessman-partner until eventually he owns all thirty-two shares. The profits of the venture are divided between the two men in proportion to their shareholdings, and the skipper will normally claim little, if any, of his part of the profits as cash-in-hand; rather, he will take his due in equity shares. However, there are many variations in these arrangements, as the following case histories illustrate.[4]

Case 1

Rupert Burns, a farmer's son, is now eighty-one years old. He tried a number of occupations, including fishing, when he was young but then became involved in building contracting and plant hire. After the war, he established a quarrying business. His first investment in a fishing boat was made in the late 1920s. This was followed by eight more purchases over the next twenty years. From 1950 to 1960 he acquired five more boats, although at any one time he owned shares in no more than seven boats. For a time in the 1950s he set himself up as a fish auctioneer, selling the catches of his own boats.

Burns started by buying smallish boats secondhand, gradually going on to bigger and newer boats until, by the 1950s, he had at least one seventy-five foot boat built new. He purchased all the boats outright; only in three cases did he sell a part of his holding to the skippers he employed. His policy, unlike most other Kilkeel investors, was to maintain exclusive ownership of his boats, to accumulate all the profit, and to reinvest it in further boats. Although he rarely permitted his skippers to buy shares, he was prepared to hire untried men as skippers. After having proved themselves in Burns's employ, these skippers would then be in a good position to negotiate a partnership with another investor.

Case 2

Alfred McLean started a fish-selling business during the war, and soon became involved in boat ownership. In 1944 he purchased a boat jointly with a young skipper and in 1945 he went into partnership in a brand-new boat with another young skipper. His involvement in the first boat lasted only a year or two, but the second venture persisted: McLean's partnership with this skipper lasted until 1965, when the skipper bought out the last of McLean's shares in a newer and larger boat they had bought in 1950. In 1965 McLean entered into two more joint ventures with other skippers, and a third partnership followed. In the 1970s he bought shares in two further boats. Thus from 1965 to 1973 McLean had shares in five boats with five skippers, all of whom eventually bought out McLean's interest to become the sole owners of their vessels.

McLean's policy has been to provide top-up capital for skippers who want to trade up to more modern secondhand boats. He takes a return on his investment through half the profits made by the boat, the other half going to the skipper. In all these cases the skipper has used his part of the profit to purchase McLean's share.

Case 3

John MacNish's father and grandfather were fishermen, though neither owned a boat. His father died young, leaving John to seek work on the schooners of the home trade, from which he managed to accumulate some savings. Later, after fishing for a few years as an ordinary deckhand and saving more of his wages, helped by a little money from his mother, he was able to form a partnership with Alfred McLean to buy a secondhand boat. In 1950 they commissioned a new boat, in which MacNish invested £700 and McLean about £2000. MacNish was now securely set up as a skipper with a modern boat, and gradually bought out McLean's share over the next fifteen years. Some time later MacNish signed over a half-interest in the boat to his son, who worked on the boat as a deckhand. When MacNish retired in the early 1980s, the son took over as skipper and assumed full control over the boat when his father died in 1984.

Through a partnership with McLean, MacNish managed to succeed from deckhand to part-owner skipper, and after twenty years had established himself as an independent skipper with a legacy to leave his son, so that he too might be an independent skipper. This pattern of enterprise is repeated, more or less, in the other cases in which skippers have formed partnerships with Alfred McLean.

Case 4

John White was a partner with McLean, but was already an established independent skipper-owner by that time. White started as a hired skipper in the late 1920s, working on boats owned by local businessmen. In 1929 he formed a partnership with one of these businessmen to buy a boat he had been working on as a hired skipper. He eventually bought out his partner and sold the boat, buying another outright in 1943. He had this boat for nearly twenty years; on it he trained his three sons as skippers. In 1960 he bought a newer boat to replace his old one, again outright. Keeping this boat, he bought another in partnership with McLean in 1965; later on he signed over the 1960 boat to two of his sons and continued to fish the 1965 boat together with his third son. By 1970 White had bought out McLean's share in the 1965 boat and was now, with his sons, the owner of two boats which could provide his sons with a livelihood, and through his continued ownership of a half-interest in the 1965 boat, will give him an investment income in his retirement.

In broader comparative terms, these partnerships between skippers and shore-based investors, which appear to have been the convention in Kilkeel, are not reported as commonplace occurrences in other North Atlantic fishing communities, although it must be admitted that the ethnological coverage is by no means complete, with reports of other Irish fishing places being particularly scarce. While this may be a common pattern in Ireland, there is insufficient published evidence to permit reliable comparison and generalisation to proceed. Yet the apparent singularity of this feature of social organisation leads one to wonder where it came from. Perhaps an explanation for it can be found in Kilkeel's history as a seaport.

It might be possible that the present-day patterns of ownership of fishing vessels in Kilkeel are derived from the port's history of seafaring that until the second world war seems to have been largely concerned with a combination of fishing and the coastal schooner trade.[5] Small merchant vessels throughout the British Isles were most commonly owned by their captains or shore-based entrepreneurs or by partnerships of captains and entrepreneurs. Ownership was seldom shared by any member of the crew other than the captain. This allowed the captain to hold unchallenged authority aboard his ship to make decisions as he saw fit in the very unstable economic conditions of the casual cargo trades. Captains who were good at making quick, instinctive decisions on the basis of fragmentary and constantly changing information would have prospered, while those who decided matters by more cumbersome procedures might have missed vital opportunities to get good cargoes. In Kilkeel, as fishing seems often to have been combined with coastal cargo sailing, according to the season, and later as fishing came to predominate and then to eclipse sail trading altogether, the fundamental conventions of ownership and management may have been transferred, little changed, from cargo sailing to fishing: this may be an explanation of the practice of sole ownership of fishing boats by their skippers, perhaps in partnership with shore-based capitalists.[6]

If so, this pattern of development contrasts markedly with other communities in the British Isles which have longer traditions of fishing and little, if any, history of involvement in coastal trading. A typical example is Burra Isle, in the Shetlands.[7] Fishing in Burra has been aimed toward the market for at least four hundred years, but nevertheless was organised like a subsistence operation. Generally, each extended household or neighbourhood provided its own boat from its own resources of capital and labour. The boat was operated in a routine and predictable regime without need of strong central direction to cope with the sorts of variables that characterise casual cargo trading. Such leadership as there was in these fishing crews was not a function of proprietorship (and this is still true today), but rather of skill, experience and the respect in which the *primus inter pares* was held by the other members of the crew. From this has evolved a pattern which in the present day is typical of long-established fishing communities in northern Europe: ownership in shares, which are frequently equal in value, among three to six members of the crew. Sometimes, as in Burra Isle, the skipper has no greater shareholding than any of his partners, and all five or six members of the crew are shareholders corporately owning the boat; there are no hired men. Burra Isle fishing boats are about the same size and catching-power as in Kilkeel. In other places in the British Isles and Scandinavia, boats worth up to £3 million are owned in this way.

Sole ownership in fishing, as in sail trading, may offer an advantage under certain economic conditions. It permits quick, uncomplicated decision-making, adaptability and flexibility in management and invest-ment strategies in which the skipper-owner can accommodate changes in the market or prospects in fishing by modifying his fishing regime or by exchanging boats. Moreover, the concentration of ownership in a single individual, with all its financial and social attractions, may be an important means by which initiative and innovation are promoted: thus an entre-preneurial spirit is emphasised and reinforced through financial and social rewards. In Kilkeel, there are some very successful skippers. Local people say that several skippers have bank accounts in the Isle of Man, and at least one of them is reputed to being well on the way to a millionaire. Certainly, many skippers live well, and there are a number of expensive cars and fine new houses in Kilkeel that belong to skippers. But for all its advantages to the skipper, sole ownership or partnerships between skippers and land-based investors is in some ways inimical to the interests of the wider community of fishermen in Kilkeel, for it creates or tends to accentuate certain organisational problems, some of which have import-ant implications for fisheries administration and public policy in the province.

First, sole ownership enables the fisherman to claim skippership by virtue of his proprietorship of the boat, without any necessary regard to his abilities as a leader, skills at finding fish, or judgement in financial matters. Seldom is it possible for a local investor, much less an office-bound bank manager or government administrator, to distinguish clearly between applicants who have had merely a modicum of good luck so far in their careers, and those who have genuine managerial talents. Unlike other places such as Burra Isle, where the lender spreads his risk over four, five or six experienced fishermen, in Kilkeel he must stake everything on one man. In all likelihood, this is one of the reasons that accounts for the fact that bankruptcies are a more regular part of fishing life in Kilkeel than elsewhere, and there have been some monumental failures of judgement. In one particularly well-known case, a skipper was able to obtain loans to buy three boats, two of them brand-new, within the space of a couple of years. He attempted to manage all three at the same time, only to go broke in a matter of months, owing his creditors no less than £1.5 million.

Secondly, the absence of co-owners in the boat's crew, or close kinsmen other than the occasional skipper's son, means that there are no effective controls of any kind, formal or informal, upon the skipper's behaviour while at sea. Some Kilkeel skippers are known far and wide for their 'cowboy' behaviour, which is alleged to include fishing out of season and in forbidden sea areas, exceeding their quotas (sometimes, it is said, by exaggerated amounts that make a nonsense of conservation measures), and landing suspect catches at times and places where fisheries inspectors are unlikely to be encountered. Such practices rarely occur in places like Shetland: the presence of co-owners and kinsmen in the crew prevents unilateral decisions by the skipper and militates against 'cowboy' behaviour. In Kilkeel, however, the men must either go along with the skipper or be sacked. That there are high rates of turnover in Kilkeel crews is perhaps not surprising.

Thirdly, as sole owner of the boat, the skipper keeps all the profits for himself. If he is a part-owner with a land-based investor, the effect is the same; none of the profit is distributed among the other members of the crew. In other places, where shares are held by three to six members of the crew, the earnings of the boat are much more evenly distributed; each partner has a share in the profits to supplement his basic wages. For a given net income to the boat, a shareholding crewman will have substantially higher earnings (by as much as 100 percent) than crewmen who, as in Kilkeel, do not own shares. In Kilkeel, ordinary crewmen on the less successful boats are forced to decide, virtually on a daily basis, whether it is more worthwhile for them to go fishing or stay ashore to collect the dole. When one considers that there is no forty-hour week in fishing and that sixteen-hour working days and eighty-hour weeks are not uncommon, the comparison between the level of fishing earnings in Kilkeel and the standard rates of state benefit is even more unfavourable. If fishing vessels in Kilkeel were owned in partnerships of four to six working fishermen rather than by a single individual, some positive economic and social benefits might accrue. The profits from fishing would be spread over a greater number of fishermen and their families, which could help to alleviate the problem of low pay. Moreover, these profits would be more likely to remain in the community than to be exported to banks in tax havens or spent on luxury goods in Newry or Belfast, thus benefiting the economy of Kilkeel as a whole. As it is, there is more observable evidence of social deprivation to be seen in Kilkeel, and a much higher reliance upon state benefits than in most other fishing communities in the United Kingdom.[8]

In conclusion, sole ownership and partnerships between land-based investors, while the typical pattern in Kilkeel, is in a broader comparative perspective probably not typical. Although this form of organisation undoubtedly offers some attractive advantages to skippers as individuals, it may be questioned whether the community at large derives as much benefit from sole ownership as other fishing communities have derived from the corporate ownership of boats. Sole ownership in Kilkeel appears to have caused some troublesome consequences that are not met in such exaggerated degree elsewhere.

Acknowledgements

The research upon which this paper is based was supported by a grant from the Economic and Social Research Council. I am indebted to my research associate in this project, Dr R.M. Dilley, for the case material presented here.

The Launch, or Men of Iron, Belfast. Oil painting by William Conor, 1923. Ulster Folk and Transport Museum collection.

15   Aspects of Shipbuilding in Belfast, Past and Present

T. JOHN PARKER

The conference theme of the maritime history of the Irish Sea coincides with the 125th anniversary of the founding of the partnership between Edward James Harland and Gustav Wolff in Belfast. The theme is commendable in its look at the overall maritime history of the Irish Sea – the history of ships and seamen, of shipbuilders, ports and harbours, of merchants and trade, of fishermen and their craft. Harland & Wolff has played a major part in this history and continues to do so today.

While this year the company is celebrating one hundred and twenty-five years, it must be remembered that it was some four hundred years ago that Sir John Perrot, lord deputy of Ireland, singled out Belfast in 1584 as being, in his opinion 'the best and most convenient place in the province of Ulster for the establishment of shipbuilding'. An early listing of ships built at Belfast places the building of two ships, a barque of twenty-five tons and a ketch of fifty tons plus sundry river craft, around 1663. Another source records that shipbuilding took place at the earlier date of 1636, when a vessel of about 150 tons was built by the presbyterian clergymen of the city. It is probable, however, that boatbuilding and repairing were carried on at the mouth of the Lagan many centuries before that date.

Shipbuilding as an industry did not get into its stride until the end of the eighteenth century, when a Scot named William Ritchie paid a visit to Belfast in March 1789, with a view to transferring his shipyards from Saltcoats in Ayrshire to the banks of the Lagan. William Ritchie returned to Belfast on 3 July 1791, bringing with him ten men and a quantity of shipbuilding apparatus and materials for the establishment of a shipyard on the Lagan. The first vessel built by Ritchie was the *Hibernia*, a vessel of 300 tons which entered the water just one year after his arrival in Belfast. In the next twenty years, Ritchie's enterprise grew and by 1812 he was able to

157

record that 'there are now employed 44 carpenters, 55 apprentices, 7 pairs of sawers, 12 blacksmiths and several joiners'.

In the first half of the nineteenth century William Ritchie's enterprise was succeeded by the wooden shipbuilding firms of Ritchie & MacLaine, Thompson & Kirwan and Charles Connell & Sons. None of these builders attempted to make engines for the few wooden steamships turned out in Belfast. The first of these, and indeed one of the earliest steamers built in Ireland, was the aptly named *Belfast* launched in 1820 by Ritchie & MacLaine with seventy horsepower engines by the local firm of Victor Coates.

It was not until the second half of the nineteenth century that Belfast became world-renowned for the construction of iron and later steel ships, both steam-powered and wind-driven. Technologically the building of iron hulls was not an extension of wooden shipbuilding, but rather a development of the expanding industry of boilermaking. Significantly the first iron vessel built on the Lagan was constructed by the engineering and boiler-making firm of Victor Coates & Co., who launched the *Countess of Caledon*, in 1838, for service on Lough Neagh.

The next notable development worth mentioning was the formation of the subsequently world-famous Queen's Island. The straightening of the Lagan involved making two cuttings which resulted in the creation of an island. Originally known as Dargan's Island, it was named after the contractor who carried out the work. In 1849 the name was changed to Queen's Island in honour of Queen Victoria who visited Belfast in that year to open the new cut, which became the Victoria Channel. At a later date the old channel of the river was filled in, but the name Queen's Island remained. Moving to 1853 there is recorded the laying out of an iron shipbuilding yard on Queen's Island for Robert Hickson & Company, owners of the Eliza Street Iron Works, Belfast.

Edward James Harland started his career as manager of Hickson's Yard in December 1854, after answering an advertisement for the post of shipyard manager. In 1858 Hickson sold his yard, his interest and goodwill to Edward Harland for the sum of £5000. With Harland in absolute control the yard grew quickly and he successfully completed three vessels in 1859 for Bibby Sons & Company Ltd. of Liverpool. They were the *Venetian*, the *Sicilian* and the *Syrian* and are listed as vessel numbers 1, 2 and 3 on the company's present order book. The pressures of running the yard grew and on 1 January 1862 Edward Harland invited Gustav Wilhelm Wolff to join him in partnership. Gustav Wolff was born in Hamburg in 1834 and was educated both in Hamburg and at Liverpool College. The capital of the new company was £2416, of which E. J. Harland contributed £1916 and G. W. Wolff £500. Wolff was an engineer and his partnership with Harland produced a spate of new ideas in shipbuilding. They were helped by the fact that the working week was 6.00 a.m. to 8.15 p.m. five days per week and 6.00 a.m. to 4.00 p.m. on a Saturday. Despite all their innovations, the partnership did not have the facility to install engines in the vessels built in the company's yard, and ships were towed to Greenock for engineering. In 1880 it was decided to build an engine works and manufacture their own propulsion machinery. Gustav Wolff retired in 1908 and died on 17 April 1913.

When Harland died in 1895 he was succeeded by W. J. Pirrie (later Lord Pirrie), a man with the push which took him and the shipyard into the international class. Harland set great store by the fact that he trained most of his men in the shipyard and this was true also of W. J. Pirrie, who had been the chief draughtsman. Pirrie was an extraordinary individual and probably even more dedicated than Harland. He died in 1924 and was succeeded by Lord Kylsant, chairman of the Royal Mail Steam Packet Company, who in turn was succeeded in 1930 by Sir Frederick Rebbeck, who remained chairman for over thirty-two years until his retirement in 1962.

There has been a remarkable growth in the size of Queen's Island since 1862. Notable developments have included the provision by Belfast harbour commissioners of dry docks of ever-increasing size, beginning in 1867 with the Hamilton graving dock. The Alexandra dock followed in 1889 and the Thompson dock in 1910. By the latter date other expansion at the Island included the Albert boiler works, the Victoria and Alexandra wharves and the construction of the new Queen's yard where the *Titanic* and other notable ships were built. In 1922 expansion was virtually completed with the construction of the Musgrave yard, the Thompson wharf and the Thompson works. It is an interesting comparison that in 1946 no fewer than twenty ships were being constructed, aggregating some 600000 tons deadweight, whereas in 1970 only four ships were being completed, but aggregating some 620000 tons deadweight.

It may be of interest to examine some of the innovations that have contributed to the reputation of Harland & Wolff. In 1859 the construction of S.S. *Venetian* for the Bibby Line was commenced as Hull no. 1. *Venetian* was the first of a 19-ship series in which Harland & Wolff broke with tradition and developed the long, narrow hull which gave greater tonnage with minimal power increase. 1868 marked the building of the gunboat H.M.S. *Lynx* and the commencement of a long association with the Royal and Commonwealth navies, which has resulted in the construction of over 200 vessels for the navy. A famous example was the aircraft carrier H.M.S. *Eagle*, completed in 1951, which, at 31100 tons displacement was for many years the largest aircraft carrier in the Royal Navy. H.M.S. *Eagle* was scrapped in 1978 after twenty-one years of active service. Today this long-standing association continues with the conversion of the aviation training ship (A.T.S.) *Argus*, which will give the navy its largest displacement ship, and the building of the auxiliary oiler replenishment vessel (A.O.R.). The first oil tanker to be built by Harland & Wolff was the S.S. *Iroquois*, completed in 1907. It was then the world's largest tanker at 11890 tons deadweight, although a far cry from today's giants of 300000 tonnes.* During the period 1910–12 the steamships *Olympic* and *Titanic* were built, followed later by *Britannic*, all of which had the largest sets of reciprocating machinery ever constructed. In 1912 the link was established with A. S. Burmeister & Wain of Denmark to manufacture marine diesel propulsion engines, originally in Glasgow and later in Belfast. As mentioned earlier, Lord Kylsant succeeded Lord Pirrie in 1923 as chairman of Harland & Wolff. He was also at that time chairman of the Royal Mail Steam Packet Company and its associated shipping lines as well as president of the chamber of shipping in London. One of his first decrees as chairman was that in future all Union Castle liners should be built at Belfast – a very convenient arrangement for the shipyard.

During the period of intensive German attack, in the second world war, the company suffered damage in varying degrees, and there is little doubt that Harland & Wolff was the most heavily-bombed shipyard in the United Kingdom. Whilst the damage was very severe, there were fortunately sufficient fitting-out berths and cranes left to enable work to proceed. The company's output of naval and merchant vessels during the six years 1939–44 (inclusive) amounted to 1052416 tons.

Wartime Output of the Yard

Naval vessels	Merchant vessels
6 aircraft carriers	1 passenger liner
2 cruisers	29 cargo vessels
2 depot ships	16 refrigerated ships
47 corvettes	30 oil tankers
29 fleet minesweepers	47 smaller vessels
9 frigates	
44 other vessels	
139 Naval	123 Merchant

Significant post-war developments have included the construction of the *Southern Cross*, completed in 1955, which was the first large passenger vessel to have all aft machinery. It is still in service as a cruise liner under the name *Azure Seas*. The S.S. *Canberra* also had aft-end machinery and was the largest U.K. passenger liner to be equipped with turbo-electric machinery of 42500

* Contemporary shipbuilding tonnage measurements are in metric tonnes.

shaft horse power. She was completed in 1961 as the flagship for P. & O.'s Australian liner service and today is still operated by the company as a cruise liner. In her recent role in the Falklands task force *Canberra* was known as the great white whale. In 1964 S.S. *Methane Progress*, built for the British Gas Council, was the forerunner of the large liquefied natural gas carriers now in service. She operated on the Algeria- Canvey Island route, transporting liquefied natural gas to the United Kingdom. This was then a revolutionary method of transporting natural gas in a liquefied state in specially insulated tanks. The gas is carried at − 160 degrees celsius and the gas boil-off is fed to the main boilers of the ship. In 1966 to the astonishment of the company's competitors, *Sea Quest*, the largest oil drilling rig built in the United Kingdom at that time, was successfully launched from three conventional slips – a feat unparalleled anywhere in the world. It is not possible, however, to leave this very brief résumé of notable achievements without some reference to the seventy-two sailing ships built in the early days of the company's history, including the famous 'Star' class of wind-jammers built by the company for J.P. Corry & Sons of Belfast. The *Star of Russia*, a full-rigged iron sailing ship, was built in twelve months by the company in 1874. One of her finest voyages was from London to Calcutta and back, loading and discharging full cargoes, in 5 months 27 days. The more usual sailing time for this route would have been 7 months 29 days. Thus, *Star of Russia*'s fast passages made a saving of 2 months and 2 days.

During the vast modernisation programme which commenced in 1968, the construction of the building dock in the old Musgrave Channel soon became the focus of attention. Not only was it to become the centre piece of all shipbuilding activities, it also ushered in a new system of ship construction. In its completed form, the building dock can permit the construction of a 1 million tonne tanker. To consider its vast size, it would accommodate 12000 mini cars or 77 million gallons of water when flooded. The new steel stockyard, including unloading quay, incorporates shot blasting and priming plants. The steel plate, coming from the stockyard, is handled through the plate shop where it is cut and prepared. The panel line consists of eight work stations where steel plates are joined together and stiffeners placed and welded automatically. Finally, there is the build-up shop where the production of block weldments up to 400 tonnes in weight are produced. Four self-elevating trailers, one of 125 tonnes payload, two of 250 tonnes and another of 400 tonnes payload, are provided to transport the finished sections to the paint hall which was built in 1974. This comprises four cells each measuring 42 x 35 metres. Weldments can be shot blasted, and painted with subsequent curing of the paint under ideal conditions – virtually unique in European shipbuilding. Each cell can accommodate the largest block or weldment envisaged for the production process. At the head of the dock the smaller module sections of 400 tonnes are assembled into blocks of up to 800 tonnes for positioning on the ship so that the ship is brought together in the dock like a Lego set.

These completed facilities are the most modern of their kind in Europe and are capable of achieving the exacting standards demanded by today's shipbuilding technology. Advanced flame cutting, welding and handling equipment, numerically controlled by tape, or computer, and also by optical means, ensures precision working from scale drawings, projected full size directly on to the steel plate.

The infrastructure to support all these new facilities has also been subject to considerable change and improvement. Computer technology, for example, has resulted in large reductions in the traditional administrative side of the programme. The adoption of the latest techniques also assists in the development of our new product range. In addition, all hull forms are developed by computer 'in-house', and stored on the computer data-base for reference in the development of manufacturing information. Micro-computers are also used in ship sales and marketing, where freighting and techno-economic evaluations, together with specially developed financial models for leasing deals and direct ship credit financing packages, are carried out. The micro-computer is also contributing to streamlining accounting facilities, engine works and planning areas of the company. Looking to the future, computers are being used in market research work in an attempt to predict likely changes in the pattern of demand for new ship types. This is far from an easy task as the marine market is characterised by constant change.

Select Bibliography

CHAPTER 2

Bertil Almgren (ed.), *Proceedings of the seventh Viking congress* (Dublin, 1973).

Gerhart Bersu and D. M. Wilson (eds), *Three Viking graves in the Isle of Man* (London, 1966).

John Bradley *et al.* (eds), *A survey of Irish archaeology to 1600* (Dublin, 1987).

Johannes Bøe, 'Norse antiquities in Ireland' in Haakon Shetelig (ed.), *Viking antiquities in Great Britain and Ireland*, iii (Oslo, 1940).

A. E. Christensen, 'Viking age rigging, a survey of the sources and theories' in Sean McGrail (ed.), *The archaeology of medieval ships and harbours in northern Europe* (B.A.R. international series, 66, Oxford, 1979).

Ibid., 'Viking age ships and shipbuilding' in *Norwegian Archaeological Review*, 15 (1982).

Ibid., 'Boat models and graffiti from the Dublin excavations' (forthcoming).

H. B. Clarke *et al.* (eds), *The comparative history of urban origins in non-Roman Europe* (B.A.R. international series, 255, Oxford, 1985).

Thomas Fanning, 'The archaeology of the Vikings in Ireland' in Bradley *et al.*, *Irish archaeology*.

Christine Fell *et al.* (eds), *The Viking age in the Isle of Man* (Select papers from the ninth Viking congress, Isle of Man, 4–14 July 1981, London, 1983).

Gillian Fellows-Jensen, 'Scandinavian settlement in the Isle of Man and northwest England, the place-name evidence' in Fell *et al.*, *The Viking age*.

Sigurd Grieg, 'Viking antiquities in Scotland' in Haakon Shetelig (ed.), *Viking antiquities in Great Britain and Ireland*, ii (Oslo, 1940).

J. E. Knirk (ed.), *Proceedings of the tenth Viking congress, Larkollen, Norway, 1985* (Universitetets Oldsaksamlings skrifter, ny rekke nr 9, Oslo, 1987).

Breandán O Riordáin, 'The High Street excavations' in Almgren, *Proceedings of the seventh Viking congress*.

Patrick Wallace, 'The archaeology of Viking Dublin' in Clarke *et al.*, *Urban origins*.

Ibid., 'The layout of late Viking age Dublin: indications of its regulation and problems of continuity' in Knirk, *Proceedings of the tenth Viking congress*.

D. M. Wilson, *The Viking age in the Isle of Man. The archaeological evidence.* (Odense, 1974).

CHAPTER 3

Calendar of the state papers relating to Ireland, 1509–1670 (24 vols, London, 1860–1911).

Conflans: de livre des faiz de la marine et navigaiges (Bibliotheque Nationale, Paris, ms français 742).

Port records of Bristol, Chester and Gloucester.

A.O. and M.O. Anderson (eds), *Adomnan's life of St Columba* (London, 1961).

Jonathan Bardon and Stephen Conlin, *Dublin, one thousand years of Wood Quay* (Dublin 1984).

Jacques Bernard, *Navires et gens de mer à Bordeaux (1400–1550)* (3 vols, Paris, 1968), and private correspondence.

Wendy Childs, 'Ireland's trade with England in the later middle ages' in *Irish Economic and Social History,* ix (1982).

John de Courcy Ireland, *Ireland's sea fisheries, a history* (Dublin, 1981).

Ibid., *Ireland and the Irish in maritime history* (Dublin, 1986).

W. P. Gerritsen *et al.*, *De wereld van Sint Brandaan* (Utrecht, 1986).

A. S. Green, *The making of Ireland and its undoing* (London, 1908).

Georges André Grosjean, *Der seeatlas des Vesconte Maggiolo* (Zurich, 1979).

The Mariner's Mirror, passim and especially 42 (1956), pp 153 *et seq.*, 71 (1985), p. 13, and 72 (1986), p. 82.

Constantia Maxwell, *Irish history from contemporary sources, 1509–1610* (London, 1923).

Michel Mollat, *La vie quotidienne des gens de mer en atlantique, IX*^{e}*–XVI*^{e} *siècles* (Paris, 1983).

Timothy O'Neill, *Merchants and mariners in Ireland in the middle ages* (Dublin, 1987).

G. E. Power and M. M. Postan, *Studies in English trade in the fifteenth century* (Dublin, 1933).

Henri Touchard, *Le commerce maritime brêton a la fin du moyen âge* (Paris, 1967).

L. D. Troadec, *Les cartographes brêtons du Conquet* (Brest, 1967).

Étienne Trocmé and Marcel Delafosse, *Le commerce rochelais de la fin du XV*^{e} *au debut du XVII*^{e} *siècle* (Paris, 1952).

D. W. Waters, *The art of navigation in England in Elizabethan and early Stuart times* (London, 1958).

Notes to Chapters

CHAPTER 1

1. Fernand Braudel, *The Mediterranean and the Mediterranean world in the age of Philip II* (2 vols, London, 1975), i, 106.
2. H. J. Mackinder, *Britain and the British seas* (Oxford, 1907), p. 20.
3. Lloyd Laing, *The archaeology of late Celtic Britain and Ireland* (London, 1975), p. 99.
4. See *Atlas of the sea around the British Isles* (London, 1981), 2.12.
5. Ibid., 2.10.
6. Ibid., 2.19.
7. Paul Johnstone, *The seacraft of prehistory* (London, 1980), p. 121.
8. Leslie Alcock, 'Was there an Irish Sea culture-province between Wales and Ireland?' in Donald Moore (ed.), *The Irish Sea province in archaeology and history* (Cardiff, 1970), p. 63.
9. Lloyd Laing, *Archaeology of late Celtic Britain and Ireland*, p. 9.
10. Ibid., p. 93.
11. Charles Thomas, *Britain and Ireland in early Christian times A.D. 400–800* (London, 1971), chapter two.
12. Leslie Alcock, *Arthur's Britain* (London, 1973), pp 130–31.
13. Lloyd Laing, *Archaeology of late Celtic Britain and Ireland*, p. 95.
14. Ibid., p. 75.
15. Charles Thomas, *Britain and Ireland*, p. 66.
16. Lloyd Laing, *Archaeology of late Celtic Britain and Ireland*, p. 246.
17. E. G. Bowen, *Britain and the western seaways* (London, 1972), pp 80–83.
18. Lloyd Laing, *Archaeology of late Celtic Britain and Ireland*, p. 374.
19. N. K. Chadwick, 'Early literary contacts between Wales and Ireland' in Moore, *The Irish sea province*, p. 73.
20. Irish Cruising Club, *Sailing directions: east and north coasts of Ireland* (Dublin, 1970 edition), p. 57.
21. Walter Harris, *The antient and present state of the county of Down* (Dublin, 1744), p. 16.
22. R. H. Buchanan, The barony of Lecale, County Down: a study of regional personality (Ph.D., Queen's University, Belfast, 1958), p. 229.
23. *Commissioners of Irish railways, second report* (Dublin, 1838), p. 69.
24. MS in author's possession.

CHAPTER 4

1. For a fuller survey see Timothy O'Neill, *Merchants and mariners in medieval Ireland* (Dublin, 1987).
2. Giraldus Cambrensis, *The history and topography of Ireland* trans. J. J. O'Meara (Mountrath, 1982), p. 58.
3. Mario Esposito (ed.), *Itinerarium Symonis Semeonis ab Hybernia ad Terram Sanctam* (Dublin, 1960), p. 25; *Il dittamondo e la rime* cited in *R. I. A. Trans.*, i (1786), p. 18.
4. J. T. Gilbert (ed.), *Chartularies of St Mary's Abbey, Dublin with the register of its house at Dunbrody and annals of Ireland* (London, 1884), ii, xv; J. F. Lydon, 'The expansion and consolidation of the colony, 1215–54' in *New history of Ireland*, ii, 170.
5. *Calendar of the justiciary rolls of Ireland, 1305–7*, p. 354.
6. *Calendar of documents relating to Ireland in the Public Record Office, London, 1293–1301*, p. 270, no. 565.
7. R. I. A., MS 12/D/12, p. 87; ibid., 12/D/8, p. 385.
8. J. F. Lydon, 'Ireland's participation in the military activities of English kings in the thirteenth and early fourteenth centuries' (Ph.D., University of London, 1955), pp 241, 258.
9. *Cal. docs Ire., 1293–1301*, no. 311.
10. *Cal. docs Ire., 1171–1251*, nos 2244–5, 2532.
11. Edward Tresham (ed.), *Rotulorum patentium et clausorum cancellariae Hiberniae calendarium* (Dublin, 1828), p. 193, no. 184 (hereafter cited as *Rot. pat. canc. Hib.*).
12. W. A. Childs, 'Ireland's trade with England in the later middle ages' in *Irish Economic and Social History*, ix (1982), pp 227–30.
13. *Cal. Carew MSS, 1515–74*, p. 85.
14. *Calendar of the close rolls preserved in the Public Record Office, 1339–41*, p. 334.
15. J. F. Lydon, *Ireland in the later middle ages* (Dublin, 1973), p. 13.
16. *Cal. close rolls, 1349–54*, p. 578; *Calendar of the patent rolls preserved in the Public Record Office, London, 1381–85*, p. 501.
17. M. K. James, *Studies in the medieval wine trade* ed. E. M. Veale (Oxford, 1971), pp 133–5.
18. Ibid., pp 151–52.
19. *Cal. pat. rolls, 1429–36*, p. 199.
20. *Rot. pat. canc Hib.*, p. 257, no. 39.
21. Ibid., p. 135, no. 162.
22. Ibid., p. 172, no. 12; ibid., p. 163, no. 107.
23. Ibid., p. 49, no. 53.
24. *Cal. pat. rolls, 1441–46*, pp 97, 58.
25. Ibid., p. 418.
26. H. F. Berry (ed.), *Statute rolls of the parliament of Ireland, reign of King Henry VI* (Dublin, 1910), pp 483 *et seq.*
27. P.R.O.N.I., Registrum Octaviani, no. 537.

CHAPTER 5

1. Charles Moncke, *Report on the customs in the northern ports of Ireland, 1637* (Belfast, 1974), unpaginated.
2. H. F. Kearney, 'The Irish wine trade, 1614–5' in *I.H.S.*, ix (1955), pp 406, 435–42.
3. E. M. Carus-Wilson (ed.), *The overseas trade of Bristol in the later middle ages* (London, 1967), pp 218–89; A. K. Longfield, *Anglo-Irish trade in the sixteenth century* (London, 1929), *passim*; D. M. Woodward, *The trade of Elizabethan Chester* (Hull, 1970), pp 7–11.
4. Woodward, *Elizabethan Chester*, pp 7–22.
5. E. A. Lewis (ed.), *The Welsh port books, 1550–1603* (Cymmrodorion Record Series, xii, 1927), *passim.*
6. Carus-Wilson, *Overseas trade of Bristol*, pp 218–89; Jean Vanes, *Documents illustrating the overseas trade of Bristol in the sixteenth century* (Bristol Record Society, xxxi, 1979), pp 13–16.
7. W. T. MacCaffrey, *Exeter, 1540–1640* (Cambridge, Massachusetts, 1958), p. 167; J. L. Wiggs, 'The seaborne trade of Southampton in the second half of the sixteenth century' (M.A., University of Southampton, 1955), p. 114.

8. Lewis, *Welsh port books*, p. xxiv; Woodward, *Elizabethan Chester*, pp 7–26; *New History of Ireland*, iii, 159.
9. *New history of Ireland*, iii, 158–9; Longfield, *Anglo-Irish trade*, pp 30–40; Vanes, *Documents*, pp 169–70.
10. Woodward, *Elizabethan Chester*, pp 7–8, 24–5.
11. *New history of Ireland*, iii, 181.
12. W. B. Stephens, *Seventeenth-century Exeter* (Exeter, 1958), p. 36; H. F. Kearney, *Strafford in Ireland, 1633–41* (Manchester, 1959), p. 157; Eileen McCracken, *The Irish woods since Tudor times* (Newton Abbot, 1971), pp 97–100; D. M. Woodward, 'The Anglo-Irish livestock trade in the seventeenth century' in *I.H.S.*, xviii (1973), pp 493–6.
13. Woodward, *Elizabethan Chester*, p. 131; D. M. Woodward, 'The overseas trade of Chester, 1600–1650' in *Transactions of the Historic Society of Lancashire and Chesire*, 122 (1970), pp 36–7; Patrick McGrath (ed.), *Merchants and merchandise in seventeenth-century Bristol* (Bristol Record Society, xix, 1955), pp 279–80; P.R.O., E. 190/1084/6–8, 13, 22; ibid., 1087/16; ibid., 1088/13.
14. From an unpublished transcription of the Ulster port books for 1613–15 by Robert Hunter: I am most grateful to him for allowing me access to his notes.
15. *New history of Ireland*, iii, 186.
16. P.R.O., 30/24/50, part 2/2, f. 46; P.R.O., S.P. 63/326/81, 82. The table presented in *Cal. S.P. Ire., 1669–70*, pp 54–5 contains many errors.
17. P. J. Bowden, *The wool trade in Tudor and Stuart England* (London, 1962), p. 27; D. M. Woodward (ed.), *The farming and memorandum books of Henry Best of Elmswell, 1642* (British Academy Records of Social and Economic History, new series, viii, 1984), p. 26.
18. John O'Donovan, *The economic history of livestock in Ireland* (Cork, 1940), p. 40.
19. Ibid., pp 40, 46–7.
20. *New history of Ireland*, iii, 162.
21. Ibid., p. 186.
22. T. C. Barnard, *Cromwellian Ireland* (Oxford, 1975), pp 42–3: Woodward, 'Livestock trade', loc. cit., pp 496–7.
23. P.R.O., E. 190/1089/11; Woodward, 'overseas trade', loc. cit., pp 39–40.
24. McGrath, *Merchants and merchandise*, p. xxi; Woodward, *Elizabethan Chester*, pp 26–34; P.R.O., E. 190/1324/4, 9, 22; ibid., 1326/8; 1327/16; Woodward, 'Livestock trade' loc. cit., pp 506–9.
25. Ibid., p. 512.
26. Woodward, *Elizabethan Chester*, pp 31–32.
27. Ibid., pp 26–30; Julian Walton, 'The merchant community of Waterford in the 16th and 17th centuries' in Philippe Butel and L. M. Cullen (eds), *Cities and merchants: Irish and French perspectives on urban development* (Dublin, 1986), pp 184–5.
28. O'Donovan, *Economic history of livestock*, p. 27.
29. Walton, 'Merchant community of Waterford', loc. cit., pp 183–9.
30. Kearney, *Strafford*, p. 137.
31. Carus-Wilson, *Overseas trade of Bristol*, pp 218–89; E. M. Carus-Wilson, 'The overseas trade of Bristol' in Eileen Power and M. M. Postan (eds), *Studies in English trade in the fifteenth century* (London, 1933), p. 195; K. P. Wilson (ed.), *Chester customs accounts, 1301–1566* (Record Society of Lancashire and Chesire, cxi, 1969), pp 149–50.
32. Wilson, *Chester customs accounts*, pp 149–52.
33. Woodward, *Elizabethan Chester*, pp 132–3.
34. Vanes, *Documents, passim*.
35. Lewis, *Welsh port books, passim*.
36. Kearney, 'Irish wine trade', loc. cit., pp 406, 435–42.
37. Woodward, 'Livestock trade', loc. cit., p. 523.
38. Woodward, 'Overseas trade', loc. cit., p. 36; D. M. Woodward, 'Ships, masters and shipowners of the Wirral 1550–1650' in *Mariner's Mirror*, 63 (1977), pp 234–5.
39. Lewis, *Welsh port book, passim*.
40. Ibid., *passim*; Longfield, *Anglo-Irish trade*, p. 212.
41. Kearney, 'Irish wine trade', loc. cit., p. 419; Hunter, unpublished transcription of Ulster port books.

42. Edward Hawkins (ed.), *Brereton's travels in Holland . . . and Ireland 1634–5* (Chetham Society, i, 1844), pp 123–5, 155, 165.

43. Woodward, *Elizabethan Chester,* pp 56–7; ibid., 'Overseas trade', loc. cit., pp 36–7; ibid., 'Livestock trade', loc. cit., pp 511–12; ibid., 'Ships, masters and shipowners', loc. cit., pp 236–7.

44. Stephens, *Exeter,* p. 17.

45. Woodward, 'Livestock trade', loc. cit., pp 512–3.

46. Woodward, 'Ships, masters and shipowners', loc. cit., *passim.*

47. Hunter, unpublished transcriptions of Ulster port books.

48. Walton, 'Merchant community of Waterford', pp 187–8.

CHAPTER 6

1. See John Appleby and David Starkey, 'The records of the high court of admiralty as a source for maritime historians', in David Starkey (ed.), *Sources for a new maritime history of Devon* (Devon, 1987), pp 70–85, and the references therein cited.

2. Eric J. Graham, 'The Scottish marine during the Dutch wars', *Scottish Historical Review,* lxi (1982), pp 67–74; J. C. Appleby and Mary O'Dowd, 'The Irish admiralty: its organisation and development, c. 1570–1640', *I.H.S.,* xxiv (1985), pp 299–326; Edwin Welch (ed.), *The admiralty court book of Southampton 1566–1585* (Southampton Record Series, xiii, 1968).

3. See the relevant volumes of the List and Index Society, especially, *Records of the high court of admiralty* (List and Index Society, 27, 1967).

4. P.R.O., high court of admiralty (examinations) 13/16, ff 188–9^v; high court of admiralty (libels) 24/40, no. 115. (Hereafter cited as H.C.A.).

5. P.R.O., H.C.A. 13/9, ff 85^v–6.

6. P.R.O., H.C.A. 13/23, ff 225–6^v, 248^v; 13/47, f. 381.

7. P.R.O., H.C.A. 13/23, ff 225–6^v.

8. P.R.O., H.C.A. 13/55, ff 3^v–4.

9. P.R.O., H.C.A. 13/28, f. 124.

10. P.R.O., H.C.A. 13/38, f. 203. The *Recovery* was forced into Aberystwyth by bad weather where her cargo was rifled by the local inhabitants.

11. P.R.O., H.C.A. 13/37, f. 30.

12. P.R.O., H.C.A. 13/45, ff 23^v–4; H.C.A. 13/43, part 2, ff 127–8^v.

13. P.R.O., H.C.A. 13/32, ff 180^v–81^v; 13/44, f. 69, 378^v; 13/53, f. 91. The *Mary Providence* was built by John Driver, a shipwright of Bristol.

14. P.R.O., H.C.A. 13/55, ff 586, 607–7^v. At the time of her arrest the *Lion* was bound from Chichester to Dublin with a cargo of malt.

15. See, for example, Ralph Davis, *The rise of the English shipping industry in the 17th and 18th centuries* (London, 1962, reprinted 1972); R. G. Lang, 'The greater merchants of London in the early seventeenth century' (D. Phil., University of Oxford, 1963); and Donald Woodward, 'Ships, masters and shipowners of the Wirral 1550–1650', *Maritime History,* 7, (1977), pp 3–25.

16. P.R.O., H.C.A. 13/55, ff 2^v–3, 4, 43–3^v.

17. P.R.O., H.C.A. 13/2, ff 121^v–3, 146^v–7^v.

18. John C. Appleby, 'The fishing ventures of Nicholas Weston of Dublin. A note of commercial contact between Ireland and Newfoundland in the sixteenth century', *Dublin Historical Record,* 39, (1986), pp 150–55.

19. P.R.O., H.C.A. 32/1834.

20. K. R. Andrews, *Elizabethan privateering. English privateering during the Spanish war, 1585–1603* (Cambridge, 1964); David J. Starkey, 'British privateering 1702–1783, with particular reference to London' (Ph.D., University of Exeter, 1985); Louis M. Cullen, 'Privateers fitted out in Irish ports in the eighteenth century', *The Irish Sword,* iii (1958), pp 171–77. J. C. Appleby, 'An Irish letter of marque, 1648', *The Irish Sword,* xv (1983), pp 218–21, provides some evidence for the 1640s.

21. P.R.O., H.C.A. 26/35, 42 and 56.

22. Gomer Williams, *History of the Liverpool privateers and letters of marque with an account of the Liverpool slave trade* (London, 1897), and references cited below.
23. P.R.O., H.C.A. 26/60.
24. P.R.O., H.C.A. 26/35.
25. C. E. Hughes, 'Wales and piracy: a study in Tudor administration 1500–1640' (M.A., University of Wales, 1937); Clive M. Senior, 'An investigation of the activities and importance of English pirates 1603–1640' (Ph.D., University of Bristol, 1972); D. G. E. Hurd, 'Some aspects of the attempts of the government to suppress piracy during the reign of Elizabeth I' (M.A., University of London, 1961).
26. P.R.O., H.C.A. 13/50, ff 405–5ᵛ, 677–8; 13/51, ff 54ᵛ–5.
27. P.R.O., H.C.A. 13/43, part 2, f. 175, 175ᵛ. Of the two pieces covered by sand, one was numbered 3215 and marked with a cross and anchors; the other was numbered 3090 but carried no mark. The former was made of brass, the latter of iron.
    This survey is based on an earlier paper presented in the Institute of Irish Studies, Queen's University of Belfast, and draws on my own work in progress towards the completion of a calendar of materials relating to Ireland among the records of the high court of admiralty, to be published by the Irish Manuscripts Commission.

CHAPTER 7

1. C. J. M. Martin, '*La Trinidad Valencera*: an Armada invasion transport lost off Donegal. Interim site report 1971–76', *International Journal of Nautical Archaeology*, 8, part 1 (1979), pp 13–38. See also C. J. M. Martin, 'The equipment and fighting potential of the Spanish Armada (Ph.D., University of St Andrews, 1983), pp 114–36.
2. Martin, '*La Trinidad Valencera*' pp 35–7.
3. *Cal. S. P. Ire., 1588–92.*
4. C. F. Duro, *La Armada invencible*, ii (Madrid, 1885), pp 337–70. A modern translation is provided by Evelyn Hardy, *Survivors of the Armada* (London, 1966).
5. P.R.O., S.P. 63/137/15 (de Luzon) and 63/137/16 (del Arbol).
6. John Laughton (ed.), *The defeat of the Spanish Armada*, ii (London, 1894), pp 217–76.
7. *Calendar of [Spanish] letters and State Papers relating to English affairs, Elizabeth, 1587–1603* (London, 1899), pp 506–10.
8. Mainly in *Cal. S. P. Ire., 1588–92.* For a general account see Colin Martin, *Full fathom five* (London, 1975), pp 194–202.
9. The topography is well shown in Robert Ashby's manuscript map of English military installations between Derry and Inch in 1601 (P.R.O., M.P.F. 335).
10. Archivo General de Simancas (A.G.S.), Contaduria de Sueldo (C.S.), 2a 280/1460.
11. A.G.S., Guerra Antigua (G.A.), 221/1.
12. Martin, op. cit., pp 118–9.
13. A.G.S., G.A., 220/61.
14. These figures are extracted from the fleet muster held at Lisbon on 9 May 1588. I have used the printed copy in the B.L. (192. f. 17 1) of the edition published at Lisbon in 1588 for Pedro Paz Salas. This copy is annotated in the hands of Lord Burghley and others.
15. F. C. Lane, *Navires et constructeurs à Venise pendent la renaissance* (Paris, 1965), pp 259–60.
16. Ruggiero Romano, 'Economic aspects of the construction of warships in Venice in the sixteenth century' in Brian Pullan (ed.), *Crisis and change in the Venetian economy in the sixteenth and seventeenth centuries* (London, 1968), pp 59–87.
17. Kostic Veselin, 'The Tobermory galleon', *Blackwood's Magazine*, 326 (August, 1979), pp 152–62.
18. Uncatalogued manuscript at Inveraray Castle. I am grateful to Alison McLeay for providing me with this information.
19. Martin, op. cit., pp 384–8.
20. A.G.S., G.A., 226/8: Don Jorge Manrique to Philip II, 19 August 1588.
21. A.G.S., C.S., 2a 280/1473.
22. *Cal. S. P. Ire., 1611–14* (London, 1877), p. 21 and *Register of the privy council of Scotland, 1610–13* (Edinburgh, 1889), p. 409. The evidence is circumstantial.

23. A.G.S., Mapas, Planas y Diagramas, V-18, 25 July 1587.
24. A.G.S., G.A., 221/156. Inventory of arms and munitions loaded aboard Bertendona's squadron, 14 May 1588.
25. Martin, op. cit., pp 363–73.

CHAPTER 8

1. P.R.O.N.I., D.856/D/73.
2. J. V. Beckett, *Coal and tobacco* (Cambridge, 1981); L. M. Cullen, *Anglo-Irish trade 1660–1800* (Manchester, 1968); Laura Cochran, *Scottish trade with Ireland in the eighteenth century* (Edinburgh, 1985).
3. P.R.O.N.I., D.501.
4. P.R.O.N.I., D.354.
5. P.R.O.N.I., D.354/735.
6. P.R.O.N.I., D.1857/1/BA/1–29, series of out-letter books 1821–1949.
7. P.R.O.N.I., D.3025.
8. P.R.O.N.I., D.1130.
9. P.R.O.N.I., D.2015/4/2.
10. P.R.O.N.I., D.671/C/12/275.
11. P.R.O.N.I., D.148.
12. P.R.O.N.I., D.1115.
13. P.R.O.N.I., D.3605. The role of the Belfast Steamship Company in the extensive cross-channel traffic of the large pauper population created in the wake of the famine in the late 1840s and 1850s is adverted to in 'Liverpool, the Irish steamship companies and the famine Irish' by Frank Neal in *Immigrants and Minorities*, 5 (1986). I am grateful to Dr Neal for his help on this issue.
14. Belfast & Ulster directory, 1850.
15. P.R.O.N.I., D.3117.
16. P.R.O.N.I., D.3117/1/EG/1–17, containing some 450–500 photographs.
17. P.R.O.N.I., D.3094; D.3095; D.3096.
18. P.R.O.N.I., D.280.
19. P.R.O.N.I., T.3349.
20. P.R.O.N.I., D.2892.
21. P.R.O.N.I., D.2982/1/4.
22. P.R.O.N.I., D.1828/4.
23. Ralph Davis, *Rise of the Atlantic economy* (London, 1973).
24. This case study, and the Cooke letter books, are thoroughly discussed in Cecil J. Houston and William J. Smyth, 'New Brunswick shipbuilding and Irish shipping: the commissioning of the *Londonderry*, 1838', in *Acadiensis* (Spring 1987), pp 95–106. The originals are in P.R.O.N.I., D.2892/2/1–2.
25. Sholto Cooke, *The maiden city and the western ocean* (Dublin, 1961).
26. P.R.O.N.I., D.1583/32.
27. P.R.O.N.I., T.2600; T.1867; D.1564; D.1389.
28. P.R.O.N.I., D.1540/1/38 and 47; D.1797; D.935/D/1.
29. P.R.O.N.I., D.2805. See also John R. Hume and Michael Moss, *Shipbuilders to the world* (Belfast, 1986).
30. L. A. Ritchie (ed.), *Modern British shipbuilding: a guide to historical records* (Business Archives Council, 1979).
31. P.R.O.N.I., D.3486.
32. P.R.O.N.I., CAB 9A/42/1; see also FIN 18 series.
33. P.R.O.N.I., D.3661.
34. Michael McCaughan, *Titanic*, (Cultra, 1982).
35. P.R.O.N.I., D.2015.
36. P.R.O.N.I., D.3158.
37. P.R.O.N.I., D.3704.
38. P.R.O.N.I., D.3465/J/3.

39. Ibid.
40. P.R.O.N.I., T.1913.
41. P.R.O.N.I., D.2015.
42. P.R.O.N.I., TRANS 2A – The complete archive of British agreements and crew lists was offered by the registrar of shipping to P.R.O. in the 1960s. The total bulk of this archive, which ran to many thousands of boxes, was so intimidating that P.R.O. decided to retain only a 10 percent sample (one box in every ten) of the post-1863 returns. The National Maritime Museum, invited to take 10 percent of the remnant, took all the returns for every tenth year beginning with 1865. Only when these samples had been extracted were other record offices invited to extract the returns of particular interest to them. Under these circumstances then, many returns of Northern Ireland interest were retained in London in both the P.R.O. and the National Maritime Museum; and, since the list of Northern Ireland-registered ships used to extract the Northern Ireland returns was incomplete, some returns of interests were unavoidably overlooked (they may have found their way to Newfoundland, where the final remnant of the class was deposited).
    The returns for the period 1835–63 were retained in their entirety in P.R.O.
43. P.R.O.N.I., H.A.R. 2.
44. P.R.O.N.I., H.A.R. 2/J.
45. P.R.O.N.I., H.A.R. 2/E/1A.
46. P.R.O.N.I., H.A.R. 1.
47. P.R.O.N.I., H.A.R. 1F/1.
48. P.R.O.N.I., H.A.R. 3.
49. P.R.O.N.I., H.A.R. 6.
50. P.R.O.N.I., U.T.A. 990/L: Irish & English traffic conference minutes 1867–1947; Irish & English livestock conference minutes 1916–35.
51. P.R.O.N.I., N7 series includes Belfast mercantile registers 1825–54; Belfast commercial chronicle Jan. 1806–Dec. 1853 (incomplete series); Taggart's mercantile journal 1817–18; 1821–22; 1824–5.
52. H.C. 1809 (113), iii, p. 597.
53. P.R.O.N.I., D.671/C.UC.
54. Anthony Marmion, *Ancient and modern history of the maritime ports of Ireland*, (London 1855), pp 316–7.
55. Quoted in Joseph Frey (ed.), *Lecale: a study of local history* (Belfast 1970).
56. P.R.O.N.I., D.162/37A–B.
57. P.R.O.N.I., D.1686/7.
58. P.R.O.N.I., D.2015.
59. P.R.O.N.I., P.M. 9/17.
60. P.R.O.N.I., D.2747; see also D.3246, minute books of Ballyholme Yacht Club (County Down) 1907–9; 1922–66.
61. John White, *Journal of a voyage to New South Wales* (London, 1790).

CHAPTER 9

1. L. M. Cullen, 'The smuggling trade in Ireland in the eighteenth century' in *R. I. A. Proc.*, 67, section C (1969).
2. R. C. Jarvis, 'Illicit trade with the Isle of Man, 1671–1765' in *Transactions of the Lancashire and Chesire Antiquarian Society*, 58 (1945–6).
3. L. M. Cullen, 'Economic development, 1750–1800' in *New history of Ireland*, iv, 190.
4. L. M. Cullen, 'The smuggling trade in the North Channel in the eighteenth century' in *Scottish Economic and Social History* (forthcoming).
5. P.R.O., Customs 1/120, f. 97, 29 Feb. 1772. Richard Field, master of the *Mary Ann* of Rush, claimed that he had been engaged in the Rosses fishery.
6. P.R.O., Customs 1/101, f. 157, 22 March 1768; ibid., 1/120, f. 82, 15 Feb. 1772.
7. L. M. Cullen, *Anglo-Irish trade 1660–1800* (Manchester, 1968), pp 153–4.
8. P.R.O., Customs 1/110, f. 93, 17 Nov. 1769.
9. P.R.O., Customs 1/118, f. 96, 16 Aug. 1771.

10. P.R.O., Customs 1/118, f. 42, 15 July 1771.
11. P.R.O., Customs 1/120, f. 68, 1 Feb. 1772.
12. P.R.O., Customs 1/100, ff 69v–70, 2 Dec. 1767.
13. P.R.O., Customs 1/117, f. 23, 10 Apr. 1771.
14. L. M. Cullen, 'Smuggling trade in Ireland', p. 163.
15. L. M. Cullen, *Merchants, ships and trade 1660–1830* (Dublin, 1971), p. 59; Custom House Library, London, selections from Scottish customs records 1928, p. 185, letter outwards, 16 May 1776; inwards, 14 May 1776.
16. L. M. Cullen, 'Ireland and Irishmen in eighteenth-century privateering' in *Course et piraterie: études presentées à la commission internationale d'histoire maritime* (Paris, 1975); Joseph Shields, 'Captain Luke Ryan of Rush' in *Dublin Historical Record,* 24 (1970).
17. Archives nationales, Paris, C^I 159, f. 41, 18 May 1782.
18. See G. Rutherford, 'The king against Luke Ryan' in *Mariner's Mirror* 43 (1957); Archives nationales, Paris, 0^{IX} 237, ff 54–5, Feb. 1781.
19. The identification suggested by Joseph Shields (loc. cit., p. 34) between the Rush men and 'the quiescent, champion-hungry catholic people of Ireland', though perhaps not lacking some basis, seems somewhat strong.
20. Shields, 'Luke Ryan', pp 27, 37.
21. Micheál O Tiomanaí, *Abhráin Ghaedhilge an iarthair* (Dublin, 1906), pp 30–32; R. J. Hayes, *The last invasion of Ireland* (Dublin, 1937), pp 17, 258–9. Miles Byrne identifies Murphy as a native of near Rush (Miles Byrne, *Memoirs* (Paris, 1863), iii, 54–8). A John Murphy is recorded as in receipt of a parliamentary fishing bounty as early as 1771.
22. P.R.O., Customs 1/117, f. 17, 30 Mar. 1771.
23. Custom House, Greenock, letterbook outwards, 1766–8, Port Glasgow and Greenock, 21 Mar. 1768.
24. O Tiomanaí, *Abhráin,* p. 79. Riocard Bairéad's poem 'Dún Domhnaill' refers to 'Caiptin Meatas a bheith ag tarraingt long tobac as Inis Géidhe'.
25. W. H. Maxwell, *Wild sports of the west* (London, 1932), ii, 169–74. Maxwell's account of the west, ostensibly set in 1829, relates as far as the *Jane* is concerned to 1820.
26. O'Malley's narrative of his life, which was formerly in the possession of the late Professor Conor O'Malley, Galway. A microfilm copy is in the National Library, Dublin.
27. L. M. Cullen, 'Privateers fitted out in Irish ports in the eighteenth century' in *Irish Sword,* iii (1957–8), p. 173. L. M. Cullen, 'Ireland and Irishmen in French privateering', pp 480–81. The original source is P.R.O., H.C.A. 26/81, f. 108, 23 Mar. 1793.
28. Shields, 'Luke Ryan', p. 27.
29. Cullen, 'Smuggling trade in the North Channel'.
30. Shields, 'Luke Ryan', p. 27.
31. Details of bounties in Irish Commons Journals, 1771–73.
32. Isle of Man Record Office, chancery court, years 1760, 1761, f. 264, 30 Mar. 1761. The year employed in the chancery records is a legal year beginning in October.
33. Isle of Man R.O., chancery court, years 1762, 1763, f. 138v, 17 Feb. 1762.
34. Isle of Man R.O., chancery court, years 1762, 1763, f. 237, 1 June 1762.
35. Isle of Man R.O., chancery court, years 1762, 1763, f. 271, 26 Sept. 1763.
36. Kenure graveyard. The tablet was erected by Rev. Edward Foster in 1827.
37. Archives nationales, Paris, G^5 62, G^5 47^x, G^5 48^x.
38. Hennessy archives, Cognac.
39. Isle of Man R.O., exchequer court, years 1759–64, 23 Aug. 1759; the events are described in a petition of Captain Littledale, dated 14 Oct. 1758.
40. Isle of Man R.O., chancery court. The references to Michael Connor occur under 9 Sept. 1763, and 2, 14, 15 and 16 Mar. and 6 May 1765. The references to John Connor are under 22 Apr. (bis) and 26 Apr. 1765.
41. Archives départementales de la Loire Atlantique, Nantes, B4635, shipping movements inwards, B4700, shipping movements outwards.
42. P.R.O., Customs 1/96, f. 86, 27 Mar. 1767. Four other vessels are identified in the report.
43. P.R.O., Customs 1/98, f. 26v, 26 June 1767.
44. P.R.O., Customs 1/106, ff 43v–4, 20 Feb. 1769.
45. P.R.O., Customs 1/101, f. 141, 16 Mar. 1768.

46. P.R.O., Customs 1/100, f. 54v, 25 Nov. 1767.
47. P.R.O., Customs 1/99, f. 106, 8 Oct. 1767.
48. Henry Atton and H. H. Holland, *The king's customs* (London, 1908), i, 345.
49. National Library of Ireland, J1969, J1949.
50. P.R.O., Customs 1/96, f. 86, 27 Mar. 1767; ibid., 1/97, f. 4, 15 Apr. 1767.
51. P.R.O., Customs 1/100, f. 73, 2 Dec. 1767.
52. P.R.O., Customs 1/109, f. 75v, 28 Aug. 1769.
53. P.R.O.N.I., Macartney papers, D.572/2/37 quoted in Cullen, *Merchants, ships and trade*, pp 60–61.
54. P.R.O., Customs 1/96, f. 86, 27 Mar. 1767; ibid., 1/98, ff 26, 80, 25 June, 17 July 1767; ibid., 1/116, f. 55, 24 Jan. 1771.
55. P.R.O., Customs 1/119, f. 47, 21 Oct. 1771.
56. Customs House Library, London, selections from customs outport records, northern England, 1924, p. 240.
57. P.R.O., Customs 1/100, ff 69v–70, 2 Dec. 1767.
58. P.R.O., Customs 1/98, ff 136v–7, 11 Aug. 1767.
59. P.R.O., Customs 1/102, ff 99v–100, 103v, 109v, (6, 9, 11 May 1768).
60. P.R.O., Customs 1/103, ff 48v–9, 23 June 1768.
61. P.R.O., Customs 1/103, f. 105, 28 July 1768.
62. P.R.O., Customs 1/117, f. 68, 24 Apr. 1771.
63. P.R.O., Customs 1/120, f. 112, 12 Mar. 1772.
64. Cullen, *Merchants, ships and trade*, p. 59.
65. P.R.O., Customs 1/103, f. 112, 30 July 1768.
66. P.R.O., Customs 1/117, f. 76v, 27 Apr. 1771.
67. P.R.O., Customs 1/98, f. 80, 17 July 1767.
68. P.R.O., Customs 1/98, f. 132, 10 Aug. 1767.
69. P.R.O., Customs 1/98, f. 158, 21 Aug. 1767.
70. P.R.O., Customs 1/100, f. 160v, 21 Aug. 1767; ibid., 1/99, f. 8v, 27 Aug. 1767.
71. P.R.O., Customs 1/100, f. 54, 25 Nov. 1767.
72. P.R.O., Customs 1/101, ff 35v–6, 27 Jan. 1768.
73. Custom House, Greenock, letterbook, Port Glasgow and Greenock, outwards, 1776–8, 29 Mar. 1768.
74. P.R.O., Customs 1/109, f. 67, 23 Aug. 1769.
75. P.R.O., Customs 1/109, f. 54, 16 Aug. 1769.
76. P.R.O., Customs 1/116, f. 131v, 4 Mar. 1771.
77. P.R.O., Customs 1/117, ff 34v–5, 12 Apr. 1771; *Waterford Chronicle*, 12–16 Apr. 1771.
78. P.R.O., Customs 1/117, f. 122, 30 May 1771.
79. Dublin, 2 Apr. 1771 in *Walker's Hibernian Magazine*, quoted in Cullen, *Merchants, ships and trade*, p. 60; P.R.O., Customs 1/117, f. 35, 12 Apr. 1771; ibid., 1/118, f. 2, 17 June 1771.
80. P.R.O., Customs 1/119, f. 14v, 4 Oct. 1771; Custom House, Greenock, letterbook, Port Glasgow and Greenock, Sept. 1768–Mar. 1772 (board to collector, copy of letter from Custom House, Dublin, 4 Oct. 1771).
81. P.R.O., Customs 1/120, ff 82, 88, (15, 20 Feb. 1772).
82. Cullen, 'The smuggling trade in the North Channel'.
83. P.R.O., Customs 1/106, f. 44, 20 Feb. 1769.
84. Custom House Library, London, selections from outport customs records, south coast, 1925 (letter of board to collector, Dartmouth, 25 Aug. 1770, quoting letter from Custom House, Dublin, 11 Aug. 1770).
85. P.R.O., ADM 1/2039, Joseph Lingin, Larne, 8 May 1733.
86. For later descriptions of the methods, see George O'Malley's description, transcribed in Cullen, *Merchants, ships and trade*, p. 57, and Maxwell's account in W. H. Maxwell, *Wild sports of the west* (London, 1832), pp 170–171, 172.
87. Custom House Library, London, selections from outport records, 1662–1829, p. 191, collector to board, Whitehaven, 14 May 1770; selections from outport customs records, south coast, 1925, p. 58 (board to collector, 23 Aug. 1770); selection from outport customs records, west coast, 1926, pp 148, 150 (21 May 1767, 7 May 1770).
88. Custom House Library, London, selections from outport customs records, south coast, 1925, p. 60 (Dartmouth, board to collector, 2 June 1774).

CHAPTER 11

1. This essay is based on information drawn from the works mentioned below and any novelty it possesses arises from the rearrangement of the information rather than the information itself. It seemed, therefore, pointless to justify every statement of easily-ascertained fact. The following books may be recommended:

C. L. D. Duckworth and G. E. Langmuir, *Clyde and other coastal steamers* (Glasgow, 1939). Ibid., *Railway and other steamers* (2nd edition, Prescot, 1968).
D. B. McNeill, *Irish passenger steamship services* (2 vols, Newton Abbot, 1969, 1971).
F. G. MacHaffie, *The short sea route* (Prescot, 1975).
A. W. H. Pearsall, *North Irish channel services* (Belfast, 1962).

CHAPTER 12

1. *Report of the inspectors of Irish fisheries... for 1874*, [C 1176] H.C. 1875, xvii, 367.
2. *Report of the inspectors of Irish fisheries... for 1870*, [C 410] H.C. 1871, xxv, 279.
3. *Report of the inspectors of Irish fisheries... for 1877*, [C 2041] H.C. 1878, xxi, 127.
4. *Cornish Telegraph*, 1 August 1866.
5. Information from the late Mr David Wilson and late Mr Tommy Donnan, Kilkeel in interviews with author in 1974.
6. See the annual parliamentary reports of the variously-titled commissioners and inspectors of Irish fisheries, 1865–1900.
7. A mease was a measurement of fish by number rather than by weight: there were 635 fish in a mease.
8. See for example, Malcolm Gray, *Fishing industries of Scotland (1790–1914)* (Oxford, 1978).
9. *Report of the inspectors on the sea and inland fisheries of Ireland for 1887*, [C 5388], H.C. 1888, xxviii, 237.
10. Ibid., and also report for 1886 ([C 5035]), H.C. 1887, xxi, 165). See also Richard Perren, *The meat trade in Britain 1840–1914* (London, 1978), pp 123–32.
11. *Report of the inspectors on the sea and inland fisheries of Ireland for 1889*, [C 6058], H.C. 1890, xxi, 241.
12. William Andrews, 'On the sea fisheries of Ireland, and with reference to trawling' in *The Journal of the Royal Dublin Society*, iv (1866), p. 300 (paper read to the society on 23 May 1864).
13. *Report of the inspectors of Irish fisheries... for 1874*, [C 1176], H.C. 1875, xvii, 367.
14. *First report of the commissioners of inquiry respecting the present state of the Irish fisheries*, H.C. 1837 (77), xxii, 1 (minutes of evidence, County Down).
15. *Downpatrick Recorder*, 18 March 1865.
16. *A picturesque handbook to Carlingford Bay* (Newry, 1846), pp 10–12. Also *The Belfast and province of Ulster directory*, v (1861–62), pp 616–17.
17. *Fourth report of the commissioners of Irish fisheries, 1822*, H.C. 1823 (383), appendix 2, x, pp 410–11.
18. *Downpatrick Recorder*, 16 July 1864, 14 January 1865, 28 April 1866, 18 January 1868.
19. *Downpatrick Recorder*, 21 February 1880.
20. Letter of 21 August 1884, office of Irish fisheries file, 1877–1912 (P.R.O.N.I., COM 9/352/472).
21. *Report of the inspectors on the sea and inland fisheries of Ireland for 1888*, [C 5777], H.C. 1889, xxii, 313. Also *Downpatrick Recorder*, 21 August 1886.
22. *Report of the inspectors on the sea and inland fisheries of Ireland for 1887*, [C 5388], H.C. 1888, xxviii, 237.
23. *Downpatrick Recorder*, 14 July 1866.
24. Calculated from the series of entries of sea fishing boats registered at the port of Newry, County Down, 1869–1900, under the requirements of part 2 of the sea fisheries act, 1868 and part 4 of the merchant shipping act, 1894. Registry books held at the customs house, Warrenpoint, County Down.
25. Information obtained by cross-referencing data in the boat registers with local directories.

26. Calculated from an account book of George Gordon, Kilkeel (P.R.O.N.I., D 899).
27. *Downpatrick Recorder,* 8 August 1876.
28. *Report from the select committee on sea fisheries,* H.C. 1893–4 (377), xv, 17. See pp 330–33 for the minutes of evidence.
29. *Report of the inspectors of Irish fisheries . . . for 1877,* [C 2014], H.C. 1878, xxi, 127.
30. For descriptions of the construction, form and rig of west Cornish luggers, see Edgar J. March, *Sailing Drifters* (Newton Abbott, 1969), pp 138–78.
31. *First report of the commissioners of inquiry into the state of the Irish fisheries,* appendix xxxiii, no. 111, H.C. 1837 (77) xxii, 1.
32. Edgar J. March, op. cit., pp 181–88.
33. O. S. Oliver, *Boats and boatbuilding in west Cornwall* (Truro, 1971), pp 19–46.
34. *Cornish Telegraph,* 28 August 1866.
35. Registered on 3 March 1869, port of Castletown, under the ownership of William and Richard Duke.
36. *Cornish Telegraph,* 12 January 1870.
37. *Manx Sun,* 19 June 1875.
38. Calculated from the entries of sea fishing boats registered at the port of Castletown under the requirements of part 2 of the sea fisheries act, 1868. Registry book held by the Manx Museum and Library, Douglas.
39. *Downpatrick Recorder,* 18 September 1875 and *Newry Reporter,* 23 November 1875.
40. Angus Martin, *The ring-net fishermen* (Edinburgh, 1981), pp 57–9. Also *Downpatrick Recorder,* 10 June 1876.
41. *Newry Reporter,* 8 September 1877 and office of fisheries file, 1877–1912, re Kilkeel Pier 1877–80 (P.R.O.N.I., COM 9/352/472).
42. *Manx Sun,* 26 June 1875 and 22 January 1876.
43. *Downpatrick Recorder,* 12 September 1885.
44. Personal communication re Campbeltown-registered luggers from Angus Martin, Campbeltown. See also Martin, op. cit., p. 57.
45. *Downpatrick Recorder,* 25 November 1876.
46. For a biographical note on Paynter, see Cyril Noall, 'William Paynter – a renowned boatbuilder' in *The St Ives Times and Echo and Hayle Times,* 18 May 1984.

CHAPTER 13

1. *Report of department advisory committee: development of fishery harbours in Northern Ireland,* [Cmd 81], H.C. (N.I.) 1927, p. 8.
2. Ibid.
3. Oral evidence, Patrick Rice, in *Report of commissioners appointed to inquire into the sea fisheries of the United Kingdom,* i, [3596–I], H.C. 1866, xvii, 638.
4. Unless otherwise indicated all the statistics presented in this paper have been extracted from figures published in the relevant annual reports of the Irish and Northern Irish fishery departments.
5. *Report of the inspectors on the sea and inland fisheries of Ireland for 1909,* [Cd 5350], H.C. 1910, xxx, 547–8.
6. *Report of the inspectors on the sea and inland fisheries of Ireland for 1911,* [Cd 6473], H.C. 1912–13, xxvii, 13.
7. This weight is based on an estimation of 1000 fish to one barrel of cured herring.
8. *Report of the inspectors on the sea and inland fisheries of Ireland for 1916,* [Cd 9018], H.C. 1918, x, 43.
9. Ministry of Commerce, Northern Ireland, *Report of sea and inland fisheries of Northern Ireland 1926–7* (H.M.S.O., Belfast, 1928), p. 7 (hereafter *Report of sea and inland fisheries*).
10. Ibid., p. 5.
11. P.R.O.N.I., COM 43/4/4: papers relating to fishery development commission (1923).
12. *Report of the inspectors on the sea and inland fisheries of Ireland for 1919,* [Cmd 1146], H.C. 1921, xii, 191.
13. *Report of sea and inland fisheries, 1928,* p. 1.

14. *Report of sea and inland fisheries, 1933–4,* p. 29.
15. *Report of sea and inland fisheries, 1926–7,* p. 3.
16. At Ardglass in 1926, 194 vessels landed herring worth £58941. In 1927, 134 vessels landed herring worth £43500.
17. *Report of sea and inland fisheries, 1928,* p. 4.
18. *Report of sea and inland fisheries, 1930,* p. 8.
19. *Report of sea and inland fisheries, 1933–4,* p. 29.
20. *Report of sea and inland fisheries, 1930,* p. 7.
21. P.R.O.N.I., AG 6/6/5: additional fishery information, Portavogie, 1936.
22. *Report of the inspectors on the sea and inland fisheries of Ireland for 1907,* [Cd 4298], H.C. 1908, xiv, 8.
23. Information from registers of fishing boats, County Down, under merchant shipping act, 1894, part 4; records held in Belfast and Newry customs houses.
24. P.R.O.N.I., COM 43/4/4.
25. P.R.O.N.I., COM 43/1/11: Thomas Cully, Portavogie.
26. *Report of sea and inland fisheries, 1926–7,* p. 10.
27. *Report of sea and inland fisheries, 1926–7,* p. 10.
28. *Report of sea and inland fisheries, 1928,* p. 3.
29. *Report of sea and inland fisheries, 1933–4,* p. 33.
30. P.R.O.N.I., AG 6/6/5; Portavogie, 1938.
31. Ibid., Kilkeel, 1938.
32. Quoted in John de Courcy Ireland, *Ireland's sea fisheries: a history* (Dublin, 1981), p. 107.
33. P.R.O.N.I., COM 43/4/4.
34. *Sailing ships of Mourne: the County Down fishing fleet and the Newcastle lifeboat* (Mourne Observer Ltd, Newcastle, 1971), p. 52.

CHAPTER 14

1. See, for example, R. F. Byron, 'Economic functions of kinship values in family businesses: fishing crews in North Atlantic communities', *Sociology and Social Research,* 60, part 2 (1976).
2. R. F. Byron, *Sea change, a Shetland society, 1970–1979* (St John's 1986), pp 87–8.
3. See, for example, James M. Acheson, 'Anthropology of Fishing', *Annual Review of Anthropology,* 10 (1981), pp 275–316.
4. This name, and all others used in these cases, are pseudonyms.
5. R. F. Byron and R. M. Dilley, 'Ulster fishermen: social bases of economic strategy' (unpublished research report, Department of Social Anthropology, Queen's University, Belfast, 1986).
6. For the development of Kilkeel as a major fishing station in the second half of the nineteenth century and an analysis of local investment in fishing boats, see Byron and Dilley, op. cit., p. 9. For the situation in this century see ibid., pp 39–51.
7. Byron, *Sea change,* p. 20.
8. Byron and Dilley, report, p. 94.

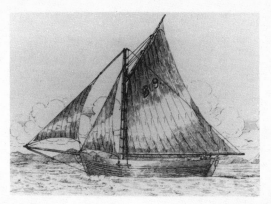

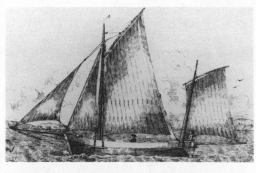

Smack (top), dandys (left), luggers (right) 1848–74, from Wallop Brabazon, *The deep sea and coast fisheries of Ireland* (Dublin, 1848) and E. W. H. Holdsworth, *Deep sea fishing and fishing boats* (London, 1874).

ACKNOWLEDGEMENTS

The editors would like to thank the following for their help and assistance in the production of this book: Professor R. H. Buchanan, Dr W. H. Crawford, Mr Eric McCleery, Mr. Anthony Sheehan, Dr Brian Walker, The Institute of Irish Studies, The Queen's University of Belfast, The Ulster Folk and Transport Museum, Cultra, County Down, and The Economic and Social Research Council, London. Thanks are also due to the various institutions who have helped with the illustrations in this volume.